The author, B. N. Pandey, is an Indian, born in 1929 and educated at the Banaras Hindu University, where he lectured for two years in Law, and then at the Bihar University for one year in History. In 1956 he joined the School of Oriental and African Studies, University of London, for higher research, and since then he has taught Modern Indian History there.

Dr. Pandey is the author of *The Rise of Modern India*, *The Introduction of English Law into India*, 'India since 1947' in *Since 1945: Aspects of Contemporary World History*, and *Shahar Ke Kutte* (a collection of short stories in Hindi). He is also the editor of *A Book of India* and joint editor of *Evolution of India and Pakistan: Select Documents, 1858-1947*

The Making of the Twentieth Century

This series of specially commissioned titles focuses attention on significant and often controversial events and themes of world history in the present century. The authors, many of them already outstanding in their field, have tried to close the gap between the intelligent layman, whose interest is aroused by recent history, and the specialist student at university. Each book will therefore provide sufficient narrative and explanation for the newcomer while offering the specialist student detailed source-references and bibliographies, together with interpretation and reassessment in the light of recent scholarship.

In the choice of subjects there will be a balance between breadth in some spheres and detail in others; between the essentially political and matters scientific, economic or social. The series cannot be a comprehensive account of everything that has happened in the twentieth century, but it will provide a guide to recent research and explain something of the times of extraordinary change and complexity in which we live.

The Making of the Twentieth Century

Series Editor: CHRISTOPHER THORNE

Other titles in the Series include

Already published

In preparation

The Break-up of British India

B. N. Pandey

Macmillan

London · Melbourne · Toronto

St Martin's Press

New York

1 9 6 9

© B. N. Pandey 1969

Published by
MACMILLAN AND CO LTD
Little Essex Street London W C 2
and also at Bombay Calcutta and Madras
Macmillan South Africa (Publishers) Pty Ltd Johannesburg
The Macmillan Company of Australia Pty Ltd Melbourne
The Macmillan Company of Canada Ltd Toronto
St Martin's Press Inc New York
Gill and Macmillan Ltd Dublin

Library of Congress catalog card no. 69–16502

Printed in Great Britain by
ROBERT MACLEHOSE AND CO LTD
The University Press Glasgow

FOR

Beni Prasad Kanoria

Contents

Plates and Maps

The cover picture shows a cartoon
from *Punch*, 14 May 1930

PLATES

between pages 112 *and* 113

The author and publishers wish to thank the following for permission to reproduce the plates: 1*a*, *b*, 2*a*, *b*, 5*a*, *b*, 6*a*, Radio
Times Hulton Picture Library; 3*a*, *b*, *Punch*; 4*a*, Paul Popper;
4*b*, 8*a*, Pakistan High Commission; 6*b*, Fox Photos; 7*a*,
Information Service of India; 7*b*, Nehru Memorial Museum
and Library; 8*b*, Camera Press.

MAPS

Abbreviations

P.I.S.P. *Partition of India Seminar Papers at the School of Oriental and African Studies, University of London.*

Select Documents *The Evolution of India and Pakistan 1856–1947, Select Documents,* edited by C. H. Philips and others.

Preface

THERE are today, broadly speaking, two schools of thought on the partition and independence of India. The first school believes that the partition of the sub-continent was not inevitable; it created many problems and solved none. It was an impractical and reactionary solution to the Hindu–Muslim problem. Not all Muslims could be transferred from India to Pakistan and not all Hindus from Pakistan to India. As a result there are more Muslims in India today than in West Pakistan. The partition created new problems which in turn caused permanent hostility and even war between Pakistan and India. The two countries have not been at peace ever since 1947; each has been spending more money on its defence than on social services for its masses. The whole of South Asia has turned into a trouble spot of the world. The partition benefited none except a small section of middle-class Muslims who found new avenues of power in politics, commerce and industry.

The second school holds that the partition was inevitable. Muslims and Hindus had lived as distinct and separate communities in a state of mutual hostility. Muslims would not have lived under a Hindu *Raj* which had to follow after the withdrawal of British power from India. If not Jinnah then some other Muslim leader would have emerged as a champion of the partition. Pakistan, thus, was not the creation of one man. It lay in the logic of Indian history. The hostility between India and Pakistan is primarily due to the fact that India did not completely accept the principle of partition.

Apparently the two schools do not seem to have any common meeting-ground. The truth, however, may not lie entirely with either school, and a host of questions can be put to the respective adherents. If the partition of India was not inevitable then why and how did it happen? Was it caused by men competing for power or by systems (colonialism, communalism, nationalism) struggling against each other for survival? If the partition of India was the only solution for the Hindu–Muslim problem then how do the Muslims and Hindus still manage to live together in the villages and towns of India and Pakistan? Why did the idea of a separate Muslim state not cross a single mind until a decade before the creation of Pakistan? Could communalism have survived if the pace of India's modernisation had been faster than it was during the British *Raj*? Could Muslim separatism have thrived without being supported by British colonialism? Why, if at all, did British colonialism in India ally with the communalism of the Muslim League and not with the nationalism of the Indian National Congress?

While not pretending to carry out a comprehensive enquiry into the thesis of each school, this work does attempt to answer some of the main questions. It is primarily a study of the social and religious reform movements, of the origins of the National Movement and Muslim separatism, and of the struggle of Indian nationalism against colonialism at the front and communalism at the rear.

The research for this work was carried out in Britain and India. Professor C. H. Philips organised for the first time a large-scale seminar on the partition of India which was held at the School of Oriental and African Studies from 1965 to 1967. Some of the participants of this study group had been involved in the events in some capacity or other – as politician, administrator, judge, general, or journalist – and their contributions have thrown new light on some facets of the subject. As a member of the seminar, I benefited immensely from the contributions and discussions of its members and I owe a deep sense of gratitude to Professor Philips for permitting me to use, for this work, the papers which were submitted during the course of the seminar.

I am grateful to my friends Dr Jagdish Raj (of the Ministry of Education, Government of India), Dr D. N. Panigrahi and Dr P. L. Malhotra (of Delhi University) for taking a keen interest in this work and securing secondary materials from various sources for my use in Delhi; to my friend and colleague Dr M. E. Yapp of the Middle East History Section for reading the typescript and generously giving me the benefit of his knowledge of Islamic institutions; to Professor Hugh Tinker for discussing with me the implications of the Mountbatten plan; to Dr S. R. Mehrotra, who read the page-proofs and offered some valuable comments on my treatment of the Congress policy; to my friend Valerie Cooper for typing the manuscript, preparing the index and helping me in various other ways in the preparation of this work; to Mr M. S. Shaw of Macmillan and Mr Christopher Thorne for their advice on technical matters, for their help in the selection of illustrations and, above all, for their kind and patient dealings with me.

School of Oriental and African Studies,   B. N. P.
University of London
April 1968

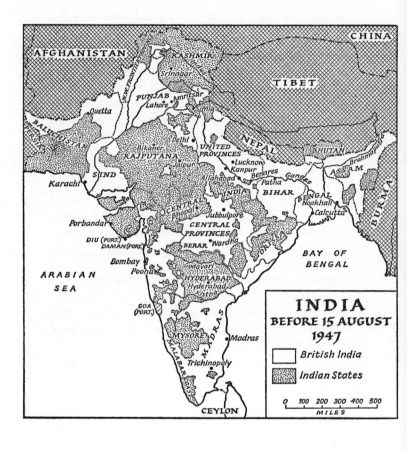

INDIA
BEFORE 15 AUGUST 1947

☐ British India
▨ Indian States

0 100 200 300 400 500
MILES

CHINA

AFGHANISTAN

TIBET

KASHMIR
Srinagar

N.W.FRONTIER
PUNJAB
Quetta
Lahore · Amritsar
Simla

NEPAL
BHUTAN

BALUCHISTAN

Delhi
Bikaner
RAJPUTANA
UNITED
PROVINCES
Lucknow
Kanpur
ASSAM

SIND
Jaipur
Allahabad · Benares
Patna
Ganges
Brahmaputra

Karachi
INDIA
BIHAR
BENGAL
Noakhali
Calcutta

Porbandar
CENTRAL
Bhopal · Jubbulpore
BURMA

DIU (PORT.)
DAMAN (PORT.)
CENTRAL
PROVINCES
BERAR · Wardha
ORISSA

Bombay
Poona
Godavari
BAY OF
BENGAL

ARABIAN
SEA
HYDERABAD
Hyderabad
Kistna

GOA
(PORT.)

MYSORE
M A D R A S
Madras

MALABAR

Trichinopoly

CEYLON

1 The Pinnacle of the Empire

As long as we rule India, we are the greatest power in the world. If we lose it, we shall drop straightaway to a third-rate power.

LORD CURZON, 1901.

THE British empire in India had reached its apogee at the turn of the nineteenth century. The Governor-General, Lord Curzon, who ruled India in the years 1899–1905 was, as he proudly avowed, 'an Imperialist heart and soul'. His administration witnessed the culmination of the main characteristics, both good and bad, of the British imperial system. Curzon was the flesh and blood symbol of empire. A firm believer in the physical and moral superiority of the British race, animated by a sense of duty, endowed with an infinite capacity for detail, fair and impartial even at the risk of incurring unpopularity, and meticulously efficient – these qualities of Curzon had gone to build up the British empire. His lack of vision, his insensitivity, his belief in the racial inferiority of the Indians, his indifference towards their aspirations, and his spite for the educated middle-class Bengali *Babus* – these created in India forces which ultimately led to the fall of the empire.

But in 1900 neither Curzon nor any other Briton, politician, statesman or administrator, could foresee that the empire would disappear in less than fifty years.

STRUCTURE

In 1901, the Indian empire contained 1,766,597 square miles and was therefore greater by 12,000 square miles than the whole of Europe, excluding Russia. Direct British rule extended over what is called British India, comprising 61·5 per cent of the Indian sub-continent and divided into seven provinces – Bengal, Bombay, the Central Provinces, Madras, the North-Western Provinces, the North-West Frontier Province, and the Punjab. The remaining 38·5 per cent of Indian territory was divided into 601 Indian states. Some of the Indian states were big (Hyderabad was larger than England and Wales and the Kashmir territory was five times bigger than Switzerland), some very rich, and a few like Mysore, Travancore and Baroda well administered by their enlightened rulers.

The population of the empire as recorded in 1901 was 294,361,056 persons, or about one-fifth of the whole world, of whom 231,899,507 lived in British India, and 62,461,549 in the Indian states.[1] Of the total population of India, 70 per cent were Hindus, 21 per cent Muslims, 3 per cent Buddhists, 3 per cent Animists, and 1 per cent Christians, the balance being made up of Sikhs, Jains, Parsis, Jews, and others.[2] With its 207 million votaries, Hinduism was strongest in Orissa, Mysore, and Madras, where it was professed by nine-tenths of the population; and in Bihar, Bombay (excluding Sind), the Central Provinces, the North-Western Provinces and in the Indian states of Central India and Rajputana. Muslims, with a total number of 62½ millions, formed more than a fifth of the total population and they were strongly represented in Kashmir, where they formed 74 per cent of the total population; the percentage was slightly lower in the Punjab, Sind and Bengal.

The Indian states were not sovereign. Constitutionally they were not part of British India and their inhabitants were not British subjects. Parliament did not legislate for the states or their people. But they owed allegiance to the British monarch and were controlled by the Governor-General, who represented the Crown in India, and in that capacity was styled the Viceroy. The external relations and the defence of the states were managed by the Viceroy. The Indian princes were not allowed even to travel abroad without first securing the permission of the Viceroy.

During the second half of the nineteenth century machinery had been developed to control the states. A Political Department under the direct charge of the Viceroy, and an Indian Political Service, manned by the members of the Indian Civil Service and Army, had been set up. The Political Department had Residents and Political Agents in all important states. This department came to assume the position of 'a government within a government'.

The Indian government had undertaken to protect the Indian princes against external attack and internal rebellion. Though technically they were independent in the management of their internal affairs, the Viceroy had reserved the right to intervene in case of mismanagement. But this right was not often exercised. The rulers occupied their feudal thrones virtually without any fear of external or internal danger. Consequently most of them had turned into irresponsible despots. To Curzon they seemed no better than 'a set of unruly and ignorant and rather undisciplined school-boys' who should be 'schooled by a firm, but not unkindly, hand'.[3]

The Indian states existed on the sufferance of the British government. But why? At any time in the course of the nineteenth century they could have been easily incorporated into British India, possibly without shedding a drop of blood. Had this been done the course of subsequent history might have been different. There were other reasons apart from the British respect for royalty and aristocracy. Most of the princes remained loyal to the British during the Indian mutiny of 1857. After the mutiny the British scholars, administrators and politicians put their heads together to find out the basic causes of this sudden and shocking uprising. It was found that the policy followed by the

Governor-General, Lord Dalhousie (1848–56), of annexing Indian states on some excuse or other was as much responsible for the outbreak as the reforming zeal of Lord Bentinck (1828–35), who had abolished *Sati* in 1829. It was thus inferred that Indians preferred their old customs, old traditions and old dynasties. So long as the British did not interfere with the social customs of the people and depose any of their hereditary Maharajas or Nawabs the empire in India would remain intact. Thus, the British government after the mutiny embarked upon the policy of 'sustaining the Native States and Princes'[4] and of refraining from the introduction of any social reform.

The feudal system of government that subsisted in the Indian states was in contrast to the government by checks and balances that was established in British India. British India had a three-tier governmental structure, each tier classified into legislative, executive and judiciary. The top level functioned in London through Parliament, the Secretary of State for India and the India Council, and the Privy Council. Parliament enacted laws for India, but only those laws which affected the Constitution of India. It had delegated its legislative authority to the Governor-General and provincial Governors in India who legislated on Indian matters in their respective legislative councils. The supreme executive power was exercised by the Secretary of State who was a Cabinet minister and responsible to Parliament. He was advised by the India Council, which was created in 1858 to act as a watchdog over him. The judicial committee of the Privy Council was the final court, hearing appeals from the decisions of the High Courts of India.

The second and third tiers consisted respectively of the central and provincial governments of India. At the head of the Indian administration were the Governor-General and his Council, and of the provincial administration the Governor (Lieutenant-Governor for some provinces) and his Council. The provincial administration functioned under the general supervision of the Governor-General in Council. But some of the provincial Governors agitated from time to time against the paternalism of the central government and asked for more freedom in matters of finance and administration.* The diversity of India impressed them more than its homogeneity and they argued that local customs could be best preserved through a system of provincial autonomy. Though not much was done by the end of the nineteenth century, the underlying trend in the constitutional developments of the twentieth century was towards the decentralisation of Indian administration.

The Indian judiciary, consisting of High Courts, one for each province, presiding over a network of district and sub-divisional courts, was independent of the executive. The independence of the judiciary, however, had been resented and occasionally assailed by the executive ever since the establishment in India in 1774 of the first British court based on the principles of English law. British administrators had opposed in vain the growth of the English legal system in India. The main reason for their opposition was that the courts, presided over mostly by British judges, treated all as equals in the eyes of the law and worked as a check on the executive. It was argued that by reducing Britons to the level of Indians the courts were undermining the superiority of the British race on which alone depended the strength of the empire in India. This line of argument, based on the racial superiority of the ruler over the ruled, was later disguised in more subtle form. The opponents of the courts argued that Indians themselves detested British judicial procedure, that the complexity of the courts was also responsible for the outbreak of the mutiny, and that a simple, patriarchal type of judicial system would dispense justice more quickly and cheaply

* Sir H. B. E. Frere (1815–84), Governor of Bombay, and Sir Henry Maine (1822–88), legal member of the Governor-General's Council 1862–69, were staunch advocates of a system of provincial autonomy.

and would be better suited to Indian conditions. The argument developed some weight due to the success of the patriarchal system in the Punjab, where all governmental power, both executive and judicial, was concentrated in the hands of one officer, the Deputy Commissioner, who was responsible only to his Divisional Commissioner and through him to the Chief Commissioner – the head of the provincial executive. The advocates of this system, chief among them Sir Bartle Frere, pointed out that the loyalty of the Punjab towards the British during the mutiny was due mainly to the patriarchal type of administration which had been established in the province. Frere argued that the administration had enveloped itself so much in rules and regulations that it was gradually becoming incapable of taking any action. The remedy, he urged, was that every official should be a 'real ruler in all things to those below him, and let him be really ruled by the functionary above him'.[5]

These arguments failed to check the growth of the English legal system in India. But they did impress upon the government the need for simplifying laws and procedure, and consequently the civil and criminal laws and procedure were codified in the post-mutiny era.

The personnel of the administration remained essentially British until the beginning of the twentieth century. Important executive posts from the top to the district level remained outside the reach of an educated Indian. Indians were admitted only to the judicial service, where a few were elevated to the bench of the High Court, and to subordinate executive posts.

However, a modest beginning in associating Indians with the administration had been made in the legislative organ of the central and provincial governments. This, of course, was dictated by the lessons of the mutiny. Syed Ahmad Khan (1817–98), then a subordinate judicial officer, who was later to found the Muslim Aligarh movement, and to become a member of the Imperial Legislative

Council, pointed out in 1858 that one of the main reasons for the outbreak of the mutiny was the wide gulf that existed between the government and the people, the adverse effects of which were felt more in the field of legislation.[6] The people, not being represented in the legislatures, had no means of protesting against a foolish measure. Bartle Frere, now a member of the Governor-General's Council (1859-62), took up Syed Ahmad Khan's suggestion at official level. Strong minutes were written, followed by correspondence between the Indian and London governments, and the outcome was the Indian Councils Act of 1861, which provided for the nomination of non-official members into both the central and provincial legislative councils.[7]

Thus the Act opened up the opportunity for Indians to sit on the Imperial Legislative Council. But these Indians were not to be representatives of the new middle class. They were to be ruling princes and landlords selected for their loyalty towards British rule and for their conservative sentiments.* Nor was the admission of Indians to the legislative councils to be interpreted as the beginning of a representative system of government in India. Sir Charles Wood, Secretary of State for India 1859-66, made this very clear:

I am as much as anybody can be for the self government of a colony of British settlers. They can manage their own affairs, and, if they mis-govern themselves, they suffer and will learn to mend their ways – but such a form of government seems to me singularly unsuited to India. The worst of all governments is a popular government of one race over another.[8]

However, the Indian Councils Act of 1892, by providing for the indirect election of non-official members to the

* Thirty-six Indian members served on the Imperial Legislative Council during the years 1862 to 1888. Of them, 6 were ruling princes and 23 landlords. *Parl. Papers 1890*, liv, pp. 104-5.

legislative councils, enabled the middle classes to enter these bodies. For example, among the elected members of the viceregal legislative council during 1895–9, there were seven lawyers and only three landlords.[9] The non-official Indian members in the legislative councils, however, remained ineffective against the joint majority of the official and non-official European members.

The steel frame of the empire was the Indian Civil Service which was at the zenith of its power and influence at the turn of the century. The personnel of the service was almost exclusively British, the 'flower of the British universities'. It was also called the 'covenanted' service, for every member of the service entered into a covenant with the Secretary of State by which he bound himself not to engage in trade, not to receive presents, and to subscribe for a pension for himself and his family. The members of this 'superior governing class' held most of the high and lucrative offices in the administration and their pension of £1000 a year was assured. They were nominated by the Directors of the East India Company until 1853 and then chosen by open competitive examination held in London. They numbered about 900 in 1900. The other branch of the service, the uncovenanted, was recruited in India by the provincial governments and its members held subordinate positions within the district administration. The personnel of this branch consisted of Europeans domiciled in India, Eurasians and Indians.

Technically the Indians were eligible to compete for the covenanted Civil Service but only a limited number of them had won through the ordeal. In order to appear at the competitive examination an Indian had first to find at least £1000 to enable him to travel to London, to stay there for some time and prepare for the examination. If he failed at the first attempt he could hardly obtain a second chance because the top age limit was fixed at twenty-two. Middle-class Indians therefore demanded that the competitive examination be held simultaneously in India and London and that the upper age limit should be raised. But the British government ignored their demands, for a variety of reasons. The government wanted to keep the 'steel frame of the empire' beyond the reach of Indians. The security of the empire rested on the Civil Service and it must, it was urged, remain British. Sir John Strachey (1823–1907), a prominent administrator and author, wrote in 1888: 'Our Governors of provinces, the chief officers of our army, our magistrates of districts and their principal executive subordinates ought to be Englishmen under all circumstances that we can now foresee.'[10] And then there were the non-official European residents in India, with their acute racial feeling, who despised all Indians. It was argued that they would not like 'to be placed in any way under the authority of natives'. Again, British members of the Civil Service were themselves opposed to Indians being admitted to their Chosen Brotherhood. Further, it was asked, who were likely to benefit from the increased employment opportunities? English-educated Bengalis, of course. The British administration seemed to have a long-standing prejudice against the Bengalis. It was believed that the Bengalis, though quick and clever, were deficient in the bolder and hardier virtues – 'in pluck, self-reliance, and veracity – the three great national attributes by which we gained, and by which we retain our hold upon British India'.[11]

Lord Kimberley, Secretary of State for India in 1886, told the Liberal Viceroy, Dufferin, that the demand for simultaneous examinations in London and in India had to be considered carefully, if only because Bengalis, 'quite unfit to rule', would benefit the most.[12]

In spite of the odds against them some Indians managed to compete and in 1900 Curzon complained to Lord Hamilton, the Secretary of State:

Some day I must address you about the extreme danger of the system under which every year an increasing number of the 900 and odd higher posts that were meant, and ought to have been exclusively and specially reserved, for Europeans, are being filched away by the superior wits of the native in the English examinations. I believe it to be the greatest peril with which our administration is confronted.[13]

Curzon thought that a racial qualification should have been insisted upon in the very beginning and lamented that it was now too late to exclude Indians from the Civil Service on that ground, for 'there would probably be a storm'.[14]

It was, however, different with the Indian army, which was organised solely on racial and communal principles and the higher posts reserved exclusively for the British. The Indians were appointed only to the ranks of jamadar, subadar, risaldar and woordi major, and they totalled 2923 in 1900.[15] Some Indian princes were given the honorary rank of captain, major or colonel but it carried with it nothing more than the privilege of wearing the British uniform.

The mutiny dictated army policy. The British element in the army was increased. Prior to the mutiny there was one British soldier to seven and a half Indian soldiers. After the mutiny the ratio was one British to two Indian soldiers, and this was maintained throughout the century. The Indians were not to be trusted and the control of arsenals and artillery was placed in European hands. The native army was to be composed of different nationalities and castes and 'mixed promiscuously through each regiment'.[16]

WEALTH

The empire's chief source of revenue was still the land, though some experiments had been made in direct taxation – income-tax and licence duty – in the later part of the century when the government faced enormous deficits. It was, however, in the field of land administration that the government had been unable to evolve a uniform system for the whole of British India. In 48 per cent of the total area the government collected revenue from the intermediaries – *zamindars* and *taluqdars*, and in the remaining 52 per cent directly from the cultivators of the land. The former was called the *zamindari* and the latter the *ryotwari* system; each having a number of regional variations. The author of the permanent *zamindari* system was Lord Cornwallis, Governor-General of Bengal, 1768–93. A believer in Whig philosophy, he considered that a permanent tenure in land would protect the landed gentry from interference by the executive, and would convert land into a regular source of investment for Indian capital. The father of the *ryotwari* system was Thomas Munro, a district officer in Madras from 1792 to 1818 and later the Governor of the presidency, 1820–7. He believed that a direct settlement of the land on the cultivator for a certain period would keep the revenue of the state elastic, because the revenue could be increased with an increase in the productivity of the land. This feature of the Munro system impressed the Directors of the Company who realised that by settling the land in perpetuity on the *zamindars* in Bengal Lord Cornwallis had virtually converted land revenue into an unexpandable source of income. As there was no middleman in Munro's system the cultivator in Madras was spared the various oppressions his counterpart in Bengal suffered at the hands of the *zamindars*.

It was never resolved which of the two systems was the better because, the interests of an alien government being not always identical with the interests of the people, the advantages accruing to the government from one system were often construed by Indian nationalists as losses to the people.

The frequent outbreak of famine was attributed to the high rate of revenue assessment. People in all ages and in all parts of the world had suffered from famines, but whereas Europe completely banished this calamity by the middle of the nineteenth century, India suffered from it more acutely and more frequently in the second half of the century than ever before. For example, there were only twelve famines in the ninety years from 1765 to 1858 but there was famine or severe scarcity in one part of the country or other in twenty out of forty-nine years between 1860 and 1908. High assessment was not the main cause for the recurrence of this calamity, though it must have been a contributory factor by lowering the purchasing capacity of the people. The main cause of the Indian famines and their disastrous consequences was the want of diversity of occupations in India, which resulted in increasingly heavy pressure on land.[17] The great mass of the population was directly dependent on agriculture, and there was no other industry from which a considerable part of the community could derive its support. The failure of rain thus deprived the agricultural labouring class as a whole, 'not only of the ordinary supplies of food obtaining at prices within their reach, but also of the sole employment by which they can earn the means of procuring it'. The Famine Commission of 1880 thus rightly suggested that the complete remedy for this condition of things was to be found only in the development of industries other than agriculture and independent of the fluctuations of the seasons.[18] In 1901, of the total population in British India less than 9 per cent was employed in industry; and about 70 per cent was dependent on agriculture.[19]

The slow pace of industrial development was partly due to the colonial economy. The establishment of British supremacy in India coincided with the industrial revolution in Britain. Britain needed raw materials for its factories and markets for its manufactures. India was virtually turned into a producer of raw materials and a consumer of British manufactures.

In spite of this the Indian *entrepreneur* class – the Parsi, the Khoja, the Bania – managed to start cotton mills in

Bombay, Ahmedabad, Sholapur and Nagpur with Indian capital and skill. At the turn of the century there were 195 mills with 42,000 looms and about 5 million spindles in India. The achievement, though modest, seems remarkable in view of the fact that no protection was given to the Indian industry against competition from Manchester. Until the Indian government obtained fiscal autonomy in the 1920s, tariff policy was dictated in the interest of British and not of Indian industries, and in this, as in other fields, British and Indian interests were more often in conflict than in unison. The growing community of industrialists, which otherwise might have been the strongest pillar of the British *Raj* in India, lost its confidence in Britain on account of her tariff and currency policies. In 1873 the rupee was steady at two shillings but then its value started to fall and in the 1890s it was worth one shilling and threepence. The Commission appointed in 1893 wisely recommended that India should adopt the Gold Standard. But the London government did not act on the recommendation and currency conditions went on deteriorating.

Next in importance to cotton were jute and tea, but these industries were started and at the turn of the century owned and managed by the British. India had a virtual monopoly in jute and the Scots owned this industry in India. The first jute mill was started in the 1850s on the banks of the Hughli river and the number increased to 22 in 1880, 36 in 1901–2 and 64 in 1914. As early as the 1830s the British started exploring the possibility of growing tea in India and working the coal mines. At the turn of the century India was exporting 137,000,000 lb of tea to Britain and producing 6 million tons of coal every year.

The growth of Indian industries, the conveyance of British manufactures from Indian docks to interior markets, the transportation of raw materials from remote areas in India to the docks for shipment abroad, the transportation of food from surplus to deficit area in times of famines, and above all the security of the Indian empire from internal and external dangers – all these were facilitated by the construction of a network of railways in India. First introduced into India in the 1850s by Dalhousie, the railroad mileage had reached 24,752 miles in 1900–1 with a total capital investment of Rs. 329 crores (over £2·6 million).[20]

POLICIES

At the turn of the century the English-educated middle class had already become a source of uneasiness to the government. It was disquieting for an imperialist to realise that the class, as a whole, was entirely the creation of the British *Raj*. But the results of the introduction of English education into India were not what had been intended by those who originally proposed it. T. B. Macaulay (the law member of the Governor-General's executive council, 1834–8) argued, and Bentinck was convinced, that the introduction of English education would not only turn its recipients into loyal subjects of the British *Raj* but might eventually induce them to embrace Christianity and thereby unshakably strengthen the foundation of the empire in India. As it turned out the English-educated Indians reformed Indian religions and customs and then led the national movements for the independence of India.

The method adopted in 1835 to impart English education was what was called the 'filtration scheme' by which 'the energies of government were devoted to the provision of superior education for the upper classes in the belief that the knowledge thus communicated would filter down to the masses'.[21] Not much progress was made with this scheme; in the 1850s there were only 1474 schools with 67,569 pupils. It was thus superseded by a more vigorous and thorough plan of education contained in the London despatch of 1854. This 'Magna Carta' of English education in India laid down the foundation of modern education there. Under this scheme universities were established in

1857, one each at Calcutta, Bombay and Madras. A network of graded schools (primary, middle and high schools)
was established all over India. The government aided
individuals in establishing all grades of schools. Arrangements were made for the training of teachers and the
education of women. On the administrative side, an
Education Department was established in each of the five
provinces under a Director of Public Instruction.

Thus the nucleus for the growth of education was
provided in the 1850s, but progress during the second half
of the century was slow and lopsided. The grants-in-aid
system failed to promote vernacular primary education to
the expected extent. The villagers, who were to benefit from
primary education, were able neither to pay for it nor to
organise local schools. After the mutiny the provincial
governments lost interest in the promotion of elementary
education. As a result in 1901 three out of every four country
villages were without a school; not much more than
3,000,000 boys, or less than one-fifth of the total boys of
school age, were receiving primary education in India, and
only one girl in forty attended any kind of school.[22]

The universities, now five with the establishment of the
Punjab University in 1882 and the University of Allahabad
in 1887, were examining bodies with no corporate existence,
controlling courses of study and setting examination papers
for the pupils of affiliated colleges. The affiliated colleges of
Calcutta University, for example, were scattered in regions
as remote as Burma and Ceylon. Higher education was
followed with too exclusive a view of entering government
service, and those who failed to obtain government
employment were ill fitted for other pursuits. Then there
was the colossal wastage. It took 24,000 candidates at
matriculation to secure 11,000 passes, 7000 candidates at
the intermediate examination to secure 2800 passes, and
4750 candidates for the B.A. degree to secure 1900 passes.[23]
In the whole system excessive emphasis was laid on

examinations, and the courses of study were too purely literary in character. Schools and colleges trained the intelligence of students too little, and their memory too much. Above all, in the pursuit of English education the cultivation of the vernaculars was neglected.

Thus the system of education that prevailed in India at the turn of the century was ill designed to produce leaders, scientists, authors, and men of action. If some of the recipients of this education became influential members of the Indian middle class it was in spite of the education they received. It is noteworthy that many top men of the middle class – the social reformers and the nationalists – were educated either in Britain or in the national institutions which had been started by the Indian educationalists.

In educational and social matters the keynote of British policy was 'perfect religious neutrality'. The government abstained from 'all interference with the religious feelings and practices of the natives' and insisted on the exclusion of religious teaching from the government schools.[24] The sudden shift to neutrality from the radical reformism of pre-mutiny days was, of course, due to the mutiny. The government would not initiate any social reform, or abolish or modify any religious custom. The suppression of female infanticide in 1870; the legalising of the remarriage of native converts to Christianity in 1866, whereby a Christian deserted or repudiated by his wife could marry again; the legalisation in 1872 of the marriage of a Brahmo Samajist who considered himself outside any recognised faith; the prohibition in 1891 of the consummation of marriage before the girl was twelve; the prohibition in 1865 of the practice of hook-swinging, by which a devotee would 'suspend himself from a raised pole by hooks pierced through the flesh of his back in order to demonstrate his religious devotion and his release from the feelings of pain' – these were some of the social legislative and regulative measures undertaken by the government in the second half of the nineteenth century. In these we find that the legalisation of the marriage of a Brahmo Samajist and the remarriage of a native Christian had nothing to do with Hinduism as such. The other measures were undertaken to prohibit certain practices which were opposed to the dictates of humanity and were in no way sanctioned or enjoined by the Hindu religion. In customs which seemed to have some sort of religious sanction, like polygamy and child marriage, the government would not interfere. The Maharaja of Burdwan and nearly 21,000 Hindus of Bengal urged the government in 1866 to enact a law for the prevention of polygamy, but the government declined to legislate because the practice at issue was a 'social and religious institution'.[25]

The Christian missionaries in India, however, opposed the religious neutrality of the government. They interpreted the mutiny in a different light. They considered the mutiny to be a 'national chastisement' caused not by attempts to spread Christianity but by 'our keeping back Christianity from the people'.[26] 'Had the mutineers of the Bengal Army possessed some insight into the principles of the Christian religion' – the Church Missionary Society submitted – 'they would never have been misled in the manner they were'.[27] Except for a few ardent Christians in the Punjab the British administrators paid no heed to these arguments. The British administration had lost its reforming zeal of the pre-mutiny period, it had forsaken its role of a progressive force in India, and had become feudal, undemocratic, racialist, and paternal, in a word unbritish, in its policy and attitude towards the people. All that mattered was the security of the Indian empire. Any measure no matter how reactionary, any alliance no matter how unfair, was to be deemed right and just if it was calculated to strengthen the foundation of the empire. This change in policy and attitude was suddenly brought about by the mutiny which, para-doxically enough, was the rising of the old order against the new, the last unsuccessful struggle of the feudal and

B

conservative forces of India against the progressive forces that had been released by British administration in the last hundred years. The British suppressed the mutiny and at the same time entered into an alliance with the forces that had caused it. The mutiny was therefore both a victory and a defeat for British rule in India.

Alliance with the feudal order – the princes, aristocrats, *zamindars* and *taluqdars*; indifference towards the wellbeing of the peasants; hostility towards the aspirations of the rising middle class; total abstention from introducing social and economic changes – these were the main features of British policy during the half-century that followed the mutiny.

The princes of India were assured by Queen Victoria 'that all treaties and engagements made with them' would be scrupulously maintained and there would be no 'extension of our present territorial possessions'.[28] The disinherited and dispossessed aristocrats were told that the Queen's government would restore them to their lands and protect them in all rights connected therewith. And the Queen assured the people of India that there would be no attempt to impose Christianity on any one of them.

The Queen's assurance to the princes was based on the moral drawn from the mutiny that the policy of annexing Indian states followed by Dalhousie was foremost among the causes of revolt. The dispossessed or aggrieved rulers like Nana Saheb, the Rani of Jhansi and the Queen Regent of Oudh had led the revolt, while the reigning princes had remained loyal to the British. Hence the inference that an alliance with the princes would be conducive to the safety of the empire. A step down from the top was the aristocracy – the *taluqdars*, the *zamindars* and the Rajas. Here the *taluqdars* of Oudh provided the moral. Before the mutiny the British administration had rightly denounced the *taluqdars* of Oudh as an incubus pressing down upon the peasants in the countryside. Consequently they had been dispossessed and their lands distributed among the peasantry, with a hope that the latter would act as the agents of agrarian progress and would remain grateful to the government. But the mutiny shattered the vision of the government. The peasantry followed the *taluqdars* against the British. Governor-General Canning (1856–62) formed the opinion that 'these village occupants deserve little consideration from us'.[29] Lord Ellenborough remarked that the government of India was chivalrous like Robin Hood in robbing the *taluqdars* of their wealth and property and giving them to the peasantry, but whereas Robin Hood managed to secure the favour of those to whom he gave, 'we managed to make them as hostile as those we plundered'.[30] The *taluqdars* were in due course restored to their pre-mutiny position with a hope that, tied together by 'mutual sympathy and trust', the Englishman and the taluqdar would stand 'as brothers before the altar of the empire'.[31] The policy of the alliance with the nobility gained such fervent adherence that Lord Lytton, Viceroy from 1876 to 1880, vainly proposed to create an Indian Privy Council and an Indian Peerage of Indian Princes and Nobility.[32]

The indulgent prince could be befriended, the ignorant, superstitious peasant could be ignored, for neither was a potential threat to the empire. But the English-educated middle class was a class apart. The Bengali *Babu* – the first to come under British influence and the first to imbibe the spirit of the modern age – who had faithfully learned the language of the Saheb, who had devoured Western literature with a special relish for J. S. Mill's *On Liberty*, who had visited England to take his Bar examination or to appear at the I.C.S. examination and had observed how much the British at home cared for freedom and the dignity of man, who had emulated the British in dress, in manner, in food and drink, now, as it seemed, stood suppliant at the doorstep of Power begging to be treated as an equal and be given a share in the administration. He was a threat to the empire; he symbolised the beginning of the end.

British hostility to the rising middle class was therefore
tinged with jealousy and fear. Each Viceroy from Canning
to Curzon had to reckon with this class and none sympathised with its aspirations. Viceroy Lord Northbrook (1872–
1876) complained to the Secretary of State, 'there is
growing up a mass of people with a smattering of English
education, just enough to make them conceited, and ape
the English habit of grumbling at and criticising everything
done by the government'.[33] Lytton in his desire to secure the
good will of the upper class wanted to tell the *Babus* plainly
'that the encouragement of natives does not mean the
supremacy of Baboodom'.[34] The Liberal Viceroy Dufferin
(1884–8) was even more antagonistic than the conservative
Lytton. He was persuaded by Richard Assheton Cross to
believe that the masses of the people in India 'do not want
to be ruled by Baboos, and it is our duty, as well as our
interest, and still more the interest of the people, that there
is to be English rule and English justice and English
consideration for the wants, the prejudices, and the habits,
religious as well as social of all classes'.[35] He had discovered
that the 'Bengali Baboo is a most irritating and troublesome
gentleman' and he thought 'we must not show ourselves at
all afraid of him'.[36] In a population of 200 millions, those
with a university education numbered less than eight
thousand. How, Dufferin argued, could this 'microscopic
minority' be allowed to control the administration.

From this fear of the educated Hindu class was born the
stratagem of 'divide and rule'. What would happen to the
empire if Hindus and Muslims united against the British
as they did in the mutiny? Secretary of State Sir Charles
Wood advised the Viceroy, Lord Elgin 1 (1862–3) that 'a
dissociating spirit' should be kept up.[37] Dufferin encouraged the Muslims to regard themselves as a distinct
political entity in India. 'Diversity of races in India, and
the presence of a powerful Mohammedan community, are
undoubtedly circumstances favourable to the maintenance

of our rule' he wrote in 1887, maintaining at the same time that 'these circumstances we found and did not create'.[38] In 1897 George Hamilton, the Secretary of State, cautioned the Viceroy Lord Elgin II (1894-9) against Hindu-Muslim harmony:

The solidarity, which is growing, of native opinion and races and religion in antagonism to our rule frightens me as regards the future. Education and the press will enhance that bad feeling and we ought to leave no stone unturned to counteract this dangerous tendency.[39]

Elgin did not share Hamilton's apprehension in full but as a measure of caution he sent a subscription to the Muslim College at Aligarh, 'whose purpose was to advance Muslim separatism'.

More than anything else the racial arrogance of the British had hurt the feelings of educated Indians and widened the gulf between the ruler and the ruled. It was believed by many that racial consciousness was the basis of the empire. Governor-General Mayo (1869-72) directed the Lieutenant-Governor of the Punjab, 'Teach your subordinates that we are all British gentlemen engaged in the magnificent work of governing an inferior race'.[40] Even Curzon, who was willing to hang a Briton for murdering an Indian, believed that Indians as a race were inferior and incapable of speaking the truth. Racial arrogance was more openly demonstrated by Britons who were not in the government – the planters and the businessmen. During the debates in 1860 on the Arms Act the European members of the legislative council pleaded that Europeans as a class should be excluded from the operation of the Act. The ground on which they based their plea was that there could be no equality between Indians and Europeans.[41] The depth of British racial feeling was revealed in the Ilbert Bill controversy of 1883. The Bill introduced in the Legislative Council by Sir Courtenay Ilbert, law member of the Viceroy's executive council, was intended to remove racial discrimination among judges. Under the existing law Indian magistrates were debarred from trying European British subjects, though the English subordinate of an Indian magistrate could try them. Viceroy Lord Ripon (1880-4) wanted to remove this 'invidious distinction'. With but a few exceptions, the whole class of the British officers in India was against the Bill. But it was the non-official Britons who organised the opposition to the Bill. Their opposition was mainly based on the ground of racial superiority. How could an Indian be elevated to the level of an Englishman and be allowed to try a Briton? The liberal Viceroy had to give way and the Bill was modified before it was passed.

The racialists of the late nineteenth century were supported by theorists. Count Gobineau, the French nobleman, was perhaps the first to put forward a theory of race (in his work, *Essai sur l'Inégalité des Races Humaines*, published in 1853). The theory was developed further by J. C. Nott and G. R. Gliddon in *Indigenous Races of the Earth* (Philadelphia, 1857). It was maintained that racial differences were basic and natural because they were based on differences in cranial structure. The size of the brain and the shape of the head, which varied from race to race, determined intellectual capacity. In other words the physical structure determined the moral and intellectual potential. The white races, it was inferred, having the most advanced anatomical structure stood at the top of the scale and the Negro at the bottom.

These theories do not hold good today but they suited the tempo of late nineteenth-century imperialism. In the case of Indians, however, the applicability of the theory was combated. In the early part of the nineteenth century British scholars had discovered the antiquity of India – its great ancient civilisation, its rich Sanskrit literature – and concluded that, among other things, Sanskrit linked the Indians with Europeans in a common racial origin: Indians were Aryans. The findings of British scholars were a challenge to the racial-superiority feeling of the British imperialists. Sir Henry Maine, a conservative, who had been the member of the Governor-General's Council, 1862–9, came to the rescue. In his book, *Village Communities in the East and West*, he argued that though Indians belonged to the Aryan stock they were a backward section of the Indo-European community, and unlike Europeans they have not progressed from the 'status to contract'. It was, therefore, a stagnant society in which reforms should be introduced with extreme caution.

Belief, right or wrong, in his racial superiority, eased the conscience of the Briton and gave him a justification for his indefinite rule in India. In 1869 Lord Mayo asserted, 'we are determined as long as the sun shines in heaven to hold India. Our national character, our commerce, demand it.'[42] In 1883, Sir James Stephen (legal member of the Governor-General's Council, 1869–72) defined the nature of the Indian government:

It is essentially an absolute government, founded, not on consent, but on conquest. It does not represent the native principles of life or of government, and it can never do so until it represents heathenism and barbarism.[43]

To hold India indefinitely under an absolute system of government was the British policy at the turn of the century. In this context the question did not arise as to what was to happen to the empire in the future. But there had been a few individual Britons throughout the nineteenth century from Thomas Munro to Gladstone, who had asked the question. Gladstone wrote in 1883:

There is a question to be answered: Where, in a country like India, lies the ultimate power, and if it lies for the present on one side but for the future on the other, a problem has to be solved as to preparation for that future, and it may become right and needful to chasten the saucy pride so apt to grow in the English mind towards foreigners, and especially towards foreigners whose position has been subordinate.[44]

But the goal of the British connection with India was not defined until 1917 and then it was too late. By 1900 there had emerged in India forces both of nationalism and communalism, of unity as well as of disruption, and the empire without vision stood as 'an isolated rock in the middle of a tempestuous sea'.

[1] *Report of the Census of India*, 1901, p. 12.
[2] *Gazetteer of India, Indian Empire*, vol. i, p. 471.
[3] Hamilton Papers, Curzon to Hamilton, 29 Aug. 1900, vol. 17, no. 38.
[4] Ibid.
[5] Martineau, *Life of Frere* (1895), i, p. 267.
[6] S. A. Khan, *The Causes of the Indian Revolt* (1873), p. 13.
[7] 24 and 25 Vict., c. 67.
[8] Wood Papers, Wood to Frere, 18 Aug. 1861, vol. 8, pp. 200-4.
[9] India Home Proceedings, vol. 5414, pp. 2327-32.
[10] Strachey, *India* (1911), p. 360.
[11] Parl. Debates, 5 May 1868, cxci, col. 1845.
[12] Quoted in Gopal, *British Policy in India* (1965), p. 171.
[13] Hamilton Papers, vol. 17, no. 17.
[14] Ibid.
[15] *Select Documents*, Curzon's Memo. 4 June 1900, pp. 519-20.
[16] Army Report, 1859, c. 2515, xiv-xv.
[17] *Report . . . Famine Commission*, 1880, c. 6591, part 1, p. 34.
[18] Ibid.
[19] Anstey, *Economic Development of India* (1957), pp. 60-1.
[20] Ibid.
[21] *Moral and Material Progress Report*, 1881-2, p. 145.
[22] *The Pioneer*, 6/7 Sept. 1901.
[23] *Progress of Education in India*, 1902-7, vol. i, pp. 34-5.
[24] Despatches to India, vol. i, 1859-60.
[25] Home Dept. Legislative, 1866, vol. 53, pp. 267-9.
[26] Quoted in Metcalf, *Aftermath of Revolt* (1965), p. 102.
[27] Ibid.
[28] *Royal Proclamations*, 1858-1919, no. 1.
[29] Quoted in Metcalf, pp. 135-6.
[30] Ibid.
[31] Ibid., 325.
[32] Lytton Papers, Lytton to the Queen, 4 May 1876, vol. 518/1, p. 134.

[33] Quoted in Gopal, p. 107.
[34] Lytton Papers, vol. 518/2, p. 49.
[35] Dufferin Papers, Cross to Dufferin, 3 Feb. 1887, Reel 516.
[36] Quoted in Gopal, p. 153.
[37] Wood Papers, vol. 10, p. 220.
[38] Dufferin Papers, Dufferin to the editor of *Pioneer*, 1 Jan. 1887, Reel 531.
[39] Hamilton Correspondence, c. 125/3, p. 45.
[40] Quoted in Gopal, p. 121.
[41] See Proceedings (Indian Legislative Council), 1860, vi.
[42] Quoted in Gopal, p. 120.
[43] Letter to *The Times*, 1 Mar. 1883.
[44] Quoted in Gopal, p. 151.

2 The Hindu Discovery of a Nation

AT the close of Curzon's viceroyalty in 1905 there stood against the British empire a Hindu nation, represented by the Hindu middle class, conscious and proud of its ancient heritage, whose members shared common problems. But the nation had been in the making ever since the establishment of the political unity of India under the British at the close of the eighteenth century. Three factors, which had operated simultaneously and separately throughout the nineteenth century, gave birth to a nation at the turn of the century. They were (a) the discovery of the civilisation and culture of ancient India, (b) the Hindu social and religious reform movements, and (c) the formation of political (or non-religious and non-social) groups and organisations.* The social reform movements were born in reaction to Christianity and they derived their confidence from the culture and civilisation of ancient India. The political organisations were born in reaction to the British *Raj* and they derived their confidence from the social reform movements. It would be an oversimplification to state that the one led to the other – that the discovery of ancient India led to the Hindu renaissance and the latter to the national movement.

* These movements were facilitated by the growth of railways in the late nineteenth century. The middle-class reformers and agitators could travel for the first time all over India and discover the country for themselves. The discovery could sometimes be very painful, as in the case of a Tamil from ever-hot Madras arriving in the bitter cold of the Punjab winter dressed in cotton garments.

HINDU RENAISSANCE

The discovery of the 'glory that was India' was mostly the work of the British scholar-administrators. The process was set in motion by one of the most brilliant scholars of the eighteenth century, Sir William Jones (1746–94), who went to Calcutta in 1783 as a judge of the Supreme Court. This orientalist studied Sanskrit, in which the Hindu scriptures and literature of ancient India were composed, and told the world that the language was wonderful in structure, 'more perfect than the Greek, more copious than Latin, and more exquisitely refined than either'.[1] He translated into English the *Shakuntala*, the masterpiece of India's greatest Sanskrit poet, Kalidasa (A.D. 400–500) and proclaimed that Indians were linked with Europeans through Sanskrit.

Jones was followed by a host of nineteenth-century Indologists who through their translations and interpretations made known to the world India's rich classical heritage. Sir Edwin Arnold (1832–1904) translated the *Gita*, the bible of Hinduism, and Tod in his *Annals of Rajasthan* celebrated the deeds of Rajput chivalry. The most outstanding was the German Sanskritist F. Max Mueller (1823–1900), who spent most of his life at Oxford in working on Hindu religious literature. Together with the discovery of India's ancient literature went the discovery of ancient monuments. The famous Ajanta caves (2nd century B.C.– A.D. 600), which had been lost to civilisation for over twelve hundred years, were by chance discovered in 1819 by a group of British officers attached to the Madras army. Curzon created an archaeological department and scientific excavation began in India, resulting in the great discovery in 1922 by Sir John Marshall and Dr R. D. Banerji at Mohenjo Daro in Sind of the remains of a great pre-Aryan civilisation which flourished in the third millennium B.C.

The discovery of India had a two-fold effect on the Hindu

reformers, who had already begun responding to the
challenges of Christianity in India. It was reassuring to
know that India had once had a great civilisation. It was at
the same time revealing to realise that the essential
Hinduism as contained in the *Vedas*, the *Upnishads* and the
Gita was nobler and subtler, and differed from the popular
Hinduism which was practised by the masses in the
nineteenth century. It was popular Hinduism with its
thousands of gods and goddesses, the idol worship, the caste
system, the *Sati* (self-immolation of widows), the untouchability, which the Christian missionaries fiercely attacked
and the English-educated Hindus found hard to defend.
The knowledge of true Hinduism provided the reformers
with a sanction to reform popular Hinduism and a weapon
with which to fight Christianity.

The era of Hindu renaissance – starting with Rammohan
Roy (1774–1833) in the late 1820s and reaching its zenith
in the missionary works of Vivekananda (1863–1902) in the
1890s – was in essence the revolt of Hindu India against
the material, moral and intellectual superiority of Britain.
The British political, naval and military structure, their
factories, railways, telegraphs and posts, their religion, their
character (perseverance, truthfulness, courage, patriotism,
self-sacrifice), the dramas of Shakespeare, the poems of
Milton and the writings of Bacon – these had impressed the
Hindu middle classes with the superiority of the British. In
consequence they had become ashamed of their traditions,
their religion, and their language and literature, and began
imitating British culture and civilisation. Some had abandoned their religion and embraced Christianity. It had
become fashionable for a Bengali youth to profess ignorance
of his mother tongue, to deride his religion, and ridicule the
ways of his ancestors. The Hindu renaissance tried to stop
this swing towards 'anglicisation' by setting the 'glory' of
India against the 'myth' of Western superiority. It found an
easy echo in the minds of the uprooted Hindus whose

complete assimilation in British culture had been made impossible by the racial arrogance of the Britons.

The strongholds of the Hindu reform movements were Bengal and Bombay, two of the three provinces first to come under full British impact. Madras, with its 91·4 per cent Hindu population* firmly rooted in the traditional stream of life, feared no threat of Christian or Islamic encounters. Most of the leaders of the movements belonged to the Brahman caste, the first of the four hierarchical castes of Hindu society.†

The main object of the reform movements was to unite Hindu society against Christianity and Islam. The Hindus in the early nineteenth century had nothing in common except perhaps their abstention from eating beef. Their religion had split up into hundreds of sects and sub-sects each with its own image of a god or goddess. Each of the four castes had got divided into many sub-castes. Then there were linguistic and geographical divisions running across the religious and caste divisions. The reform movements attempted to achieve the religious and social unity of the Hindus by reviving a common God, a common history, and possibly a common language. The reformers went over 3000 years back in Indian history to find out from the various vedic scriptures a concept of Hindu religion which could be superior to Christianity and Islam and acceptable to all Hindus. The task was made easier for them by the intricate style of ancient Sanskrit in which the Hindu scriptures were composed, and which made them liable to different interpretations. The Muslim period of Indian history (roughly from A.D. 1100 to 1765) was ignored as an unhappy interlude, and the Hindu period (from 3500 B.C. to A.D. 1100) was acclaimed as the golden age in history, not only

---

* By 1881 census of India.

† The other three castes of Hindu society were the Khattriyas (the warriors), the Vaisyas (the traders), and the Sudras (the menials). Below the caste system were the untouchables.

of India but of the whole of mankind. Sanskrit, which had already received the testimony of Jones as superior in some ways to Greek and Latin, was hailed as the mother of all languages. But as it was no longer the language of the masses, attempts were made to cultivate its direct offsprings (Bengali, Hindi and other languages of North India) as mediums for the expression of subtle ideas and feelings. The Hindu poets, philosophers, and scientists were recovered from ancient India and set against their Western counterparts. Kalidasa, the great Sanskrit dramatist, was first hailed as the Shakespeare of India; later when the Hindu renaissance became more aggressive Shakespeare was called the Kalidasa of Britain.

The reform movements can be broadly classified into two, the revivalist and the non-revivalist. The revivalist reformers tried to restore Hinduism to its ancient purity. They claimed that true Hinduism was the best of all religions and fit to become the universal religion of the world. They expounded true Hinduism to prove that it did not sanction any of the evil customs of present Hindu society. The non-revivalists were not concerned about the true religion of the Hindus. In fact some believed that the ancient civilisation of the Hindus was not worth reviving.* They accepted Western standards and applied them in reforming the Hindu society. Thus, though the revivalists and the non-revivalists had the same end in view, the former took their inspirations from ancient India and the latter from the modern West.

The Bengali Brahman, Rammohan Roy, was the father of both the revivalist and the non-revivalist reform movements. He revived Hinduism as contained in the *Upnishads*.†

* The leading non-revivalist reformer was the Maratha Brahman, M. G. Ranade (1842–1901), who founded the Indian National Social Conference in 1887.

† Supposed to be 108 in number, the *Upnishads* are philosophical treatises composed during 900–500 B.C. They are a part of the vedic literature.

It was a religion without forms, prophets and miracles. He considered it superior to all religions of the world. In order to propagate the religion of the *Upnishads* Roy founded in 1828 the Brahmo Sabha (the Society of God) which later became Samaj. He attacked idol worship, Brahman priesthood, the caste system, and above all the practice of *Sati*,* as customs and practices which were not sanctioned by true Hinduism. At the same time Roy accepted the material superiority of the West, the modernising influences of British rule in India, and pleaded for the introduction into India of English education, English legal and political institutions, and English capital and skill.[2]

Roy's synthetic view of life, based on Indian religion and Western science, could not be maintained by his followers in the Brahmo Samaj. The Samaj stood against Christianity and attracted many young and brilliant Bengalis during the leadership of the Bengali Brahman, Debendranath Tagore (1817–1905). But when the Westernised Bengali Brahman K. C. Sen (1838–84) took over its leadership the Samaj became an Indianised version of Christianity. Sen aimed at disarming Christianity by embracing Christ as the fulfilment of India's devotional striving. To disprove the notion that the West was, and always has been, superior to the orient, he asserted the Asiatic origins of Christian civilisation.[3] But Sen was not a Christian and as a Brahmo he did not consider himself a Hindu either.† He sought solace in the cult of universal religion which Brahmo Samaj was to represent for him. The ideal of universal religion was incomprehensible to the average Hindus and unacceptable to the proud Christians. Even the Brahmos were reluctant to accept Sen's Indianised Christianity, and the Samaj was finally split up in 1878, which marked the

* *Sati* or the practice of widow-burning was finally abolished in Bengal province in 1829 during the administration of Lord William Bentinck (1828–35).

† It was at his initiative that the Native Marriage Act of 1872 was passed to legalise a Brahmo as distinct from a Hindu marriage.

downfall of both Sen and the Samaj. The Brahmo Samaj movement remained mainly confined to Bengal; even there it never caught the imagination of the masses.

It was the revivalist reformers who attempted to transform Hinduism from a passive and compromising way of life to an aggressive missionary religion. They broke the ground for the growth of Hindu nationalism. The foremost revivalist was the Gujrati Brahman, Dayanand Saraswati (1824–83), the founder of the most powerful of all nineteenth-century Hindu reform movements, the Arya Samaj (the Society of the Aryans). He rejected both the material and moral superiority of the West and endeavoured to unite the Hindus on the basis of a common religion – the vedic religion as embodied in the four *Vedas* of the Aryan Hindus,* which he upheld as the best religion, or rather the only true religion, of the world.[4] He put forward his theory of the infallibility of the *Vedas* by asserting that the fundamental principles of all sciences were revealed by God in the *Vedas*.[5] Accordingly every scientific discovery and invention of modern times must be found expressed, germinally at least, in the *Vedas*. The science of the West then, he argued, was but the realisation of the scientific programme anticipated by the seers of the East thousands of years ago.

To restore Hinduism to its vedic purity Dayanand attacked the non-vedic social and religious customs – the idol worship, polytheism, caste system and untouchability, Brahman supremacy and superfluous rituals. His was a militant religion which made no compromises. On one hand he attacked Islam and Christianity and on the other the Hindu orthodoxy, and even the Brahmo Samaj which by its over-reverence for Christianity had a denationalising influence on Hindu society.[6]

Dayanand wrote and preached in Hindi which he wanted

* Rigveda, Yajurveda, Samaveda and Atharvaveda. Rig is the earliest of the four vedas composed during 1500–900 B.C.

to be the common language of the people. He founded his Arya Samaj in Bombay presidency in 1875. But the tenets of the Samaj did not appeal to the 'emancipated rationality and scholarly sobriety of the educated groups in Bombay'.[7] Bengal was still under the influence of the Brahmo Samaj. Madras, being safe against Islam and Christianity, was not visited. Dayanand moved to the north in 1877 and founded his Samaj at Lahore in the Punjab where the Arya Samaj movement became the strongest.* There were two main reasons for its popularity among the Hindus of the Punjab. First, the Hindus formed the largest minority population in the Punjab and thus were more conscious of their identity.† The aggressiveness of Arya Samaj suited their temperament and gave them a sense of identity against the Sikhs and the Muslims. Secondly, the Hindus in the Punjab had been influenced by Sikhism and Islam and were thus more prone to accept the monotheism of Arya Samaj. Hinduism there was more flexible in creed than elsewhere; the caste system was not rigid, and powerful groups like the Jats, who were to provide a large segment of the Arya Samaj membership, were not dominated by the Brahmans.[8]

More than any other Hindu reform movement the Arya Samaj antagonised the Muslims. The *Suddhi* movements of the Samaj, which was designed for the reconversion and purification of converts to Islam and Christianity, terrified the Muslims, most of whom had been converted to Islam from Hinduism.‡ Arya Samaj also became the champion of cow-protection which frequently led to Hindu-Muslim riots. The Samaj thus became a contributory factor in the growth of Muslim separatism at the close of the last century. At the same time it fostered the rise of Hindu communalism in the

* Within a decade after Dayanand's death in 1883 the membership of the Samaj rose to 40,000. See Lajpat Rai, *The Arya Samaj* (1967).

† According to 1881 census the Muslims were 51·4 per cent of the population, the Hindus 40·7 and the Sikhs 7·6.

‡ Between 1907 and 1910 the Arya Samaj reconverted to Hinduism 1052 Muslim Rajputs. See Lajpat Rai, *The Arya Samaj*, 121.

Punjab. It did not preach openly against British rule but later in the first decade of the twentieth century it played a 'conspicuous part in the seditious agitation' against British rule.[9]

Arya Samaj and Brahmo Samaj were the only two significant reform movements in the nineteenth century. Each had a religious philosophy and a social programme. But there were also individual reformers who, though they did not belong to either of the Samajs fell broadly into one of the two categories of revivalists and non-revivalists. Then there were the conservatives who endeavoured to preserve Hindu society as it was. No sooner was a reform association established than an orthodox body was founded to oppose it. In Calcutta the Dharma Sabha was founded in 1830 to oppose Rammohan Roy's Brahmo Samaj and the abolition of *Sati*; in Bombay the Association for the Preservation of the Hindu religion (Hindu Dharma Vyayasthapaka Mandali) was founded in the 1860s to oppose the Widow Remarriage Association; in Madras the Theosophical Society* was founded in 1879 to preserve all that was Hindu; in the Punjab the Eternal Religion Society (Sanatan Dharma Sabha) was founded in 1895 to oppose the Arya Samaj. The orthodox movement reached its peak in the foundation of the Hindu Mahasabha in the first decade of the twentieth century.

These three streams of Hindu movements – revivalists, non-revivalists, conservatives – originating from the time of Rammohan Roy, united in Vivekananda at the turn of the last century. The English-educated disciple of the Bengali mystic Ramkrishna Paramahamsa (1836–86) who had been highly esteemed by the Bengali educated class as 'a symbol of their revolt against English cultural superiority',[10] Vivekananda represented Hinduism at the Parliament of Religions held in Chicago in 1893. It was there that he

* Founded first in New York in 1875 by Colonel Olcott and Madame Blavatsky.

made his mark. The *New York Herald* wrote that he 'is undoubtedly the greatest figure in the Parliament of religions. After hearing him we feel how foolish it is to send missionaries to this learned land.' He placed Hinduism on a high pedestal, preached the philosophy of Vedanta, gained converts to Hinduism in America and Britain, and returned home triumphantly.

Vivekananda was at once the antithesis and fulfilment of the Hindu renaissance. He was not an iconoclast like K. C. Sen or Dayanand. He expounded the essential Hinduism of the Vedanta. At the same time he accepted without apology some of its popular forms, image worship and caste system. Giving a rationale to image worship he asserted: 'Brothers! If you are fit to worship God without Form, discarding any external help, do so, but why do you condemn others who cannot do so.'[11] In the same breath he condemned the meaningless rituals and 'touch-me-not' religion of the conservatives. Opposed to radical social changes, he pleaded for slow reform through education. Yet he fulfilled the purpose of the Hindu renaissance. He declared that Indian spirituality was a unique force which must conquer the world. He acclaimed the religious, moral and intellectual superiority of the Hindus and opposed the social Europeanisation of the Indians: 'We must grow according to our nature. . . . If you find it impossible for the Europeans to throw off the few centuries of old culture which there is in the west, do you think it is possible for you to throw off the culture of shining scores of centuries?' He taught India self-respect and inspired his fellows to accept 'their own traditional culture, their own traditional values, their own traditional way of life'.[12] He insisted that 'the ideals of strength and freedom necessary for nationalism could be found within the Hindu tradition'.[13] He aroused emotional patriotism and called Indians to be proud of being an Indian and proudly proclaim, 'I am an Indian, every Indian is my brother'. His call fell on receptive ears.

The spell of the superiority of Western civilisation was dispelled, shame was cast off, fear conquered, factional rivalries ignored, and there was born in the minds of the middle classes the idea of a Hindu nation.

Looking back at the turn of the century one could very well ask what tangible results the half-century of social reform movements had achieved? The thousand gods of the Hindus were still alive. An Arya Samajist was still marrying his daughter within his own caste. A reformist of Bombay could be seen doing a private penance for having taken a cup of tea at the house of a beef-eater. The law prohibiting child marriage was more often defied than observed. There were young and childless widows in the villages who had never heard of the Widow Remarriage Act. The untouchables were still not touched. Interdining and intermarriage were not to be thought of. The priests were still there as intermediaries between God and man. The astrologer was still telling the villager when he should set out on his journey, which the cat round the corner could stop any moment just by crossing the road. None of these practices had been rooted out. The masses were untouched by the reform movements. And the middle-class man was a reformer only on platforms, in public meetings and processions. He discarded the role of a reformer at the doorstep of his house. Not much was achieved in concrete terms. The results of reform movements, however, lay in another direction. They had succeeded in arousing among middle-class people a common feeling of belonging to a large Hindu community and a common pride in their rich past. On these emotions were firmly laid the foundations of a nation.

EMERGENCE OF NATIONALISM

The non-revivalist reformers, the revivalist reformers including Vivekananda, and the conservatives, respectively inspired the three types of political movements – the moderate and constitutional, the extremist and terrorist, and the Hindu reactionary.

The moderates gave birth to the national movement and led it unchallenged down to 1905. They considered the British connection with India as providential, and, possessed of an ardent faith in the British sense of justice, they hoped to secure political reforms through constitutional agitation. They wanted to see India as a self-governing colony or Dominion within the Empire. Theirs was a secular national movement based on Hindu-Muslim unity. Outstanding among the moderates was Gopal Krishna Gokhale (1866–1915).

The extremists considered British rule disastrous for India. They had no faith in the British sense of justice and considered revolution as the only means of attaining complete freedom, nothing short of which they wanted for India. They derived their inspiration from the Hindu scriptures. They were not antagonistic to Muslims but theirs was essentially a Hindu nationalist movement. All terrorists were extremists but not all extremists were terrorists. The extremists became powerful around 1905. Their outstanding leader was Bal Gangadhar Tilak (1856–1920).

The Hindu reactionaries had no political programme. Their main concern was to safeguard Hindu society against the Muslims on the one hand and the Hindu secularists on the other. They were loyal to British rule. Theirs was not a nationalist movement and they lacked leadership.

The political petitioners and agitators were not also the reformers, and vice versa, though both belonged to the middle class. The Indian middle class had emerged under the British impact; the personal lives or the jobs of its members had been moulded noticeably by Western influences. The class included small landholders, businessmen, doctors, teachers, clerks, subordinate government officers, journalists, industrialists and lawyers.[14] They spoke a common language – English; they were conscious of a common heritage, and when in the later part of the century they started sharing common problems they turned into nationalist agitators. But in the beginning they were mere petitioners. They had learned in their English schools that the British at home were permitted to criticise their own rulers, therefore they started loyally petitioning the government for the redress of their grievances.

But the middle class did not enter politics until after the mutiny. In pre-mutiny days there existed only a few political associations of the landed aristocracy. The first political association was formed in Bengal in 1837 and called the Zamindary Association. As the name suggests it was founded to promote the interests of the landlords who then considered themselves the natural leaders of the society. In 1843 the Bengal British India Society was founded to advance the interests of 'all classes of our fellow subjects'. These two associations had both non-official English and Indian members. But the association of the Indians with the English based on common economic interests was wrecked on the grounds of racial differences. In 1850 when Bethune, a law member of the government of India, introduced a Bill in the legislative council to remove racial discrimination in the judicial process, the non-official English as a whole opposed the Bill. Consequently the Bill was dropped and the short-lived association of the Indians with the British came to an end. The Indian landlords then formed in 1851 the British Indian Association which had no English members. The racial rebuff sharpened their awareness of being Indians first, and the members of the new Association boldly petitioned Parliament in 1852 to improve the system of administration in India. The petitioners regretted that the British connection with India had not been profitable for Indians and demanded improvement in the judicial administration, relaxation of the pressure of the revenue system, admission of Indians to the higher administrative services, encouragement of indigenous manufactures, protection of the life and property of Indians from molestation by the British, and above all, the establishment of a representative legislative body in India, free from executive control and empowered to manage all Indian affairs except political and military which could be controlled by the Governor-General in Council.[15] The petition laid the pattern for demands which were more frequently renewed in the later part of the century by the moderates, and never granted by the government. The Association, however, ceased to represent the political ambition of the Indian people after the mutiny. It reverted to its original character and in 1859 petitioned Parliament, demanding among other things a permanent settlement of land for the whole of India which would create a class of landlords who would, as shown by the mutiny, remain loyal to the British government.[16]

The middle-class Bengali could neither afford Rs. 50 (nearly £4), the annual membership fee for the Association, nor subscribe to its policy. Sisir Kumar Ghose, the founder of the newspaper *Amrit Bazar Patrika* in 1868, and his brother Motilal Ghose, were the first Bengali agitators who attacked the landlords as vehemently as the government, the latter for having blocked the advancement of educated Indians either in the government or in the professions. Sisir Kumar Ghose demanded that the 'Indian Nation' be given a democratic, representative government, in particular a Parliament on the lines of the British Parliament. Political groups were organised in the Bengal districts and to coordinate them all, the Indian League with a Rs. 5 annual membership fee was founded in 1875.

At this stage there entered into Bengal politics Surendranath Banerjea (1848–1925). A Brahman and the son of a doctor, Banerjea had been one of the first Indians to be admitted to the Indian Civil Service in 1871. In 1874 he was dismissed from the service for his failure to correct a false report prepared in his name by a subordinate. It was too severe a punishment, for an English member of the I.C.S. would not have been dismissed for such an oversight. Banerjea appealed in vain, and failing also to be admitted to the Bar he returned to India an embittered man, convinced that 'the personal wrong done to me was an illustration of the impotency of our people' and determined to spend his life 'redressing our wrongs and protecting our rights, personal and collective'.[17] In less than three years after his dismissal he became a leader and caused a change of heart in the educated Indians 'from blind loyalty to British rule to stubborn resistance against its evils'.

Realising the need for a strong political organisation and not finding Ghose's Indian League popular with the middle class, Banerjea founded the Indian Association in 1876 with the objects of (a) creating a powerful public opinion in India towards political questions, (b) uniting the Indian people on a common political programme, and (c) promoting Hindu-Muslim unity.* The following year Banerjea started his campaigns for raising the age limit for the I.C.S. examination and for holding simultaneous examinations in London and India. He toured northern India, addressed several meetings and opened several branches of the Indian Association. He soon became an all-India figure and his name excited 'as much enthusiasm among the rising generation in Multan as in Dacca'. The Civil Service question united the Indian middle class on a common platform. The Indian Association, however, did not become an all-India organisation, 'probably because the organisational technique employed was one of spawning branch associations and linking up with already organised

* Bengal had taken the lead but Bombay and Madras had not been far behind in starting political organisations. In Bombay, the Bombay Association had been founded in 1852 and Poona Sarvajanik Sabha in 1870, in Madras the Native Association in the 1850s; the Madras Mahajana Sabha was founded in 1884. None of these associations, however, attained the importance of Banerjea's Indian Association.

bodies in other provinces; this method could not create an all-India leadership primarily loyal to the Indian Association'.

The need to form an all-India political organisation was realised during the Ilbert Bill controversy of 1883.* In order effectively to oppose the Bill the European community formed a Defence Association with branches in different parts of the country. They also raised over a lakh and fifty thousand rupees to protect 'what they conceived to be their interests, and to assert their special privileges'. Their organisation and their resources achieved success for their cause. The Indian middle class watched the struggle with interest. They realised the importance of combination and organisation. If they wanted to promote their interests they must combine into an all-India organisation. The reaction was quick. Before the year was out the first National Conference was organised by S. N. Banerjea and held in Calcutta from 28 to 30 December. 'It was', as he observed, 'the reply of educated India to the Ilbert Bill agitation, a resonant blast on their golden trumpet.'[18]

The same year, on 1 March 1883, a retired British Civilian, Allan Octavian Hume (1829–1912), son of the Radical M.P. Joseph Hume, had urged the graduates of Calcutta University to organise an association for the mental, moral, social and political progress of India.[19] While serving the Indian government, Hume had observed that there was a surging tide of intellectual, social and economic discontent in the country, and realised that this must be controlled and channelled if it was 'not to ravage and destroy but to fertilise and regenerate'.† In 1884 Hume conceived the idea 'that it would be of great advantage to

* See pp. 21–2.

† Being passed over for a young man in the Civil Service and deprived of his post as Secretary to the government in 1879, Hume got frustrated and retired from the government in 1882. However, his 'hunger for recognition and influence' forced him to stay in India and organise Congress. Anil Seal, *The Emergence of Indian Nationalism* (1968), p. 270.

the country if leading Indian politicians could be brought together once a year to discuss social matters'.[20] He did not then desire that they should discuss politics. His idea was that the Governor of the province where the politicians met should preside over them. This, he thought, would establish great cordiality between the official classes and the non-official Indian politicians. With these ideas in his mind he met the Viceroy Lord Dufferin in early 1885. The Viceroy suggested that as there was no body of persons in India who performed the functions which Her Majesty's Opposition did in England, 'it would be very desirable in the interests as well of the rulers as of the ruled that Indian politicians should meet yearly and point out to the Government in what respects the administration was defective and how it could be improved'. He further suggested that such an assembly should not be presided over by the Governor because in his presence the people might not like to speak their minds. When Hume placed the two schemes, his own and Dufferin's, before the leading politicians of the country, the latter unanimously accepted Dufferin's scheme.

Preparations began to hold the assembly in 1885, and invitations were issued to those leaders of the country who were 'well-acquainted with the English language'. The Conference was held in Bombay on 27 December and only a few days before it was held it was named the Indian National Congress. Seventy-two delegates attended the first Congress. When these gentlemen assembled 'in their morning coats, well-pressed trousers, top hats and silk turbans', they or Lord Dufferin could hardly have realised the historic role they were playing. The birth of the Congress was the beginning of an all-India movement.

For nearly twenty years the Congress movement was not opposed to the British rule. The keynote of the organisation was 'unswerving loyalty to the British Crown'. The early Congress leaders believed that 'the continued affiliation of India to Great Britain' was absolutely essential to the interests of 'our own National Development'.[21] When in his presidential speech to the Congress of 1886, the Parsi leader of the Congress, Dadabhai Naoroji (1825–1917), put the question: 'Is this Congress a nursery for sedition and rebellion against the British government?', the delegates cried 'no, no'; when, continuing, he asked, 'or is it another stone in the foundation of the stability of that Government?' the answer was 'yes, yes'.[22]

The fundamental objects of the Congress as defined by Hume in 1888 were threefold:

First: the fusion into one national whole of all the different and till recently discordant elements that constitute the population of India;

Second: the gradual regeneration along all lines, mental, moral, social and political, of the nation thus evolved; and

Third: the consolidation of the union between England and India, by securing the modification of such of its conditions as may be unjust or injurious to the latter country.[23]

Self-government was not the goal of early Congressmen. Possibly they aspired to the extension of British citizenship to all Indians. At any rate, the future of the British connection was not defined or discussed until 1905. The Congress was either timid and realistic or was under the influence of its British supporters. It demanded isolated reforms: that the legislative councils be expanded 'by the admission of a considerable proportion of elected members'; that the competitive examinations 'be held simultaneously, one in England and one in India', and 'the maximum age of candidates for entrance into the covenanted Civil Service be raised to not less than 23 years'; that there should be 'a complete separation of judicial and executive functions'; that trial by jury should be extended to those parts of India where it was not in force; and that army expenditure should be reduced and Indians be given commissions.[24] These were some of the main demands of the Congress.

The Congress was committed to achieve its objects through constitutional means, through representations to the government of India and to Parliament. The leaders of the Congress firmly believed in the British sense of justice. Parliament and Britons at home, it was thought, would introduce reforms in India when they were told that such reforms would be conducive to the welfare of the Indian people. 'Nothing is more dear', Dadabhai Naoroji assured his people, 'to the heart of England – and I speak from actual knowledge – than India's welfare; and if we only speak out loud enough, and persistently enough, to reach that busy heart, we shall not speak in vain.'[25] With this faith in the British sense of justice the Congress took steps to organise public opinion in Britain. It found active supporters in over a dozen prominent public men in Britain, including retired civil servants like Sir Henry Cotton (1845–1915), Sir William Wedderburn (1838–1918); some radicals like Keir Hardie, S. K. Ratcliff, the future Labour Prime Minister Ramsay MacDonald (1866–1937), Charles Bradlaugh, Dr V. H. Rutherford; some journalists and writers like H. W. Nevinson, William Digby (1849–1904) and Wilfred Blunt. With the active support of Bradlaugh, Wedderburn and Digby, the British Committee of the Indian National Congress was formed in July 1889 and Wedderburn was elected chairman. He retained that office until his death in 1918. A journal, *India*, was started in 1890 under Digby's editorship to provide the British public with accurate information about Indian conditions. To meet the expenses of the British Committee and *India*, Congress sent Rs. 50,000 every year to Britain from 1889 to 1900 when it was reduced to Rs. 30,000.* In twenty years after its inception the Congress had four Britons as its president – George Yule, 1888; William Wedderburn, 1889; Alfred Webb, 1894; Henry Cotton, 1904. This close

* The British Committee of the Congress ceased to function in 1920 and the publication of the journal *India* was suspended in 1921.

alliance between the Congress and the non-conservative forces in Britain was further manifested in the election in 1892 of one of the Congress leaders, Dadabhai Naoroji, to the House of Commons on the Liberal ticket. The Congress in India was financially supported by some industrialists like Tata, some Rajas of British India like that of Darbhanga, and some Indian princes like those of Baroda and Kolhapur.[26]

Politically supported by left-wingers in Britain, financed by the capitalists and the landed aristocracy in India – the middle class, loyal to the Empire, Congress movement had but few years of contentment. Even its modest demands were at cross-purposes with the 'imperial responsibilities' of the Indian bureaucracy. The Indian government reasoned that to concede any of the main demands of the Congress would endanger the continuation of the British *Raj* in India. Congress propaganda in Britain failed to stir the British Government and Parliament into defining their policy towards India. Fearing the 'effects of democracy at home on the Indian empire or those of an utterly un-English autocratic' Indian Government upon that democracy, the Indian question was 'held at an arm's length', and the Commons even feared to debate Indian issues lest India might be lost on the floor of Parliament.[27]

The Indian Civil Service remained unresponsive to the aspirations of the Congress. The non-official British community kept on expressing its racial superiority and arrogance on each occasion when the Indians demanded equality of treatment. The Viceroys simply ignored the Congress hoping that their indifference would cause its death. Lord Dufferin withdrew his blessings soon after they were given. In 1888, three years after the birth of the Congress, he was complaining that it is 'the product only of that infinitesimal section of the Indian community' which had been 'tinctured either directly or indirectly with an infusion of European education, European political ideas, and European literature'.[28] The Congress, he asserted, did not represent either the aristocratic section or the masses of Indian society. His sentiments were echoed by Lord Curzon in 1900 who believed that 'the Congress is tottering to its fall, and one of my greatest ambitions while in India is to assist it to a peaceful demise'.[29]

The Congress was not dying in 1900. There was coming forward in the Congress a group of people who did not believe either in the invulnerability of the empire or in its blessings. The failure of the Congress to attain any of its objects had made this group of men realise the futility of constitutional means. They believed that the British held India for their own benefit and therefore they would not concede anything unless forced through mass movement, direct action, revolution, even terrorism. The British imperial government, they argued, 'is not of whites and blacks, but only of white people, and it is consequently for the benefit of the whites alone'. They thus believed that nothing short of complete independence for India would be good for the Indian people. They drew their political inspirations from indigenous sources, from Indian religion, from the *Gita* and the *Vedas*, from Dayanand and Vivekananda. They accused the moderates, who still controlled the Congress, of timidity; denounced their Europeanisation and their suppliant ways. Theirs was a radical, extremist form of nationalism. They grew in strength and became a formidable challenge to both the British *Raj* and the moderate leadership in the Congress on the partition of Bengal issue in the years 1905–6.

Curzon's 'grand folly' of partitioning the largest province of Bengal for administrative convenience as well as for the political purpose of weakening Hindu Bengali nationalism had important consequences. It led to an unprecedented Hindu agitation in Bengal. The Bengali leaders were aggrieved at the division of their community, speaking the same language and sharing the same culture, into two separate provinces – West Bengal with a Hindu, and East Bengal and Assam with a Muslim majority. Perhaps the main reason for their resentment was that they were not consulted and their protestations were disregarded after the partition scheme was finalised. Even Curzon's successor, Lord Minto, who accepted the partition as a 'settled fact', admitted that 'local feeling has been treated with some want of sympathy in aiming at what in the official mind is considered necessary for administrative machinery'.[30] The partition of Bengal was turned into a national cause, and the anti-partition movement which soon started was the first movement in which the government and the Viceroy concerned were openly and bitterly attacked. A new weapon of agitation was used – the boycott of British manufactures and the use of home-made goods. The extremists took the opportunity to popularise their own tenets, and they gave a wider construction to the term boycott so as to mean total abstention from the use of anything British and from rendering any help to the British Government. Tilak, the leader of the extremist party, pointed out to his audience in 1906 that a handful of Britons could not rule India without the help of the Indians. Boycott as a political weapon would therefore mean:

We shall not give them assistance to collect revenue and keep peace. We shall not assist them in fighting beyond the frontiers or outside India with Indian blood and money. We shall not assist them in carrying on the administration of justice. We shall have our own courts, and when time comes we shall not pay taxes. Can you do that by your united efforts? If you can, you are free from tomorrow.[31]

Twenty-five thousand people listened to Tilak in Calcutta. His lieutenant records in his diary that Tilak was respected like a God.[32] The rift between the extremists and the moderates became imminent in the 1906 Calcutta session of the Congress. It was, however, saved by the election to the Congress presidency of Dadabhai Naoroji, who was respected as the Grand Old Man of India by both the moderates and the extremists. With a view to conciliating the extremists the moderate Naoroji boldly defined the goal of the Congress. It was to attain for India 'self-government or *Swaraj* like that of the United Kingdom' or the Dominions.[33] The moderates were opposed to the extremists' definition of boycott. But since they were not sure of their victory at the Calcutta session they managed to postpone to the 1907 session the passing of a formal resolution on the subject. To further conciliate the extremists Dadabhai did not call upon the Viceroy after the Congress session. Minto observed:

Naoroji much to my surprise went off home without attempting to see me. I fully expected he would ask for an interview which I would gladly have given him and I suspect his not doing so was out of regard to extremist susceptibilities.[34]

After the Calcutta Congress of December 1906 both the moderate and the extremist leaders began explaining to the people the tenets of their respective parties. The politicians in both camps knew there was going to be a fight between them for control of the Congress at its 1907 session. The moderate Gokhale, who had by then emerged as the leader of the Congress was, more than anybody else, concerned about its future. He feared that the government would brand the Congress movement as seditious and suppress it if the extremists came to control it. At the same time he was aware that, feeding on the general anti-British feeling which was then prevalent in the country, the extremists were growing in strength and power. He knew that Congress's adherence to constitutional means had hitherto yielded no results but he believed that a change-over to violence and a total boycott of the British *Raj* would be disastrous. In this dilemma his only hope was the Liberal ministry which had been formed in 1905. He earnestly hoped that the Liberals, who had been the ardent supporters of the Congress aspirations, would now introduce some political reforms, and he would be able to show to his opponents in the Congress that constitutionalism had at last borne some results. The speedy introduction of constitutional reforms, he calculated, would pacify the extremists as well as the terrorists who had increased their underground activities since the partition of Bengal. So circumstanced and so conditioned, Gokhale, in 1907 was on the one hand frantically appealing to the Liberal Secretary of State for India, John Morley (1838–1923) for the earliest introduction of political reforms in India, and on the other hand entreating his people to keep faith in 'the genius of the British people' who would deliver 'political freedom' and 'constitutional liberty'.[35] He reiterated that to attain self-government within the empire was the creed of the Congress.

Gokhale's belief in the divine providence of British rule stemmed from his excessive awareness of the inequities and inadequacies of Hindu society. None but India herself was responsible for her subordinate political condition. Through education and association with British democracy alone could India rise into a modern nation. The fact that from the beginning of his public life Gokhale had warm associations with the British partly accounted for his attitude towards them. He had visited Britain, he had many friends in Britain, and he had succeeded in becoming what he resolved in 1898 to become – a member of the Bombay Legislative Council from 1899 to 1901 and of the Imperial Legislative Council since 1901.[36] Partly because of his frail physique he was without the capacity to endure sufferings or to incur great risks in life. He lacked enthusiasm.[37] The regeneration of India was a long process. He conceived his generation working 'at a stage of the country's progress when our achievements are bound to be small, and our

c

disappointments frequent and trying', and he hoped that it will be given 'to our countrymen of future generations to serve India by their successes'.[38] He also lacked bitterness. Those who were not with him were not necessarily against him. He was an intellectual who put himself in everybody's shoes and held no strong convictions. His background and temperament qualified him to pilot the gradual evolution of a society with no jerks, stirrings or breaks. But he could not lead a revolution.

Tilak, leader of the extremist (they called themselves nationalist or new) party, was the opposite of Gokhale. Steeped more in the lore of Hinduism and proud of the Indian heritage, he viewed British rule as 'a predatory foreign incubus rather than a blessing'.[39] From the beginning of his public career he was opposed to the peaceful constitutional method of the Congress and he had been imprisoned in 1897 for inciting violence and sedition. His sufferings had endeared him to Indians and in 1907 at the age of fifty-one (ten years older than Gokhale) he was speaking to his people with more confidence and courage than his rival. He ridiculed Gokhale for hoping that the Liberals would deliver the goods. What if the Liberals were out of power next year? Was India to wait 'till there is another revival of liberalism?' After all what could a Liberal government do? Whether Liberal or Conservative, 'rest sure that they will not yield to you anything'.[40] There was only one remedy and that was not 'petitioning but boycott'. He thus asked: 'prepare your forces, organise your power, and then go to work so that they cannot refuse you what you demand'.[41]

In Tilak's ethical relativism it was the motive rather than the action itself which determined the guilt. From this it followed that a political murder with a higher motive was different from an ordinary murder. On this point he differed basically from Gokhale and the latter's political disciple Gandhi who believed that the means must be as noble as the ends. Thus Gokhale's comments on his rival's character were:

Mr. Tilak has a matchless capacity for intrigue and he is not burdened with an exacting conscience. As a result, he is often able to play for his own hand when to all appearances he is fighting for a principle only. His great talents, his simple habits, his sturdy and dauntless spirit and above all the cruel persecution which he had to bear at the hands of the government have won for him the hearts of millions in all parts of the country. And this general affection and admiration make it comparatively easy for him to play his game.[42]

The philosophers of Tilak's party were Aurobindo Ghose (1872–1950) and Bipin Chandra Pal (1858–1932). Aurobindo Ghose, only thirty-five in 1907, had in 1890 passed the written examination for the Indian Civil Service but failed in the horse-riding test. He came back to India disappointed, started his career as a teacher and by 1905 soon became a revolutionary. Thus the Bengal government felt that it was a great blunder on the part of the home authorities not to have admitted Ghose to the I.C.S.[43] Ghose appeared on the Indian political scene in 1906 like a flash and soon in 1910 retired to Pondicherry (then a French colony in India) to become a spiritualist. He criticised the moderates for accepting the Western concept of nationhood which implied a common political sentiment and an economic and territorial type of nationalism. For him the nation was a spiritual being which was to be organised not on the basis of common self-interest but on the basis of common feeling that 'we are all sons of one common mother'.* Absolute freedom was necessary for the growth of a nation.[44]

B. C. Pal, a journalist, discussed at length the impracticability of aspiring to self-government within the empire.

* It was the Bengali novelist Bankimchandra Chatterji who in his novel *The Anandmath*, published in 1882, first conceived the nation as a mother. The novel incorporated his famous poem *Bande mataram* (Mother I bow to thee) which soon became the *Marseillaise* of the nationalist movement throughout the country.

Self-government within the empire was a contradiction. There would always be a conflict between British paramountcy and Indian independence. Britain would never treat India as she did her white colonies.

The nationalists thus challenged both the creed and the method of the Congress. They proposed that Lajpat Rai (1865–1928), or Tilak should be the president of the 1907 session of the Congress. They also wanted to hold the Congress session at Nagpur where they were hopeful of influencing the session to their advantage. The moderates finally realised that the extremists could not be persuaded to subscribe to their creed and method. Hence they must be kept out of the Congress. They changed the venue of the Congress session from Nagpur to Surat where with the help of the local delegates they hoped to outmatch the extremists. They also got their own man, Dr Rash Bihari Ghose (1845–1921) nominated to the presidency.

In the last week of December 1907 extremists and moderates gathered in different camps at Surat. The battle commenced on 27 December when the Congress met. Over 1600 delegates were present. When the name of the president designate was formally proposed and then seconded the extremists raised the battle cry. 'Waving their arms, their scarves, their sticks, and umbrellas', they rose to their feet and 'shouted without a moment's pause'.[45] The sitting was suspended. Next day they met again. Tilak wanted to speak on the nomination for the president. When his request was not granted he proceeded to the platform to assert his right to speak to the delegates. He was denied this by the Chair, and while he was on the platform a shoe was thrown at him.* That 'Maratha shoe' missed Tilak and fell on Surendranath Banerjea. The supporters of Tilak

* The fact that the shoe was thrown at Tilak by a delegate belonging to the 'moderate camp', and not at the moderate Chairman by an extremist is established in Jayakar, *The Story of my Life* (1958), vol. i, p. 82, and also in the diary of Khaparde.

then became violent and started 'striking at any head that looked to them moderate'. The Congress was suspended *sine die*. It met again, however, in December 1908, but without the extremists. They had been excluded.

The partition of Bengal led, on the one hand, to the split in the Congress and on the other to the growth of Muslim separatism. Terrorism and Hindu communalism grew in the same period but with a different motivation.

[1] *The Works of Sir William Jones* (1807), iii, p. 34.
[2] Ram Mohan Roy, *English Works* (1906), 2, pp. 113-16.
[3] *Sen's Lectures in India*, pp. 33-4.
[4] Lajpat Rai, *The Arya Samaj* (1967), p. 70.
[5] *Encyclopaedia of Religion and Ethics*, 2, p. 59.
[6] Dayanand, *Satyartha Prakash* (1915), ch. ii.
[7] Heimsath, *Indian Nationalism* (1964), p. 125.
[8] Ibid., p. 126.
[9] V. Chirol, *Indian Unrest* (1910), pp. 111-12.
[10] Andrews and Mookerjee, *Congress* (1967), p. 17.
[11] *The Complete Works of Vivekanand* (1922), iii, p. 460.
[12] *Vivekanand Centenary Volume* (1963), p. 523.
[13] Dalton, D. G., 'The idea of freedom in the political thought of Vivekanand, Aurobindo, Gandhi and Tagore', p. 99 (unpublished London University Ph.D. thesis).
[14] See Misra, *The Indian Middle Classes* (1961), pp. 12-13.
[15] Andrews and Mookerjee, p. 58.
[16] *Select Documents*, pp. 101-2.
[17] Banerjea, *A Nation in the Making* (1925), p. 33.
[18] Ibid., pp. 85-6.
[19] Wedderburn, *Allan Octavian Hume* (1913), p. 66.
[20] *Select Documents*, pp. 138-9.
[21] Wedderburn, p. 53.
[22] *Report of the 2nd Indian National Congress* (1886), p. 53.
[23] *Select Documents*, p. 141.
[24] Ibid., pp. 151-2.
[25] *Speeches and Writings of Dadabhai Naoroji* (1910), p. 18.
[26] Gokhale Papers, file 442, Ranade to Gokhale, 25 Jan. 1897; Hamilton Papers, D/570/2, vol. 14, p. 63-7.
[27] John Seeley, *The Expansion of England* (1883), pp. 190, 304.
[28] *Select Documents*, p. 145.
[29] Ibid., p. 151.

[30] Morley Papers, vol. i, Minto to Morley, 13 Dec. 1905.

[31] T. de Bary, *Sources of Indian Tradition* (1958), p. 722.

[32] Khaparde, Diary, 1906.

[33] Sitaramayya, *The History of the Congress* (1946), i, p. 54.

[34] Morley Papers, vol. v. Minto to Morley, 16 Jan. 1907.

[35] *Select Documents*, p. 163.

[36] Gokhale Papers, File 203, part i, Gokhale's Resolution, 5 Feb. 1898.

[37] W. Blunt, *My Diaries 1900–14* (1920), part ii, pp. 219–21.

[38] *Speeches of Gokhale*, p. 957.

[39] Wolpert, *Tilak and Gokhale* (1962), p. 297.

[40] *Select Documents*, p. 161.

[41] Ibid., p. 162.

[42] Gokhale Papers, file 203, Gokhale to Natesan, 2 Oct. 1906.

[43] Das, *India under Morley and Minto* (1964), p. 114.

[44] A. Ghose, *The Doctrine of Passive Resistance*, pp. 69–70.

[45] Nevinson, *The New Spirit in India* (1908), pp. 247–58. Nevinson, the correspondent of the *Manchester Guardian*, was present at the Congress session of 1907.

3 The Growth of Muslim Separatism

BIRTH OF THE MUSLIM LEAGUE:

By the beginning of the nineteenth century political consciousness had filtered down to the middle stratum of Hindu society, but it was still confined to the upper class of the Muslim community. Thus the early conflicts between Hindu and Muslim interests were essentially the conflicts of classes; the Muslim aristocrat distrusted the Hindu as much as he did the Muslim *Babu*. When the Muslim middle class entered politics its nature and course had already been determined by the higher class. It was conservative, communal, and loyal to the foreign government. Liberal and nationalist Muslims, not satisfied with the framework of Muslim politics, had to join either Congress or the terrorists.

The reasons for the late growth of the Muslim middle class were various. At the advent of British rule the bulk of the Muslim community was economically backward. Of the total population, the ancestors of only ten per cent had come from outside India; the rest had been converted to Islam mostly from the lowest strata of Hindu society. Poor they were before and poor they remained after their conversion to Islam. The richer section of the community had monopolised the military, executive and judicial offices under the Muslim governments and held rent-free lands. Trade, commerce, industry and agriculture were carried by the Hindu bourgeoisie. With the growth of British administration in India the Muslims were gradually replaced by the British in the higher and by English-speaking Hindus in the subordinate services of the government.

Starting with a crippling handicap the Muslims, due to their religious conservatism, political jealousy and cultural backwardness, unlike the Hindus, were slow at taking to British ways by accepting English education and all that it promised. For example, in Bengal, the first province to come under full British impact, the Muslims, most of whom were poor peasants and weavers, stood aloof and let the Hindus reap the fruits of their new learning. By the middle of the nineteenth century, the Muslims, who formed one-third of the population of Bengal, occupied a few minor posts in the government, and a very few had entered the new professions.[1] Between 1852 and 1868 there were no Muslim covenanted officers or High Court judges, and in all the government-gazetted appointments of the province, the Muslims filled 92 places out of 1338. Of 240 Indian pleaders admitted to the Calcutta Bar during the same period only one was a Muslim.

The areas where the Muslims had established themselves as the upper class – the North-Western Provinces, the Punjab, Hyderabad – were the areas 'least or last affected' by the British system. When some of these areas came under British rule, the Muslim upper class took to British ways as readily as the Hindus. For example, in 1850 the Muslims in the North-Western Provinces held 72 per cent of the judicial positions open to Indians, including almost all the senior posts of the *Sadr Amin*, although they comprised only 12 per cent of the population of the province.[2] Throughout the country, however, the balance numerically was in favour of the Hindus because the areas under the dominance of the Muslim upper class were few and far between.

The government's attitude towards the Muslims, initially jealous and later hostile on account of the Wahhabi movement and the mutiny of 1857, was partly responsible for the slow growth of the Muslim middle class. The Wahhabi movement, named after its founder Ibn Abd al-Wahhab (1703–87), began in eighteenth-century Arabia with a view to restoring Islam to its original purity and order. In India the movement was started by Sayyid Ahmad Barelawi (1782–1831) and it was at once religious and political. The Wahhabis in India wanted to purge Islam of all its accretions, corruptions and superstitions which they thought were mostly borrowings from Hinduism. Their preachings made the Muslims in India more conscious of their separateness from the Hindus. Politically the Wahhabis preached Holy War against the infidel governments – the Sikhs in the Punjab and the British in Bengal. The movement lingered on till the 1870s, long after the death of Sayyid Ahmad, and the Wahhabis organised various rebellions and a network of conspiracies against the British government, culminating in the murder of the Viceroy Lord Mayo in 1871 by a Wahhabi convict in the Andaman Islands.

It was, however, the mutiny which further inflamed matters. The government became decidedly hostile to the Muslims after 1857 and repressed the Muslim upper class which had attempted to revive the Mughal empire. All over the North-Western Provinces 'a Mohammedan was another word for a rebel'. The Muslims were not to be educated and were to be kept out of the administration and out of the medical, legal and other professions.[3] This anti-Muslim policy was pursued for over a decade after the mutiny, at a time when the Hindu middle classes were developing, and beginning to wield some power.

Repression of the Muslims came to a halt in the 1870s. This change in government policy was brought about mainly by two people – a British official W. W. Hunter and an upper-class Muslim Syed Ahmad Khan (1817–98). Hunter published in 1871 his important book – *Indian Mussalmans*. In this he showed that whereas the Wahhabi movement had aroused anti-British feeling among the lower classes of the Muslims, the anti-Muslim policy of the government had alienated the upper classes. Thus the whole of the Muslim community was simmering with anti-British feeling, and a dangerous situation had been created. He criticised the 'government's past policy as inexpedient' and pleaded for a more lenient attitude. The government, he pointed out, could win over an influential section of the community to loyalty, by establishing for them educational facilities.

In 1873 Syed Ahmad Khan's work, *The Causes of the Indian Revolt*, which had been published in Urdu fifteen years earlier, was translated into English by two British officials and republished. In this work Khan had tried to exonerate the Muslims and show the real causes of the mutiny – the lack of understanding between ruler and ruled. The organisation of the army, he held, had also been responsible for the uprising. The British had failed to use Hindu-Muslim differences to ensure the loyalty of the army. They had put them together in the same regiment with the result that in course of time the differences had got smoothed away and they had come to consider themselves as one body. Hunter and Khan influenced the government, and before long 'British favour for well-to-do Muslims was a recognised Indian institution'. Khan succeeded not only in 'weaning the government from its policy of suppression to one of paternalism' but also in weaning the Muslim community from its policy of opposition to the government, 'to one of acquiescence and participation'. To secure the absolute loyalty of the Muslims towards the British he worked to separate them from the agitating Hindu middle class. Khan was thus the originator of both Muslim revival and Muslim separatism.

Born in an aristocratic family, Syed Ahmad Khan came in contact with the British at the age of twenty-four when he entered the service of the East India Company. The mutiny occurred when he was in British service. He thus opposed the mutiny, but he found himself in a distressing situation afterwards. From the conflict between his personal liking for British rule and the anti-Muslim policy of the government arose the urge in him to work for a *rapproche-ment* between the British and the Muslims. He devoted the decade after the mutiny to this task. His visit to England in 1869 profoundly influenced his subsequent public life. He was over-impressed by the upper-class British culture with which alone he came in contact during his brief stay, and wrote home generalising:

I can truly say that the natives of India, high and low, merchants and petty shopkeepers, educated and illiterate, when contrasted with the English in education, manners and uprightness, are as like them as a dirty animal is to an able and upright man. The English have every reason to believe us in India to be imbecile brutes.[4]

He was received in England by nobility and high officials and decorated by the Crown. This strengthened his loyalty to the British and at the same time aroused in him a class consciousness. He returned home in 1870 with a deter-mination and an antipathy; determination to persuade his co-religionists to be loyal to the *Raj* and to accept English education and British ways, and antipathy towards the 'people of low rank'.

Syed Ahmad had realised that the greatest objections which his co-religionists had to sending their boys to government colleges were 'the absence of Islamic education in these colleges and the danger that the boys' faith might be corrupted in them'. He had further realised that Muslims could not get into the government service or professions without an English education. He therefore founded at Aligarh in 1875 the Mohammedan Anglo-Oriental College, which subsequently grew into Aligarh University. In this college the students were to be given an English education but they were also to learn Arabic and receive religious instruction as compulsory subjects.[5] The college was soon patronised by the Nizam of Hyderabad and the Amir of Afghanistan, and visited from time to time by the Viceroy and the Governor of the province. It was successful in producing not only Muslim candidates for the government services, but Muslim political leaders. It became the centre of what is called the Aligarh Muslim movement – culturally progressive and politically conservative.

What Hume, Wedderburn and Cotton were to Congress, Theodore Beck, T. Morrison and W. A. J. Archbold, the first three British principals of Aligarh College, were to the Aligarh Muslim movement. Beck, the first principal of the college and Syed Ahmad's loyal adviser, calculated that it would be in the best interests of both the British *Raj* and the Muslims if the latter separated themselves completely from the Hindu middle-class political movements, especially the Congress, and remained loyal to the British. Syed Ahmad was led to realise that in a country where the Hindus were in the majority and educationally far ahead of the Muslims, the holding of competitive examinations for admission into the I.C.S. and the introduction of representative institutions would virtually mean the establishment of a Hindu *Raj*. From this it followed that the Muslims must not join the Congress and should oppose the introduction of democratic institutions in India.

Badruddin Tyabji (1844–1906), a middle-class Muslim who later, in 1896, became a judge of the Bombay High Court, was in 1887 elected President of the Indian National Congress. His election was held to show that the Congress was a secular movement representing all Indians irrespective of religion. It was also hoped that his election would encourage the Muslims to join Congress in large numbers. In essence it was a challenge to Syed Ahmad, Beck and the Aligarh school. Syed Ahmad reacted and wrote to Tyabji on 24 January 1888:

The fact that you took a leading part in the Congress at Madras has pleased our Hindu fellow subjects no doubt, but as to ourselves it has grieved us much.

I do not understand what the words 'national Congress' mean. Is it supposed that the different castes and creeds living in India belong to one nation, or can become a nation, and their aims and aspirations be one and the same? I think it is quite impossible and when it is impossible there can be no such thing as a national Congress, nor can it be of equal benefit to all peoples. . . . I object to every Congress in any shape or form whatever – which regards India as one nation on account of its being based on wrong principles, viz., that it regards the whole of India as one nation.[6]

Syed Ahmad projected at the Congress his theory of two nations, that the Muslims and Hindus formed two different nations, that they could not 'sit on the same throne and remain equal in power'.[7] The extension of representative government in India, he argued, would result in Congress rule which would virtually mean the rule of the Hindu middle class – the Bengali *Babu*. 'Men of good family', he asserted, 'would never like to trust their lives and property to people of low rank, with whose humble origins they are well acquainted'.[8]

Beck raised the alarm. Writing to Tyabji on 7 May 1888, he warned that if the Congress went on propagating the doctrine that the poverty of the Indian people was due to British rule, the poor, proud and fanatical Muslims of the North-Western Provinces and the Punjab would rise in revolt against the government and the results would be disastrous for the Muslims, whose well-being really depended on their loyal co-operation with the British.[9]

Tyabji held his ground for some time. Admitting that India was not one nation, he pointed out to Syed Ahmad that there were some problems which were common to all communities, and Congress should deal only with those problems. Muslims, he suggested, should act from within rather than from without the Congress.[10] But soon Tyabji began to stagger under Anglo-Muslim pressure and he suggested to Hume on 27 October 1888 that, in view of the opposition to it from the Nizam and other principal men of the Muslim community, the Congress should be prorogued

for five years and then if it was not supported by the
Muslims it should be abolished.[11] Hume, however, pulled
him up by pointing out that over one million middle-class
Muslims were with the Congress and not more than one
hundred thousand really 'opposed to us'.[12]

Failing to separate the entire Muslim community from
the Congress, Syed Ahmad and Beck formed in August
1888 the United Indian Patriotic Association whose
membership was open to members of both Hindu and
Muslim upper classes – Muslim Nawabs and Hindu Rajas.
This upper-class organisation was established in opposition
to the middle-class Congress and its main objects were to
inform Parliament and the British people of the opinions of
Muslims and those Hindus who were opposed to the
Congress, and 'to strive to preserve peace in India and to
strengthen British rule'. Hindu and Muslim aristocrats
supported the Association and in certain parts of the
country resolutions were passed to express loyalty to the
British government and opposition to the Congress. But
Beck wanted to go further and separate the Muslims
completely from the Hindus. Thus with Syed's support he
founded in 1893 the Mohammedan Anglo-Oriental
Defence Association of Upper India, the membership of
which was confined to Muslims and Britons. The main
object of the Association was to prevent political agitation
from spreading among the Muslims. A branch of the
Association was started in London, and Beck told the
English people in 1895 that friendship between the British
and the Muslims was possible but not between the Muslims
and the Hindus; that the Muslims would never accept a
government 'in which the Hindu majority would rule over
them'; and that Indians did not like a democratic system,
they preferred monarchy. Until his death in 1899 Beck
worked incessantly to stimulate Muslim separatism and the
circumstances were favourable to him. It was the time when
Tilak had revived the Hindu religious festivals (Sivaji and

Ganpati) in Bombay for political purposes, when the
anti-Muslim Arya Samaj movement was extending from
the Punjab to the North-Western Provinces, when the cow
protection movement was getting stronger in Bombay and
the north, and when the British government, in order to
counteract the Congress movement, was well disposed to
follow the old Roman policy of *divide et impera*.

An additional support to the Muslim revival was given
by the barrister Ameer Ali (1849–1928), who belonged to
an aristocratic Muslim family of Bengal. He had founded
in 1878 the Central National Mohammedan Association
with the objects of promoting the loyalty of the Muslims
towards the government and their political regeneration.
Ameer Ali travelled far and wide and opened several
branches of his association in India. His Association
supported the Congress in 1885 but seceded from it in the
following year. Ameer Ali, however, was not openly hostile
to the Congress. In fact the Bengali Muslims, as compared
to the north Indian Muslims, were less communal. This
might have been due to their closer cultural affinity with
the Bengali Hindus, and also because militant Hindu
religious movements like Arya Samaj did not spread to
Bengal. But communal harmony was broken when the
province was partitioned on 16 October 1905.

Two factors were mainly responsible. The first was the
use of Hindu religious symbols and slogans by the anti-
partitionists, who were mostly Hindus. This gave a
somewhat religious colouring to the movement and in effect
aroused the antipathy of the Muslims towards it.[13] The
second factor was the pro-Muslim policy of the government
which prompted the officials to arouse Muslim hostility and
opposition to the anti-partition movement. Sir Bampfylde
Fuller (1854–1935), who was appointed in 1905 the
lieutenant-governor of the new province, was instrumental
in shaping the policy of the government. In November 1905
he assured the Viceroy, Lord Minto, that the Muslims of

the new province favoured partition 'and are losing no opportunity of showing their respect for the new government'.[14] The Viceroy was disturbed by the anti-partition movement and the Congress agitation, and he was willing to consider devices which might counteract the nationalist movement. But the Viceroy was cautious; his lieutenant-governor was not. Fuller openly pursued a pro-Muslim and anti-Hindu policy. He tried to win over the Muslims by appointing them into the government services and helping them enter trade and commerce. He played off 'the two sections of the population against each other' and aroused animosity between the two communities.[15] With a religious zeal he opposed the agitation against partition. Orders were issued banning meetings and processions and the schools, which could not stop their students participating in the anti-partition agitation, were closed. The Secretary of State for India and the Viceroy were not prepared to give a public impression that the government was patronising the Muslims against the Hindus. Fuller resigned in August 1906 and the Viceroy accepted his resignation with great relief. Fuller's fall was taken by both the Muslims and the officials as a victory for the Hindus. To the pleasant surprise of the Viceroy, the Muslims sent to him messages of sympathy for Fuller. Minto at once informed Morley that this strong Muslim feeling for Fuller was going to be 'useful to us'. He commented: 'It shows, at any rate that there are two sides to the question of "Partition", and though the Mohammedan population is slow to move, it is quite evident that any reconsideration of "Partition" would raise a dangerous Mohammedan storm.'[16] L. Hare, Fuller's successor, assured the Viceroy that the Muslims would combine to a man against the boycott and the anti-partition movement.[17] Having won over the Muslims to their side the government realised the necessity of continued assistance to them in order to counteract the 'one-sided agitation'. Minto advised Hare to move with caution and 'instead of publicly calling upon the Moslems to accept services, offer them without publicity'. Minto was pleased to find 'the first confirmation of his theory that revolutionary ideas would subside with the rise of communal disturbances'.[18] He had carefully studied the separatism of the Aligarh school and he was willingly converted to the idea that the people of the Indian empire did not form one nationality and therefore it would be risky to introduce into India popular representation on any large scale.[19]

In his analysis of the Bengal situation – the anti-partition movement resulting in communal riots – Gokhale, the Congress leader, put the blame on all three parties – the Hindus, the Muslims and the officials.[20] The officials who had been bitterly attacked by the Hindu press, sometimes unfairly, became decidedly anti-Hindu after the humiliation they suffered by Fuller's downfall. By committing Morley to the statement in Parliament 'that boycott was the cause of these Hindu-Mohammedan disturbances in East Bengal', the officials armed themselves with new power to repress all preaching of boycott on the ground that it led to breaches of the peace. They suppressed whatever appeared to them as a Hindu agitation and ignored, sometimes encouraged, the 'Muslim rowdies' to preach even 'a holy war against the Hindus'. The anti-Hindu attitude of the officials provoked the Hindus to preach more aggressively the theory of boycott and complete independence for India. They quite wrongly assumed that the Muslims were with them. Partly on religious grounds, partly on economic (the boycott of Liverpool salt had adversely affected poor Muslims) and mainly on account of the pro-Muslim policy of the government, the majority of Muslims were against the anti-partition agitation. Reporting to Gokhale from a village in East Bengal on 27 January 1907, Srinivasa Sastri wrote that the Muslims on the whole, except a few educated ones and the weavers, were against the boycott movement. Among them the anti-Swadeshi feeling was universal. This opposition to the country's cause, Sastri pointed out, was 'the work of a band of *Maulavis* paid by the Nawab of Dacca and helped by the police'.[21]

The Anglo-Muslim *rapprochement* arrived at in the crucial years 1905–6 led to the birth of the Muslim League in December 1906. In August of that year Morley told the House of Commons that he was contemplating the introduction of constitutional reforms in India on the lines desired by the Congress, admitting at the same time – 'I do not say that I agree with all that the Congress desires'. The conservative Muslims of the Aligarh school reacted almost immediately. What would happen to the Muslim interest if Morley introduced representative institutions as demanded by the Congress? On 4 August 1906, Nawab Mehdi Ali Khan (better known as Mohsin-ul-Mulk), the secretary of Aligarh College, wrote a letter to the principal of the college, W. A. J. Archbold, who was then staying at Simla, asking him to consider whether 'it would be advisable to submit a memorial from the Mohammedans to the Viceroy, and to request His Excellency's permission for a deputation to wait on His Excellency to submit the views of Mohammedans on the matter'.[22] Minto was in Simla with his private secretary Dunlop Smith. As Minto had already formulated his policy towards the Muslims, it took no persuasion on the part of Smith and Archbold to secure his willingness to receive the deputation. Mohsin-ul-Mulk's letter was on the Viceroy's table four days after it was written, and Minto writing to Morley on 8 August subtly warned him not to ignore the apprehension of the Muslims that their interests 'may be neglected in dealing with any increase of representation on the Legislative Councils'.[23] The period between 8 August and 30 September was spent by Archbold, Smith and Minto in deciding the composition of the Muslim deputation, the form and contents of their address, and the contents of the Viceroy's reply to the deputation, and on all these matters the advice of Hare from East Bengal was sought and obtained. The deputation of thirty-five, led by the Aga Khan, presented their address to the Viceroy on 1 October 1906. In the address the deputation demanded that if representative institutions were extended to India the government should take into account the 'political importance' of the Muslim community and 'the value of the contribution which they make to the empire', and accordingly safeguard their interests in the municipal and local boards and provincial and imperial legislative councils.[24] In his most sympathetic reply to the address Minto assured them that he was in complete agreement with the views of the deputation.[25]

The Viceroy was quite anxious to know the reaction of the Hindu Bengalis to the Muslim move. The nationalist newspaper *Amrita Bazar Patrika* commented on 4 October:

The whole thing appears to be a got-up affair and fully engineered by interested officials. . . . So the all-India Mohammedan Deputation is neither all-India, nor all-Mohammedan, nor even a Deputation, properly so called. It is only an instrument in the hands of the officials to whitewash their doings.[26]

Strengthened in his stand by Muslim separatism the Viceroy advised Morley that 'India is quite unfit for popular representation in our sense of the word'.[27] Morley congratulated Minto on his success and added that the Muslim deputation could be used to derange the plans and tactics of the pro-Congress Liberals and Radicals in Parliament.[28]

Encouraged by the patronage received from the government, the leading members of the Muslim deputation assembled at Dacca in Eastern Bengal on 30 December 1906 and formed a political association styled the All-India Muslim League. The League was set up with the objects of promoting among the Muslims of India feelings of loyalty to the British government and of protecting and advancing the political rights and interests of the Muslims.[29] At the same meeting the newly-born League passed a resolution supporting the partition of Bengal and condemning the boycott movement.[30]

The emergence of Muslim politics 'made Minto master of the situation'.[31] He could now convince the Liberal Secretary of State for India that the Indian unrest was predominantly Hindu and, therefore, one-sided. There were now two parties to reckon with, the Hindus and the Muslims, and their demands and aspirations were different from each other.

Minto's policy had a determining influence on the constitutional reforms which were finally introduced in 1909. But its immediate results were the intensification of terrorist activities and the rise of the orthodox Hindu party.

GROWTH OF TERRORISM

Hatred born of helplessness breeds violence. The loyal constitutional methods of the Congress had yielded no results and the organisation itself had been slighted and ignored by Curzon. Showing utter indifference to the sentiments of the Hindu Bengalis the government had partitioned Bengal. And to counteract the anti-partition movement and boycott, Minto had succeeded in winning over the upper-class Muslims to his side. In this state of helplessness the thought of violence came easily to the young men of India. In adopting violent methods of revolution the terrorists were following European examples, particularly those of Russia and Ireland. The defeat of Russia in 1904 by Japan had freed their minds from the spell of European invincibility. They derived justification for their acts from the writings and speeches of the leaders of the extremist party in the Congress. Tilak had differentiated political from ordinary murder. Murder committed and punishment suffered for the sake of the motherland were noble deeds to be proud of. The Hindu Bengali novelist Bankimchandra Chatterji had created the mother-image of India. The Mother was in chains. Her sons must suffer and sacrifice to set her free. Thus inspired by religious emotionalism and initiated in Western revolutionary methods, the terrorists soon became a menace to the British Raj.

Starting in the plague year of 1897 with the murder of two British officers, Rand and Ayerst, in Bombay and animated by the anti-partition and boycott movements in 1905–6, the wave of violence turned into a terrorist movement in 1907. The fiftieth anniversary of the mutiny was to fall on 10 May 1907. The British were apprehensive and tense. Early in the year there had grown up among the cultivators of the Punjab a strong resentment against the government over the Punjab Colonisation Bill. The Bill was intended to stop further fragmentation of land in the Chenab colony by providing for inheritance by primogeniture. The inhabitants of the colony – mostly ex-soldiers who had been given lands in this irrigated area for their services – considered the government's measure as an unjustified interference in their old customs. Protest meetings were addressed by the Punjabi leaders Lajpat Rai and Ajit Singh. Unrest followed. In April the chief court of the Punjab upheld the conviction and sentence that had been passed on the editor of the weekly *Punjabee* a year before for publishing seditious articles. The provincial government reported that the terrorists were causing disaffection in the Indian army by urging the Punjabi soldiers to rise against the British and make up for what they had not done in 1857. The provincial government 'in order to make an impressive show of force before 10 May struck at Lajpat Rai because he was the most prominent political worker in the province'.[32] Lajpat Rai and Ajit Singh were deported to Mandalay in Burma.

It was Bengal where the terrorists worked according to a system. Terrorist *Samities* (Societies) were organised, literature on the manufacture of explosives was smuggled in from foreign countries and the members were trained, disciplined and drilled in secrecy. In December 1907 an attempt was made on the life of Sir Andrew Fraser, Lieutenant-Governor of Bengal. He escaped. He escaped again when a second attempt was made a year later. The district officers and prosecution witnesses directly or indirectly connected with the discovery of a conspiracy or the conviction of a conspirator, were terrorised. B. C. Allen, the district magistrate of Dacca, was killed in December 1907. A bomb intended to kill D. H. Kingsford, who as chief presidency magistrate had tried cases against revolutionary Bengali newspapers, *Yugantar*, *Bande Mataram*, *Sandhya* and *Nabaski*, by mistake fell on the wrong railway carriage at Muzzafarpur on 30 April 1908, and killed two innocent European ladies, Mrs and Miss Kennedy. Soon the government discovered a widespread conspiracy in Bengal. Bombs, dynamite and cartridges were found in a suburb of Calcutta. Aurobindo Ghose, the extremist, and his brother were suspected of being ringleaders but due to lack of evidence Aurobindo could not be convicted. Nandalal Banerjee, a police inspector, who had caught one of the two terrorists involved in the Muzzafarpur bomb case, was shot dead in November 1908. In the same month an attempt was made on the life of the Viceroy from which he very narrowly escaped.

In these years the Indian revolutionaries were also trying to establish bases outside India, in London, in New York, in Paris. Shyamaji Krishnavarma (1857–1930), having had a good education in India and England, had finally established himself in London and started in 1905 a monthly, *Indian Sociologist*, which preached violent revolution against the government with a view to attaining complete freedom. With the same object in view he had in 1905 started the Indian Home Rule Society in Highgate, London. Some of the future revolutionaries including V. D. Savarkar (1883–1966) were then being trained in London.

Revolution was followed by repression. In Minto's

analysis the free press was mainly responsible for inflaming sedition in India. Starting with the prosecution of the seditious vernacular newspapers in 1906 the government kept on tightening the restrictions through the years, culminating in the passing of the Indian Press Act of 1910. Deportation without trial was frequently resorted to, sometimes unjustly as in the case of Lajpat Rai. Public meetings in northern India were restricted by the Regulation of Meetings Ordinance of May 1907. Severe restrictions on the use of explosives were imposed by the Indian Explosive Substances Act of June 1908. And finally Tilak, the 'father of Indian unrest', was arrested in June, and tried and sentenced in July 1908 to six years' imprisonment for publishing in his *Kesari* articles containing inflammatory and seditious comments on the Muzzafarpur murders. Minto was not concerned as to whether Tilak's conviction was right or wrong or the punishment too severe. He thought that his conviction would have a 'beneficial effect' on the situation.[33] And to soothe the conscience of the Liberal Morley, who was about to introduce reforms in India, Minto wrote:

As to the repressive legislation. It is all-important that it should precede your announcement of reforms . . . we must give the medicine first, and then do all we can to take the taste away. If we were to follow up your announcement with stiff legislation and deportation we should make a fatal mistake.[34]

The prospect of reforms, the birth of the Muslim League and the recognition by the government of communal interest, the rise of terrorism – these encouraged some Hindu Rajas* to come forward and register their loyalty to the government and in turn be recognised as a body of persons representing the orthodox Hindu community.[35]

The Hindu orthodoxy did not succeed in creating a

* The Maharajas of Banaras and Darbhanga were the main sponsors of this movement.

central association for all India. In the Punjab, however, there was formed in 1907 the Punjab Provincial Hindu Sabha which in later years grew into the all-India Hindu Mahasabha. Writing to Wedderburn in September 1909 on the political situation in India, Gokhale rightly observed:

The situation is further complicated by the fierce antagonism between Hindus and Mohammedans that has been rekindled by the open partiality which the Hindus generally believe, has been shown by the Government to the Mohammedans in working out the details of the Reform Scheme. This antagonism has already led in upper India to a movement for the formation of a Hindu League and the Punjab where the relations between the two creeds are the worst is taking the lead in the matter. The movement is frankly anti-Mohammedan, as the Moslem League is frankly anti-Hindu, and both are anti-national.[36]

But the main impetus to the growth of communal and class organisations, as against the secular national movement of the Congress, was given by the Morley-Minto Reforms of 1909.

THE SEPARATE ELECTORATE:

The Reforms of 1909 were the joint work of Minto and Morley. The two differed widely in their politics and outlook. The Conservative Viceroy Minto, while recognising that a new spirit swept over India, endeavoured to counteract it by 'encouraging the more conservative and loyal elements in Indian society'. He considered the national movement of the Congress to be disloyal and subversive and set against it the forces of communalism. Believing that India was conquered by sword and could be retained only by the sword, he believed more in repression than in conciliation. The Liberal Secretary of State for India, John Morley, was in his seventies when he took office. He was cautious and timid. Though he was conscious that it was Indian bureaucracy and not English democracy which was 'the real menace to the empire', he himself fell under the pressure of bureaucracy. He believed that if the reforms did not save the Raj 'nothing else will'. But the reforms he could manage to introduce in India lacked vision; they were a 'series of expedients' to meet the particular situation. They bore the stamp of Minto more than of Morley. However, both men were convinced that the welfare of India depended on the permanence of British administration, that in the foreseeable future the Indian government was to remain autocratic, and that the representative form of government was unsuited to India. Morley asserted in Parliament that to give universal suffrage to India and to treat her 'on the same footing as our self-governing colonies like Canada', was a 'fantastic and ludicrous dream'.[37]

It was on Morley that the moderates in the Congress, Gokhale in particular, had pinned their hopes.[38] In order to influence him and to put before him the Congress's points of view Gokhale visited London in 1905, 1906 and again in 1908. Writing from London in May, 1908, he observed:

Whatever the shortcomings of the bureaucracy and however intolerable at times the insolence of individual Englishmen, they alone stand today in the country for order and without continued order, no real progress is possible for our people.[39]

Placed between the officials and the extremists and trusted by neither, Gokhale and his colleagues were losing the 'necessary public spirit and energy of character, to hold together effectively for long'.[40]

Talks on reforms were first started by Morley in June 1906. Minto begged Morley to let the initiative rest with him lest the Indians should think the reforms were the outcome of pressure from London. Morley agreed. The reforms were discussed in 1906; some, which needed no parliamentary enactment, were implemented in 1907; the remainder were finally announced by Morley in December 1908, and nearly a year after in November 1909 enacted as the Indian Councils Act. There were two main features of the Morley-Minto reforms: first, the admission of two Indians to the Council of the Secretary of State in London and one Indian each to the Executive Councils of the Governor-General and the Governors; and second, the expansion of the legislative councils.

The Congress had for long demanded the appointment of Indians to the Executive Councils. For the first time Morley conceded the demand in principle. But there was opposition from all sides. Minto and his Executive Council, all but one of the provincial Governors and councillors, the non-official Europeans in India, *The Times*, the India Council, the King and the Prince of Wales – all were opposed to the admission of Indians to the bodies they thought ought to be exclusively British and 'white'. But Morley was determined on this issue. He soothed the critics by his arguments. The promotion of an Indian to the highest rank would satisfy the vanity of the Indian people. And what harm could a lone Indian in the council do? He could be given an unimportant portfolio. Morley kept on pressing the matter until Minto gave way.

Morley made the first appointments to his own council. In July 1907 two Indians were appointed to the Council of the Secretary of State for India. A Hindu, K. G. Gupta, a senior member of the Indian Civil Service, and a Muslim Nawab Sayyid Ali Bilgrami, a Leaguer from Hyderabad; both were Morley's choice. Realising that only one Indian, and for that reason a Hindu, would be appointed, the Muslim leaders – Aga Khan, Ameer Ali and Bilgrami – opposed the very idea of appointing an Indian to the Executive Council of the Governor-General. This was tactfully overcome by Morley. The difficulty lay in selecting a Hindu for the Executive Council. Morley would have accepted Gokhale, the obvious choice. But Minto would not have any Congressman and definitely not Gokhale. Explaining his objections to Morley he wrote:

A Congresswallah is to my mind quite out of the question, not on account of any objections that you or I or the European community might raise, but because of the interpretation that would be given to the appointment by the vast majority of the native population, – which would be that it was a surrender to ideas which are undermining our power. . . .[41]

Minto's choice lay between Ashutosh Mukherjee, Vice-Chancellor of Calcutta University and a High Court judge, and S. P. Sinha, a barrister and Advocate-General. In finally recommending Sinha for the post, Minto wrote to Morley: 'Please do not think me terribly narrow! but Sinha is comparatively white, whilst Mookerjee is as black as my hat! and opposition in the official world would not be regardless of mere shades of colour.'[42] Sinha was appointed on January 1909 as the law member of the Executive Council.

Morley and Minto found Gupta and Sinha 'very useful'. The announcement of the appointment of the Indians to the councils in 1907, however, was not received with enthusiasm by the Congress and the Hindus. This was, as Gokhale explained, due to the deportation of Lajpat Rai earlier in the same year.[43]

In expanding the imperial and provincial legislative councils the Morley-Minto reforms introduced for the first time in Indian politics what is commonly called the communal electorate, which in a way foreshadowed the birth of Pakistan. On this issue Minto, who was committed to provide separate electorates for the Muslims, and Morley, whose liberalism would disapprove of dividing Hindus and Muslims in politics, disagreed in the beginning. Minto's policy of weakening the national movement of the Congress through the Anglo-Muslim alliance depended on securing special electorates for the Muslims. It was necessary for him to win. He did.

Minto wrote to Morley in 1907 stating that the 'only

representation for which India is at present fitted is a
representation of communities as I said in my reply to the
Mohammedan Deputation and only to a very small extent
in that direction'.[44] Morley agreed in principle that 'the
Muhammedan community is entitled to a special
representation', commensurate not only with its number but
also political and historical importance. But then he had
no idea as to how it could be secured. The Muslims could
have special representation on the legislative councils
through nomination, through election from mixed electorates or through separate communal electorates. It was
only when Minto suggested separate electorates that Morley
gave serious thought to the matter and put forward his
scheme of mixed electoral colleges.[45]

Minto and the Muslim League opposed Morley's scheme.
It was argued that large Hindu majorities in an electoral
college would enable Hindus to elect not only their own
man but a Muslim as well, 'and that being so a Mahommedan may be elected representative of advanced Hindu
political inclinations, and not at all of bona fide
Mahommedan interests'.[46] Minto and the Muslim League
were aware that the emerging Muslim middle class would
be more inclined to join Congress than a conservative
league, and the Congress, in order to show that it was
representative of all classes, would elect some Muslims from
such mixed electoral colleges. Minto insisted that the
Muslims must have separate electorates, electing Muslims
only, and also be entitled to contest elections from the
general electorates.

Morley gave up his scheme. He agreed in May 1909 to
the two demands of the Muslim League, that they should
elect their own representatives to these councils in all the
stages and that they should have a number of seats in
excess of their numerical strength. These demands were
finally embodied in the Indian Councils Act of 1909. Under
the Act the Imperial Legislative Council was to consist of

the officials and non-official members. The officials were to remain in a majority. The total of the non-official members nominated and elected was not to exceed sixty. The Act doubled the number of the Indians in the provincial legislative councils and created in each a non-official, nominated and elected, majority. Elections to the legislative councils were to be indirect, except in the case of the landlords and the Muslims; the franchise was very limited. The legislative councils, however, were essentially advisory, with no control over the executive, 'and the result was to increase the demand for self-government rather than to diminish it'.

The Act of 1909 was a victory for Muslim separatism. The Viceroy received the gratitude of the Muslim upper class:

The hearts of the Mahomedans of India were filled with deep gratitude to the Government, and they saw that, in the new Councils, not only would their interests be safe-guarded owing to the presence on them of a sufficient number of their own real representatives, but that the state of things thus created would secure the stability of the British Government, which they look upon as their very own, and would prevent the Hindu dream of *Swaraj* from being realised.[47]

The rules which were framed by the government of India under the Act were equally biased in favour of the Muslims. The Imperial Legislative Council was to have a total of 27 elected members of whom thirteen were to be elected by the general electorates, six by special landholders' con-stituencies in the six provinces, six by separate Muslim constituencies, and two by chambers of commerce. In this set-up the Muslims, apart from safely electing six members from the Muslim constituencies, could elect a few more Muslims from the rest of the constituencies.[48]

When the elections to the Imperial Legislative Council were held in January 1910, eleven Muslims were returned, only a few less than the total number of the Hindu members.

It was 'not only unjust but monstrously unjust'. Even Minto realised that the scale had been tipped too much in favour of the Muslims:[49]

I am afraid when the position is clearer we may fairly be accused of having neglected the even-handed justice to which we owe so much in India. . . . I should say that, if the Government of India was biased in any direction, it was towards Mahommedan interests.

Morley washed his hands of the matter by putting the blame on Minto – 'it was *your* speech about their extra claims, that first started the Mahometan hare'.[50]

Why did the Congress not oppose the communal electorate? Only S. N. Banerjea and Madan Mohan Malaviya (1861–1946) raised their voice against it, but finding no support from Gokhale they could go no further. Malaviya urged Gokhale to protest against the increased weightage given to the Muslims otherwise it would cause dissatisfaction among the Hindus which would soon deepen into discontent.[51] But Gokhale had a different vision of the future. Explaining his sentiments on the matter he wrote to an English friend in January 1909:

Personally I have always been, as you are aware, in favour of separate Mahomedan representation. To my mind the most important thing just now is not to let any section feel any real or reasonable grievance, so that the new arrangements may be started with the utmost goodwill on all sides. And as regards Mahomedan representation particularly, what I value above everything else is to free the community from dependence upon Government nomination. When this is done, their interests are generally so far identical with ours that they are bound before long to come and range themselves by our side.[52]

Perhaps Gokhale could not do otherwise than pin his hopes on the future. The twenty-five-year-old national movement had yielded nothing but doubtful results. The Congress had been split and Muslim separatism set against it. But a harder struggle lay in the future for now there were three parties in the arena – Congress, the Muslim League and the British.

1 Hunter, *Indian Mussalmans* (1871), p. 145.
2 Metcalf, p. 301.
3 Smith, W. C., *Modern Islam in India* (1943), p. 163.
4 Graham, *Sir Syed Ahmad Khan* (1885), p. 125.
5 *Select Documents*, pp. 183–4.
6 Tyabji Papers, file S.
7 Syed Ahmad Khan, *The Present State of Indian Politics* (1888), p. 31.
8 Ibid.
9 Tyabji Papers, file B.
10 Ibid., Tyabji to Syed Ahmad, 18 Feb. 1888.
11 Ibid.
12 Ibid., Hume to Tyabji, 5 Nov. 1888.
13 Wasti, *Minto* (1964), p. 29.
14 Minto Papers, M. 968, vol. i, no. 11.
15 Morley Papers, vol. iv, Minto to Morley, 15 Aug. 1906.
16 Ibid., vol. iii, Minto to Morley, 22 Aug. 1906.
17 Ibid., 2 Sept. 1906.
18 Das, p. 159.
19 Morley Papers, vol. i, Minto to Morley, 3 Jan. 1906.
20 Gokhale Papers, file 203, part i, Gokhale to Wedderburn, 24 May 1907
21 Sastri Papers, serial no. 5.
22 Morley Papers, vol. iii.
23 Ibid.
24 Ibid., The Mohammedan Address.
25 Mary Minto, *India, Minto and Morley* (1934), p. 47.
26 Quoted in Das, p. 173.
27 Morley Papers, vol. iii, Minto to Morley, 4 Oct. 1906.
28 Ibid., vol. i.
29 League's Resolution, quoted in Das, p. 178.
30 Ibid.
31 Ibid., p. 179.
32 Gokhale Papers, file 296, letter to the *Times of India*, 21 May 1907.
33 Morley Papers, vol. xi, Minto to Morley, 19 Aug. 1908.
34 Ibid., 1 Dec. 1908.
35 Minto Papers, vol. i, no. 259.
36 Gokhale Papers, file 203, part ii.
37 Quoted in Das, p. 183.
38 Gokhale Papers, file 203, part i.
39 Ibid.

40 Ibid.

41 Morley Papers, vol. x, Minto to Morley, 11 June 1908.

42 Ibid., vol. xii, 9 Nov. 1908.

43 Gokhale Papers, file 203, part i, Gokhale to Vamanroy, 23 July 1908.

44 Morley Papers, vol. v, Minto to Morley, 23 Jan. 1907.

45 Morley. Despatch of 27 Nov. 1908. Quoted in Das, p. 232.

46 Morley Papers, vol. xii, Minto to Morley, 31 Dec. 1908.

47 Minto Papers, vol. i, no. 157, Safi to Dunlop Smith, 30 Apr. 1909.

48 Gokhale Papers, file 203, part ii, Gokhale to Wedderburn, 3 Dec. 1909.

49 Quoted in Das, p. 248.

50 Ibid., p. 249.

51 Gokhale Papers, file 319, Malaviya to Gokhale, 4 Mar. 1909.

52 Ibid., file 203, part ii.

4 The Struggle for Unity, 1910–1928

THE politics of both the Muslim League and Congress remained confined to the upper stratum of society until 1919. The League was run by titled gentry, Nawabs and landlords who wanted to serve the Muslim cause only so far as it did not affect their own position either socially or in relation to government.[1] Congress was very much 'an English-knowing upper-class affair where morning coats and well-pressed trousers were greatly in evidence'.[2] It met once a year during Christmas week, passed resolutions and then went to sleep until next December. Its annual session was more of a social gathering 'with no political excitement or tension'. In both Congress and League circles the moral superiority and physical strength of the British *Raj* remained undisputed. Only a common cause and fearless leadership could unite the two communities into a national movement. The cause and the leadership came, but from two different sources and with different ends in view. The Muslims found a cause in the preservation of the Turkish Empire, whose Sultan was the spiritual head of Muslims all over the world. From the Congress ranks emerged the fearless Mahatma Gandhi. That the pan-Islamic movement should be led by a nationalist Congress was a contradiction. That the 'Islam in danger' movement of the Muslims be led by a non-Muslim was perhaps a greater contradiction. The 'unholy' alliance lasted for four years and it created more problems than it solved.

ISLAM IN DANGER, 1910–19

The policy of Syed Ahmad Khan – to remain loyal to the

D

British *Raj* and not to join the Congress – was faithfully carried on until 1914 by his disciples in both Aligarh College and the Muslim League, respectively the centre and organ of Muslim politics in India. The Aga Khan, who spent most of his time on the French Riviera, in his brief visits to India preached loyalty to the *Raj*. Viqar-ul-Mulka (1841–1917), who in 1907 succeeded Mohsin-ul-Mulk as secretary of Aligarh College, would not advise his co-religionists to join Congress even when, as in 1911 when the partition of Bengal was revoked, he realised it was futile to rely any longer on the British government.[3]

A series of factors, however, led to a change in Muslim attitudes from a pro-British to an anti-British cast. In 1910 the Muslim League removed its headquarters from Aligarh to Lucknow – away from the anti-Congress and pro-British influences of both the British principal and the orthodox secretary of Aligarh College. In its annual session of the same year held at Nagpur the League was inclined to confer freely with Congress on the solution of the Hindu-Muslim problem. The possibility of holding a conference of Hindu and Muslim leaders had earlier in the year been discussed in London between the Aga Khan and Wedderburn, the Congress president for the 1910 session which was held at Allahabad.[4] The conference of forty Muslim and sixty Hindu leaders was held in January 1911 at Allahabad. It yielded no practical results but it did show that the Muslim leaders were willing to confer with Congress on matters affecting the common life of both communities. However, at this stage almost all the Muslim leaders were pro-British and some of them blamed the Hindus for the general economic backwardness of the Muslim community.[5]

Before the year was out the Muslim attitude began to change. In October–November 1911 Italy went to war with Turkey in Tripoli. The Sultan of Turkey was also held to be the spiritual head, the Caliph, of the Muslim world. His empire included a part of south-eastern Europe and almost the whole of the Near East. There was, of course, no love lost between the Christians of South-eastern Europe and their overlord the Sultan. Even the Arabs cared little about this outdated religious bond between them and the Sultan. But those who most resented the temporal and spiritual authority of the Sultan were the Young Turks, the movement which in due course was to depose him and abolish the Caliphate.

But the Indian Muslims had been living as a minority in a predominantly Hindu country and, for the last hundred years or more under a Christian government. The Muslims in India were on the whole poorer than the members of the majority community. Usually the filthiest part of a town or a city would be inhabited by Muslims or Untouchables. The Hindu community was self-contained. No non-Hindu could embrace Hinduism. For these reasons, and in order to maintain their separate identity, the Muslims in India had become more fanatically observant of their religious rituals and bonds than Muslims anywhere else in the world. For an Indian Muslim the offering of prayers to Allah was not only a solemn duty but also an assertion and declaration of his rights against the Hindus.

The news that a Christian power was at war with the Caliphate aroused first among the few middle-class Muslims sympathy and concern for the safety of Turkey. Then followed in November–December 1911 the announcement at the Delhi Durbar of the revocation of the partition of Bengal. For the first time the ruling monarch of Britain was visiting India. This occasion was chosen to placate the Hindus, especially of Bengal, who had been agitating against the partition ever since it was effected in 1905. This 'masterstroke of policy', as Gokhale termed it, gave to the Hindus not only a 'sense of relief but a new note of hope and gladness in their hearts'.[6] But the Muslim leaders took it as a betrayal of trust on the part of the British government. They were shocked, sullen and aggrieved. The revocation of the partition meant to them the loss of a Muslim majority province and the reinstatement of Hindu supremacy in the political and economic life of Bengal and Assam. The ground was thus paved for the growth of anti-British feeling among the Muslim middle class.

In 1912 Turkey became involved in the first Balkan war. In the same year Russia, then an ally of Britain, perpetrated massacres in Persia. To the Indian Muslims it seemed as if the whole of the Christian world was against the Crescent, which was struggling for survival. Britain was identified as the leader of the Christian powers. Anti-British feeling was increasing among the expanding Muslim middle class, whose members were equally opposed to the upper-class Muslims who had hitherto followed a pro-British policy. The leaders of the middle-class Muslims at this stage were Shibli Nomani (1857–1914) and Muhammad Ali (1878–1931) from the United Provinces, and A. K. Azad (1888–1958) from Bengal. All three were orthodox Muslims who believed that religion should be the basis of politics, and they were advocates of Pan-Islamism. They were at the same time anti-Aligarh and anti-Muslim League. In his journal *Al-Hilal* which he had started at Calcutta in July 1912, Azad attacked Aligarh College as a citadel of reactionaries and in one of his speeches called the men of Aligarh 'heretics and hypocrites' who had in the last forty years co-operated with the 'satans of Europe to weaken the influence of the Islamic Caliphate and Pan-Islam'.[7] Shibli Nomani attacked Aligarh College as 'an institute for training in slavery'.[8] They attacked the Muslim League because it had no goal and did not represent the aspirations of the Muslim middle class. These men were more in sympathy with Congress, perhaps not so much for its nationalism as for the fight it had so far waged against the British *Raj*.

The complacency of the Muslim League was broken. To try to prevent these angry men from joining Congress the

League in 1913 defined for the first time its goal, which was to achieve for India a 'suitable' form of self-government within the British Empire. The term 'suitable' smacked of meekness and Shibli Nomani commented that it was simply a cloak for the old pro-government policy.[9]

Of the three, Muhammad Ali played the leading role in arousing among educated Muslims sympathy and concern for Turkey, 'the greatest Muslim power on earth'. Educated at Aligarh and Oxford, Ali had failed the I.C.S. examinations and had also failed to obtain an appointment at Aligarh College, owing to the opposition of its English principal, Theodore Morrison. He had personal reasons for being anti-British. He was deeply religious, aggressive and unscrupulous.[10] Of the various emotions which motivated his public career from 1912 until his death, his pan-Islamism was perhaps the strongest. He organised a medical mission which left Bombay for Turkey on 6 November 1912. His anti-British feeling was further intensified when the government disapproved of the proposal to name the projected Aligarh University a Muslim university. Any act of the government having the remotest effect on Muslim institutions and rituals was now construed as a deliberate aggression against Islam. The demolition of a portion of a mosque at Kanpur by the Public Works Department was used by Ali to arouse anti-British feeling among the ordinary Muslims of that city.

On 30 May 1913 the first Balkan War was concluded by the Treaty of London. According to this Treaty Turkey ceded all her dominions in Europe west of the Enos-Media line and also the island of Crete. The Indian Muslims regretted that their Caliph should be forced to lose territory but they hoped that Turkey would not be involved in any future war, for the division of their loyalty between Turkey and Britain was painful for the average educated Muslim. Ali knew that in the event of a war between Britain and Turkey, he and his followers would have to take sides and that they would certainly support Turkey, no matter how just or unjust her reasons for entering into war against Britain.

On 4 August 1914, Great Britain declared war on Germany. Ali's fears came true. On 31 August he sent a wire to the Sultan of Turkey:

Placing our faith and confidence which we the Indian Muslims have in the Khilafat, we respectfully urge upon your Majesty either to support Britain or to keep neutral in this war.[11]

On 4 November 1914, Turkey joined Germany against Britain. The decision of the Caliph could not be questioned. Ali and his followers ranged themselves with Turkey against the *Raj*. Anti-British feeling mounted but the Muslims had no strong political organisation either to express their feelings or to launch a movement against the British government. The Muslim League was meek and loyal to the British. The Muslims thus gathered round individual leaders but none of them had the vision, strength or resources to canalise Muslim emotions into a movement. In December 1914 Muhammad Ali and his brother Saukat Ali sent a team of Muslims to tribal areas on the North-West Frontier to secure arms from the gun factories which could be used against the British. The team returned without success. Then they pinned their hopes on the neighbouring Muslim state of Afghanistan. Letters were sent to the King of Afghanistan entreating him either to attack India or to persuade Germany to attack India.[12] In May 1915, the Ali brothers were arrested for openly justifying Turkey's entry into the war against Britain. A. K. Azad was likewise interned. The Muslims were left helpless. A leader with courage and vision was needed and he was in the making. In March 1915 M. K. Gandhi (1869–1948), who had returned to India in January of the same year from South Africa, while speaking to Calcutta students said: 'Politics cannot be divorced from religion. . . . If I were for sedition I would speak out for sedition and think loudly and take the consequences.'[13] The courage of this newcomer to Indian politics at once impressed Muhammad Ali and he said, 'Gandhi alone can be our man'. Four years were to pass before Gandhi became India's man.

There is perhaps no other great politician in the modern world who had such a large following as Mohandas Karamchand Gandhi, or was so reverently respected by the masses he led, or whose private life was so public and whose public life so much controlled by 'his inner voice', or whose advice was so widely sought on problems affecting all aspects of human life, but who was so little understood by either his followers or his opponents, and whose impact on the social, political and economic life of the country he served until his assassination has been so slight. When baffled in their understanding of this great man or alarmed at his rejection of modern industrial civilisation, his followers often found solace in the thought – after all he is a Mahatma, beyond the reach of average human comprehension. He will forgive us if we cannot shape our life after his image, for his ideals are unattainable by us the little ones. Consequently the Mahatma was more often worshipped than followed.

Gandhi's early life, however, was more ordinary than that of some of his disciples. Born into a Vaisya family (the third in the Hindu caste hierarchy) at Porbandar, now in the state of Gujerat, he inherited the vegetarian dietary habits and non-violent temperament of his caste and province which were under the influence of Jainism, one of the religions of India which believes suffering and deprivation to be the best means of attaining salvation. He was an average boy at school; his timidity verged on cowardice and his shyness made him an introvert from quite early in his life. He was married at the age of thirteen and was, in his own words 'a lustful, though a faithful husband'. At the age of nineteen, in 1888, he went to London for legal studies leaving behind his wife and family. While in London he adopted Western dress, took a few lessons in dancing and elocution but, realising that this self-indulgence was expensive and futile, he soon gave them up. He made the acquaintance of a young woman without first telling her that he was already married. But before 'taking improper liberties with the young lady' he plucked up the courage to tell the truth and sever the relationship.[14] His general reading consisted largely of books on religion and he was particularly impressed by the *Bhagavad Gita* and the New Testament 'which went straight to my heart'. Like most young men of his age Gandhi was searching for truth but perhaps with this difference – that he was also endeavouring all the time to live by truth. One of the injunctions of Hinduism, that there should be harmony between thought and conduct, became for Gandhi one of the main purposes of his life. But the urge to be truthful both in thought and action emerged from his desire to overcome his basic fearfulness. The turning point in his life was his interview with the Political Agent of Kathiawar on his return from England after completing his legal studies. His brother, who for some time had been the Secretary and Adviser of the Hindu ruler of Porbandar, was charged with giving wrong advice when in that office. The matter was being considered by the Political Agent, an English officer whom Gandhi had met in London. Gandhi's brother asked him to use his friendship with the Agent, meet him and put in a good word on his behalf. Gandhi did not like the idea for it seemed to him improper. But his brother insisted and Gandhi sought an interview with the Political Agent which the latter granted. At the interview Gandhi found that although the officer owned to the acquaintance he did not like it to be abused. He refused to listen to Gandhi's case and desired him to leave his house. Gandhi insisted – 'but please hear me out'. The officer became more angry and asked his servant to 'show him the door'. Gandhi was still hesitating 'when the servant came in, placed his hands on my shoulders and put me out of the room'.[15] The young barrister's pride and vanity were hurt and he was crestfallen. He thought of suing the officer for insult and assault, but he was advised by Sir Phirozshah Mehta to pocket the insult because 'he will gain nothing by proceeding against the Sahib, and on the contrary will very likely ruin himself'. The advice was as bitter as poison to him but he swallowed it. 'Never again', Gandhi said to himself, 'shall I place myself in such a false position; never again shall I try to exploit friendship in this way.'[16] He admitted later, 'This shock changed the whole course of my life'.

Gandhi might have asked himself, 'How can I be fearless and free?' and taken stock of his background, and physical and moral self: orthodox in breeding, frail and unattractive in physique, but possessed of an inner quest for truth and an unshakeable belief in its ultimate victory. If he could find truth and live by it, if his conduct was as just as his thought, then he would be able to conquer his fear, make up for his inadequacies, and stand forth in the world with unbounded confidence and firmness. From then on he was to be constantly searching for and experimenting with truth. He accepted some old values and human virtues as contained in Hindu and Christian scriptures, but later in his public life a host of new problems, economic and political, were to emerge for which he had to find answers. His task became doubly complicated because of his total rejection of machine-age civilisation. He was thus obliged to reconstruct a social system or way of life. But he did not do it systematically, thinking peacefully in his study or a museum like a social and political philosopher. His life soon became public and he had to find answers when the problems arose. He had to do his own thinking and acting. He was to be his own Marx and Lenin and that too in the brief span of fifty years of his working life. It was a difficult task, even for a Mahatma. In this task Gandhi succeeded, but barely. His life and thoughts from 1919 to 1948 show contradictions, inconsistencies and incoherence. What was called Gandhism in his lifetime ceased to exist after his death as a way of life. And his way of life had its dangers too. What he considered truth might not be truth or could be only a relative truth, but by virtue of the power he was to hold over the masses he could, and he did, impose his convictions on them.

Soon after his unhappy encounter with the Political Agent Gandhi accepted employment with an Indian firm in South Africa and left for Natal in 1893. On his arrival in Natal he realised that Indians were racially discriminated against and subjected to various kinds of humiliations. Those who were indentured labourers were subjected to poll tax, and all, including Hindu and Muslim businessmen, were virtually prevented from travelling in first- and second-class railway compartments. They could not stay in hotels, were not allowed to walk on the pavement after 9 p.m. and all of them, whether labourers or shipowners, were called 'coolies' (porters) by the white settlers. Being in a helpless position the Indians had become reconciled to this way of life and had learned to pocket insults without protest.

Gandhi, dressed in a frock-coat and a small Indian turban and conscious of being a barrister, had to learn his lessons the hard way within one month of his arrival. He was asked to take his turban off when in a Court, he was assaulted by a policeman when found walking on a pavement after nine in the evening, he was refused accommodation in hotels and was pushed out of a first-class railway compartment by the guard and a constable because his fellow passenger, a European, did not like to travel with a coloured man. He refused to go to a third-class compartment and the train steamed off leaving him and his luggage scattered over the platform. In that winter night while shivering more from humiliation than cold Gandhi thought of his duty: should I fight for my rights or go back to India? Realising that the event symbolised the deep disease of colour prejudice he decided to 'root out the disease and suffer hardship in the process'.[17]

He spent twenty-one years of his life (1893 to 1914) in South Africa fighting for the rights and dignity of his countrymen. It was during this period that he conceived and organised *Satyagraha* (non-violent passive resistance) against the unjust laws and regulations of the government. While opposing the Registration Law of the Transvaal government in 1906 he declared: 'There is only one course open to those like me, to die but not to submit to this law.' To die but not to kill for the truth, that is to seek redress through self-suffering, was the essence of *Satyagraha*. He raised an 'army' of truth-seekers, Indian men and women, who defied the law non-violently, and courted arrest and imprisonment with no malice and hate towards their enemy. He organised the last *Satyagraha* in 1913 against the judgment of the Cape Supreme Court delivered on 14 March 1913 which, in effect, withdrew recognition from all Hindu and Muslim marriages which were not solemnised according to Christian rites and registered by the Registrar of Marriages. The movement was a success, General Smuts gave in and a compromise was reached. Smuts said of Gandhi later in his life: 'It was my fate to be the antagonist of a man for whom even then I had the highest respect.'[18] In May 1917 indentured immigration from India, against which Gandhi drafted the first petition in 1894, was finally stopped.

Throughout his fight against the race laws in South Africa and later in his struggle for Indian independence, Gandhi tried to establish the moral superiority of Indians in contrast to the material superiority of the British. He was convinced that the sufferings of his countrymen would not only strengthen their own character and self-respect but would also cause a change of heart among the British, who, in due course, would not only be cured of the disease of racialism but would be so ennobled as to concede independence to India. The moderate success he achieved in South Africa confirmed his belief in non-violent passive resistance. His success was partly due to the fact that Indians in South Africa, being in a minority, formed a compact group. Thus when he finally left South Africa in 1914 he had more faith in the British system of government and the British character than he had either before or after. On his way back to India he reached England on 6 August, two days after the war had broken out. He felt that Indians residing in Britain ought to help in her hour of need. He thus planned to organise an Indian ambulance corps but owing to a serious attack of pleurisy he was obliged to return to the warmer climate of India. Had this not happened he might have lost his life defending the empire which he was later to shake to its foundations.

On his return to India in January 1915, Gandhi found his country strange to him. He had spent less than four years in India between 1888 and 1915. His success in South Africa had made him vaguely known among Indian leaders who, now that he was with them, found him remote and odd. Gandhi followed the advice of his political *guru*, Gokhale, and kept out of Indian politics for one year. During this period he was only to tour India and observe political trends. If he had entered politics in 1915 or 1916 he would not have stood far above the bottom in the political hierarchy. It was therefore a remarkable feat that the remote man of 1915–16, then known in government circles as a social reformer and among the Congress leaders as a philosophical anarchist, should become in less than four years the leader of the nation. How did it happen? Or how did he do it? The answer is – Gandhi's courage and technique of openly defying the authorities. Gandhi had devoted twenty-one years of his life to attaining *Abhaya* (fearlessness) and forging the method of *Satyagraha*, which was as constitutional as it was revolutionary. The fundamentally constitutional nature of the British *Raj*, the traditional character of the Indian people, and the dilemma of Indian politics, provided both the circumstances and the time for the rise of Gandhi.

The first bold impression Gandhi made on the minds of Indians was in April 1917. At the invitation of some local men Gandhi had gone to Motihari, the headquarters of Champaran district in the province of Bihar, to enquire into the grievances of tenants against the English indigo planters. In Champaran district the planters, with the support of the law and of government officials, had virtually become the landlords, forcing the tenants to grow indigo on the most fertile quarter of their individual holdings. The ignorant, timid and poor peasants lived completely at the mercy of the ruthless planters. Audacious cultivators who defied the planters were harassed; 'their houses were looted, crops destroyed and stray cattle let loose on their lands'.[19]

Soon after his arrival in Motihari with a team of Bihar lawyers, Gandhi was served with a government order to leave Champaran. He declared that he did not propose to comply with the order or to leave Champaran until his enquiry was finished. Thereupon he was served with a summons to appear on trial for disobeying the government order. The news of the order and summons spread like wildfire and the villagers gathered in their thousands outside the court-house to glimpse the man who had the courage to defy the government order and was willing to go to jail and suffer for their cause. Both the magistrate and the prosecution counsel were on tenterhooks and they had nearly postponed the trial when Gandhi, the accused, interfered, pleaded guilty and requested them to try him. Gandhi then made a statement explaining why he refused to leave Champaran and added:

I venture to make this statement not in any way in extenuation of the penalty to be awarded against me, but to show that I have disregarded the order served upon me not for want of respect for lawful authority, but in obedience to the higher law of our being, the voice of conscience.[20]

Strange words, strange feelings, but therein lay the challenge to the hitherto accepted supremacy of the government's orders, rules and laws. The executive and legal measures of the government could be disobeyed if they were unjust or improper according to the natural law. The manner in which such measures were to be defied was even more strange. Not by constitutional agitation or armed rebellion but through sufferings at the hands of the 'oppressors'. Explaining his non-violent resistance some time later, Gandhi wrote:

I seek entirely to blunt the edge of the tyrant's sword, not by putting up against it a sharper-edged weapon, but by disappointing his expectation that I should be offering physical resistance. The resistance of the soul that I should offer instead would elude him. It would at first dazzle him, and at last compel recognition from him, which recognition would not humiliate him but would uplift him.[21]

The magistrate, being at a loss, postponed judgment. When Gandhi reappeared to receive the sentence the magistrate informed him that the Governor of the province had ordered the case against him to be withdrawn and that he was at liberty to conduct his proposed enquiry. Gandhi at once became a hero of the Champaran peasants. He started the inquiry, the government appointed a commission, eventually most of the cultivators' grievances were redressed, and the planters' *Raj* in Champaran came to an end. But one of the significant results of Gandhi's civil disobedience was that the peasants of Champaran and the educated middle classes of India became less fearful of the *Raj* and the Englishman.[22] For Gandhi it was a great political success. He captured the attention of the Indian leaders as a man of action and from now on his activities were watched by all, hopefully and with admiration.

Less dramatic but equally rewarding were Gandhi's 1918 *Satyagrahas* in the Bombay presidency. He intervened in wage disputes between the labourers and the owners of the Ahmedabad cotton textile mills.[23] In this case both the parties were Indian. While he was negotiating with the mill-owners the labourers went on strike. He supported them and asked them to depend upon their soul-force. With no strike-dole available the workers complained that it was easy for Gandhi to ask them to live on their soul-force and starve while 'he himself was well-dressed and well-fed'. Stung by these remarks Gandhi abandoned all his clothes except the loin cloth which he wore throughout the rest of his life. In appearance and dress he was from now on to look and live like the peasants and labourers of India. And then he went on a 'fast unto death' which immediately induced the mill-owners to give way because they did not want to take the responsibility for his death. This 'fast unto death' shows among other things that Gandhi was, by 1918, aware of his popularity among the people and knew that they would not let him die. Later in his public life when Gandhi once asked one of his lieutenants, Sardar Vallabhbhai Patel (1875-1950) to fast, the latter replied: 'Why should I fast? If I fast people will let me die. They are your friends and they exert themselves to end your fast. Not for me.'[24]

Owing to a widespread failure of crops in the Khaira district of Bombay the harvest was less than the legal limit and the cultivators were thus entitled to a remission of the land revenue which was withheld by the government. Gandhi organised the *Satyagraha* and asked the cultivators to refuse to pay the land revenue and remain prepared for the forfeiture of their lands.[25] The government gave way and a compromise was reached.

The success of these local *Satyagrahas* had given Gandhi enough confidence and by the end of 1918 he was ready to organise, if need be, a nation-wide non-violent passive resistance. But he was, until 1918, a supporter of the British government. He attended the war conference convened by the Viceroy in Delhi in June 1918, and he had personally organised recruiting campaigns to help the government during the war. He believed that if the Indians helped the British in their hour of crisis, 'India would become the most favoured partner in the Empire and racial distinctions would become a thing of the past.'[26] Thus, a cause for a national campaign against the government was not yet in sight. At the same time, Gandhi was aware of the new trends towards unity that had taken place in Muslim and Congress politics between 1915 and 1918. He had realised early enough in South Africa 'that there was no genuine friendship between the Hindus and the Mussal-mans'.[27] Hence he was tempted by the situation that had arisen out of a closer alliance between Muslim and Congress politics, and was naturally inclined to foster their proximity into a permanent union.

But the task was not so easy. There was, indeed, among middle-class Muslims a general feeling of hostility towards the British government. But in the Congress there were different groups with different shades of opinions and it was doubtful whether the nationalists of Congress would support the Pan-Islamism of the Muslims. Besides, Gandhi had so far worked on his own, outside the Congress and the Muslim League. Beneath the surface unity of Congress there was a silent struggle among its leaders for all-India leadership. If Gandhi wanted to capture the leadership of Congress and to unite the Muslims and Hindus into a national movement he needed a national cause. This is what he was looking for, and at the end of 1918 he found one. But before passing on to 1919 when Gandhi plunged into national politics it would seem worth while to look back briefly over League and Congress politics since 1915.

After the Surat split in 1907 the moderates secured a firm grip over Congress and held it under tight control until

1915. This they did by drafting a new constitution for Congress in April 1908. Article one of the constitution defined the objects of Congress which were to secure, through constitutional means, self-government for India within the Empire.[28] All who wanted to be or remain members of Congress were to accept Article one of the constitution. The extremists, as expected, did not accept and therefore they remained excluded from Congress until December 1915. Another reason for moderate supremacy in Congress was the extremist leader Tilak's imprisonment for sedition in 1908 for six years. When Tilak was released in June 1914, his health was bad and he was far less extremist in his political views. Negotiations with Gokhale for the re-entry of Tilak's party into Congress were started in 1914 by the English theosophist, Mrs Annie Besant (1847–1933), who had by then shifted her activities from the spiritual and social to the political life of India.[29] But Gokhale, partly due to his own fears and partly due to pressure from Sir Pherozshah Mehta, was reluctant to let the extremists into the Congress. Gokhale died in February and Mehta in November, 1915. In December of the same year, therefore, the Congress at its Bombay session modified its constitution to enable the extremists to rejoin the Congress. Tilak and his followers joined Congress in 1916, after eight years of exclusion, and it was the united Congress which held its significant session in Lucknow in December of the same year.

The outbreak of the First World War in August 1914, and the entry of Turkey against Britain, further stiffened Muslim hostility towards British rule. There was a growing desire among middle-class Muslims to join hands with Congress against the British. The Muslim League was willing to modify its separatism and come to an agreement with Congress. The future creator of Pakistan, Muhammad Ali Jinnah (1876–1948), was in 1915 an ardent Congressman, a nationalist, an ambassador of Hindu-Muslim unity, aspiring to be, in his own words, 'the Muslim Gokhale'. When in 1913 the Muslim League defined its objectives and expanded its vision for the first time, Jinnah joined it but on condition that he would not be induced to be disloyal to the larger national cause.[30] He remained a leading member of Congress and of the Imperial Legislature to which he had been elected by the Muslim electorate of Bombay. With a view to bringing the League nearer to Congress he managed to hold the League's annual session of 1915 at the same time and place as that of Congress. Thus, the separate sessions of the League and Congress were held in December at Bombay, and they continued to be so held, in the same month and at the same place, until 1919. The change in the League's policy from anti-Congress to pro-Indian and the proposed *entente* between the progressive Muslims and Congress, 'were viewed with suspicion and dislike by the reactionary and autocratic officials of the Bombay government', who secretly planned with the aid of some reactionary Muslims the complete dispersion of the League's session, which was to be held after the conclusion of the Congress session so that the Muslim members of the Congress could attend it.[31] In this they succeeded, the session of the League was dispersed, but held subsequently behind the closed doors of the Taj Mahal Hotel. The Congress and League, however, succeeded in starting negotiations for an agreement, which was concluded in 1916 at their Lucknow sessions, and hence commonly called the Lucknow Pact. The scheme was a full constitution for India demanding, among other things, self-government at an early date.[32] The important feature of the scheme was the agreement on the mode and percentage of Muslim representation in the provincial and central legislatures. Congress agreed that the Muslims should continue to be elected by their separate electorates, a system which was introduced in 1909 and soon after vehemently criticised by the Congress. Tilak and Jinnah, however, hoped that the scheme of separate electorates would have but a short life and a time would come when the Muslims needed this no more and there would be no distinction in political life between Hindu and Muslim.[33]

Thus in December 1916, while the war was still continuing, the Congress-League scheme presented a united India to the British *Raj*. This, of course, among other factors, was responsible for galvanising the British government into formulating the next set of reforms for India. But in 1916, before the Lucknow Pact was made, Tilak and Mrs Besant, being unsure of the turn Congress politics might take, and with a view to laying additional pressure on the British government, started their Home Rule movements.[34] Tilak in April, and Mrs Besant in September, founded separate Home Rule Leagues, the object of both being to secure self-government for India within the Empire. There might have been other reasons – perhaps the personal ambition to capture Congress or to remain in control of some sort of political movement – which motivated Mrs Besant to start her League outside Congress. The 'obstreperous old harridan' as *The Times* called Mrs Besant, was perhaps a little vain, 'influenced by a passionate desire to be a leader of movements', but in the first six months she enlivened the national movement through her speeches and writings, decrying her own countrymen for their misdeeds in India and at the same time extolling the glorious past of India: 'Let India remember what she was and realise what she may be; then the sun [will] rise once more in the East, and fill the western lands with lights.'[35] In June she was interned, perhaps foolishly, by the Madras government. This made her a national heroine. Indian nationalists of all different parties rose in a wave of sympathy for this old lady of sixty-nine, and many joined her Home Rule League who would not have done so otherwise. On her release in September she was given a hero's welcome and was elected to the highest national post, the Presidency of

Congress, for its 1917 session which was held in Calcutta.

Mrs Besant's release was occasioned by a change in the Indian policy of the British government. The need for defining British policy towards India and introducing further reforms had arisen in the first years of the war. India had generously helped Britain with men and money to fight a war for 'freedom' and 'nationality'. India had been, in Curzon's words, 'sending out civilised soldiers to save Europe from the modern Huns'.* From this had arisen a willingness in government circles to reward India for her help. Then there were pressures exercised on the government by a group of people in Britain called the 'Round Table', by the Congress-League scheme and by Mrs Besant's Home Rule League. In March 1917, Austen Chamberlain, Secretary of State for India (1915–17), cautioned the Viceroy that the war fought by the allies in the name of 'freedom' was bound to have an effect on the Indian mind, and 'what would have seemed a great advance a little time ago, would now satisfy no-one and we should, I think, be prepared for bold and radical measures'.[36]

In May 1917 the London government was urged by the Viceroy to announce immediately British policy in India.[37] In July, Edwin Montagu, a Liberal, replaced Chamberlain as Secretary of State for India. He soon evolved a formula for the Indian problem, got it sanctioned by the Cabinet on 14 August, and then made in the Commons on 20 August the famous declaration of British policy in India:

The policy of His Majesty's Government, with which the Government of India are in complete accord, is that of the increasing association of Indians in every branch of the administration and the gradual development of self-governing institutions with a view to the progressive realisation of responsible government in India as an integral part of the British Empire.[38]

* India had also participated in the Imperial War Conference held in December 1916.

In over 150 years of British rule in India this was the first time that British policy in India had been formally defined. The declaration, however, did not indicate when in future India would actually become a self-governing dominion. It did by implication suggest that India in 1917 was not fit to be a self-governing nation. The future thus depended on the set of reforms which the government would be introducing in a year or so. To confer with the Viceroy and the Indian political parties on the nature of the reforms to be introduced, Montagu arrived in India in November 1917. On the 26th of the same month the leaders of both Congress and the League met the Viceroy and the Secretary of State for India and placed before them their demands as contained in the Congress-League scheme. Montagu then visited Bombay in December where he met the leaders of the Home Rule Leagues – Tilak, Mrs Besant and Jinnah. Their demands were the same as those of Congress. In fact the Leagues were doing propaganda for 'the old-fashioned Congress'. Then Montagu met the leaders of communal organisations whose demands were in conflict with those of Congress and the Home Rule Leagues.* Encouraged by the government's policy of safeguarding the political interests of the minorities, as evinced in the creation of separate electorates and the reservation of seats for the Muslims, there had been a rush since 1909 among the petty local leaders, who could not otherwise carve out a career in national politics, to create and organise communal organisations where they did not exist, and then come forward to the government with demands for special privileges. The leaders of these organisations impressed upon Montagu that India was not fit for democracy, because there existed in India wide gulfs between the various castes and classes, and the great majority of the

* The names of some of them were: Anjuman-i-Islam, Indian Christians, Lingayats, Depressed Classes, Deccan Ryots Association, Marathi-speaking Hindu backward classes.

people were uneducated.[39] Montagu was to some extent impressed by their arguments. He noted in his diary that the 'great giants' of Indian politics are by generations removed 'from the rest of India' because of 'the thinness with which we have spread education'.[40] He remarked that if democracy was introduced 'this would be only another indigenous autocracy'.

While Montagu consulted the Indian leaders on the impending reforms, and political life was beginning to settle down in a congenial atmosphere, the government of India, on 10 December 1917, appointed a committee, with Mr Justice Rowlatt from England as its president, to 'investigate and report on the nature and extent of the criminal conspiracies connected with the revolutionary movement in India' and to advise as to the legislation 'necessary to enable Government to deal with them'.[41] The appointment of the Rowlatt Committee, the publication of its report in April 1918, and the incorporation of its recommendations in the Government of India Acts, passed in March 1919 in the teeth of the united opposition of the Indian leaders, were perhaps the most unimaginative and ill-timed of all the measures of the government of India. Though not so intended by the government of India, these measures virtually forestalled what was intended to be achieved by Montagu's visit to India in 1917, the publication of the joint Montagu–Chelmsford report in July 1918, and the incorporation of the report in the Government of India Act.

Had the Indian bureaucracy not been as it was – isolated from the people it governed, suspicious, stubborn, assertive and autocratic – the Rowlatt Committee would not have been appointed in the first place, and in the second place the legislation to give effect to its recommendations would have been either withheld or postponed to a more suitable date. There were, indeed, reasons for inquiring into the problem of sedition. Indians, mostly Sikhs, who had emigrated to Canada and the U.S.A. since the end of the last century, had started a revolutionary party, the *Ghadr* Party, in 1913 at San Francisco to overthrow the British government in India by force of arms.[42] Within a few months the Party had gained support among Indian settlers in South-East Asia, Africa, Canada and Europe. The plan of the *Ghadr* leaders was to smuggle arms into India, to open arms factories in India, and to persuade Indian soldiers in the army to rise against the British. After the outbreak of the war they were supported by Germany with arms and money. The *Ghadr* Party, however, did not get much support from Indians in India and its final attempt to organise a rebellion in the Punjab in February 1915 failed miserably. Its leaders were apprehended, some hanged and others given various terms of imprisonment. By the summer of 1915, the *Ghadr* uprising had virtually petered out in the Punjab. The same year the government of India armed themselves with the Defence of India Act under which the provincial governments were empowered to try conspirators summarily by special tribunals whose verdicts were to be final. This Act was adequate to deal with stray conspiracies in Bengal and the Punjab. The dire necessity to have a fresh look at the problem did not exist in 1917.

Congress met in August 1918 at a special session in Bombay to consider the proposals for reforms as contained in the Montagu–Chelmsford Report published in the previous month. To all except Gandhi the Report seemed to promise less than expected. Gandhi, who in less than a year was to lead the nation against the *Raj*, felt quite contented with the proposals which, he thought, 'gave India as much as she could chew'.* The liberal politicians who had been in control of Congress since 1908, and were fast losing their grip on it since 1916, were for accepting

* But Gandhi was ignored and a suggestion that he be made the President of the special session of Congress was instantly dismissed by Mrs Besant on the grounds that he was not a politician.

what was given and fighting for the rest. The majority in Congress, then led by Mrs Besant, demanded that India should have a fully responsible government within fifteen years and, in order to accelerate the process, more powers should be transferred now to Indian hands than proposed in the Report.[43] The liberals, knowing what the decision of the Congress would be, did not attend its Bombay session, and formed at the same time a separate party of their own, to be called the National Liberal Federation. Congress, with a view to bargaining for more, rejected the proposals as inadequate, but behind this tough attitude lay the general willingness to accept what was finally given through Act of Parliament. The year ended peacefully with hopes for better things to come in 1919 but nobody knew that it was merely a lull before the storm.

1919. Two Bills incorporating the recommendations of the Rowlatt Committee were introduced in the central legislature. The Bills placed unlimited power in the hands of the executive and police to determine which offences constituted a conspiracy against the government. They then provided for the rapid trial of the accused. There was to be no committal procedure; the person accused was not to be represented by a pleader; there was to be no appeal from the sentence passed. The Bills were vehemently opposed by all elected non-official members of the legislature, including liberals like S. N. Banerjea, Srinavasa Sastri (1869–1946), and Tej Bahadur Sapru (1875–1949), who had parted company with Congress the previous year. Jinnah declared that a government which enacted such a law in peacetime forfeited its claim to be called a civilised government. Sastri warned the government that they would have no Indian behind them if they passed the Bills into Acts.[44] But the government ignored these protests and with the solid support of the official members the Bills were passed into Acts on 3 March. With anger and in helplessness some members including Jinnah resigned from the Imperial legislature.

It was at this juncture – when all Congressmen whether liberal or radical, all sections of the Muslim middle class whether orthodox or progressive, were harbouring in different measure hostility and discontent towards the British *Raj* – that Gandhi made his bold entry into national politics. He had taken the Rowlatt Bills 'as an open challenge' and a good enough cause for *Satyagraha*. Before the Bills were passed into Acts Gandhi had organised in February a *Satyagraha* Committee, the members of which were to take a pledge to 'refuse civilly to obey these laws and such other laws as a committee to be hereafter appointed may think fit, and further affirm, that in this struggle we will faithfully follow truth and refrain from violence to life, person or property'.[45] In his plan to start a mass civil disobedience movement Gandhi was opposed by Mrs Besant who feared that this might lead to violence and loss of respect for law and order.[46] It was a clash for leadership and Gandhi, rising fast on the wave of popular discontent, won. Mrs Besant lost her popularity and leadership. With Bombay won over to his support, Gandhi made a tour of Madras in March. With what he had done for Indians in South Africa, who were mostly from Madras, he had 'a special right over' the people of Madras.[47] Madras was conquered for the *Satyagraha* campaign, and among the many converts Gandhi made there was C. Rajagopalachari. While in Madras, Gandhi decided the nature of the civil disobedience movement and the date on which it was to start.[48] 30 March was first fixed, then changed to 6 April. On that day a general *hartal* (a closing of all shops and places of business as a sign of mourning) was to be observed. It was to be a day of self-purification as well. The people were to take a bath in the sea or river, fast and pray. Then civil disobedience was to be offered 'in respect of such laws only as easily lent themselves to being disobeyed by the masses'. The salt-tax, for example, was an unpopular government measure, and it could be easily disobeyed by the masses who could prepare salt from sea water in their own houses. Gandhi's grand strategy, and possibly his greatest achievement, was to bring the lower middle class and the masses into the national movement, which had hitherto been the preserve of the upper middle class. The technique he used was to give the political movement a religious colour in order to make it more acceptable to the people of India. Hence the rituals of bath, fast and prayer.

The cities of India began to seethe with processions and meetings. In Delhi on 20 March the police fired on a procession of Muslims and Hindus. The next day, the orthodox Arya Samajist Shraddhanand led the procession, offering his chest to the police to fire at. His courage won him the gratitude of the Muslims who took him to the famous Muslim mosque, the Jama Masjid in Delhi, and heard him speak from the pulpit. Never before had a Hindu spoken from the pulpit of a Muslim mosque. United more by common hostility than anything else Hindus and Muslims marched hand in hand, drank water from the same cup, and together shouted *Bande Mataram* (Hail, Motherland) and *Allaho Akbar* (God is Great). The notification of the change of date did not arrive in Delhi in time, hence 30 March was observed there as the day of the complete strike. On 6 April, the whole of India 'from one end to the other, towns as well as villages' observed a complete *hartal*.

Gandhi became the Mahatma but the people began to grow violent. The mob attacked the police in Bombay and Ahmedabad. When Gandhi appeared before the crowd in Bombay they hailed him as Mahatma but continued throwing stones at the police station.[49] He rushed to Ahmedabad where a police sergeant had been killed and martial law declared. There he decided that the people were still not fit for non-violent civil disobedience. Calling it his 'Himalayan miscalculation' Gandhi suspended the civil disobedience movement in April and for self-purification, fasted for three days.[50] But a greater tragedy had by then been enacted in the Punjab.

Sedition, the phobia of Punjab government officials, was mainly responsible for the massacre on 13 April of over 500 of the 20,000 unarmed Indians who had assembled for a meeting on a piece of wasteland in Amritsar, called the Jalianwala Bagh. The meeting ground was enclosed on all sides by houses and had only a few narrow exits and one main entrance. The killing was done by ninety soldiers at the command of General Dyer. The purpose of the firing was to disperse a crowd which had unlawfully assembled. This purpose could have been achieved by the mere approach of soldiers with guns to the entrance or by firing a bullet or two in the air. Instead 1650 rounds of ammunition were fired continually for ten minutes at a crowd which was all the time struggling to disperse through the narrow exits. Dyer wanted to prove the determination and strength of British power to crush any uprising against the *Raj*. The killing of hundreds, he calculated, would terrorise the whole of the Punjab into meek submission to British authority.

The average British official did not understand Gandhi's non-violent *Satyagraha* and suspected that it was a mere camouflage 'to cover some vast secret design which would burst out in violent upheaval one day'.[51] The rumours that the Bolsheviks and the Egyptians were supporting a widespread conspiracy in the Punjab had overstrained the nerves of the Punjab officials. But their fears were unfounded. The Intelligence Bureau of the government of India soon reported in May that 'no traces of organised conspiracy have been found in the Punjab'.[52]

Possessed as they were by a mutiny complex the Punjab authorities declared martial law. During the martial law regime, from 15 April to 9 June, they indulged in further excesses to humiliate the people, who were flogged, made to crawl lying flat on their bellies, and marched miles under the scorching heat of the sun to salute the Union Jack. In securing the necessary approval of the Indian government for their measures, the Punjab government used the 'bogey of the Frontier' – the proximity of the Punjab to the Indian Frontier.

The Punjab 'atrocities' were condemned by all political parties in India, and a demand for an official inquiry into the conduct of the responsible officials gained strength. The government of India therefore appointed on 14 October a committee consisting of four British and three Indian members (called the Hunter Committee after its president, Lord Hunter) to inquire into the Punjab and Bombay disturbances.

To show its sympathy for the sufferings of the people of the Punjab the Congress decided to hold its 1919 annual session in Amritsar.

A great antipathy towards the Indian government had grown when on 23 December 1919 the Government of India Act was finally passed by Parliament. The Congress leaders had prepared their angry speeches and were now on their way to Amritsar for the Congress session. To soothe the bitterness of the people towards the Indian government, the British government once again invoked the Proclamation of the King-Emperor. The symbol of the Crown as being above parties and governments had come to be accepted even by the Indian leaders. The Proclamation of King George V was thus issued on 24 December. Granting an amnesty to the political prisoners the King-Emperor desired that 'so far as possible, any trace of bitterness between my people and those who are responsible for my government should be obliterated'. These sentiments of the King 'created a most favourable atmosphere in Amritsar' and it seemed to the leaders of the Congress that 'British democracy would triumph over the British bureaucracy in India' and 'British justice would triumph over British prestige'.[53] Tilak, who was on his way to Amritsar, cabled from a railway station his 'grateful and loyal' thanks to the King-Emperor and offered his 'responsive co-operation' to the working of the Act.

The Government of India Act of 1919 introduced for the first time a semi-democratic system of government in the provinces.[54] The Provincial government was divided into 'Reserved' and 'Transferred' subjects. The Reserved subjects, which included police, justice and land-revenue administration, were to be controlled by the Governor and his councillors. The Transferred subjects were to be administered by ministers responsible to the provincial legislature and included education, public health and public works. The Governor remained the head of the administration but he was to be guided by the advice of his ministers in the administration of the Transferred subjects. The structure of the central government remained authoritative; the Viceroy and his Executive Council were to be responsible to the London Cabinet and not to the Indian Parliament. All the same the Act created a legislature at the centre – a Legislative Assembly of 146 members to be elected every three years and a Council of State of 61 members to be elected every five years. The Act maintained the system of General and Special electorates for the elections to central and provincial legislatures; the Hindu members to be elected from the general, and the Muslims (also Sikhs in the Punjab and Christians in Madras) from the separate electorates. The Act further provided for the appointment of a statutory commission every ten years to inquire into Indian conditions and recommend further constitutional reforms to be introduced into India for her gradual advancement towards fully responsible government.

To accept the Act with or without conditions or to reject it were the decisions which faced the Indian leaders who had assembled at Amritsar in the last week of December for the annual sessions of both the Congress and the Muslim League. There was vagueness in the Congress deliberations on this issue. None stood for full acceptance with gratitude. That would amount to placing complete faith in the British government and forgetting the Rowlatt Acts, the Amritsar tragedy and the predicament of the Caliphate. It would further imply the acceptance of the British government's view that Indians were not then fit to have a fully responsible government. Tilak's stand, therefore, was for acceptance with conditions and clarifications. Likewise none of the leaders pleaded for the outright rejection of the Act which marked a definite departure in the policy of the British government and had created new hopes for the future. Hence the resolution of C. R. Das (1870-1925) embodied more of an emphasis on the competence of India for responsible government and the inadequacies of the Act rather than on its straightforward rejection. An equally vague compromise solution was found by Gandhi and Jinnah and finally approved by Congress. Reaffirming that India was fit for full responsible government and yet the Act of 1919 was 'inadequate and unsatisfactory', and urging the British Parliament to take early steps to establish full responsible government in India, the Congress, in response to the sentiments expressed in the Royal Proclamation, agreed to work the Act so as to secure an earlier establishment of full responsible government.[55]

The Congress session was thus concluded on a happy note. At the session it had become clear that the majority of the delegates, 'and even more so the great crowds outside', looked to Gandhi for leadership.

IN THE SHADOW OF THE MAHATMA, 1920-2

The peaceful political life following the conclusion of the Amritsar Congress session was cast off in less than a month. Gandhi, who in December stood for co-operation with the government, soon changed his opinion and told his people that 'co-operation in any shape or form with this satanic government is sinful'.

This change was mainly caused by two events that took place early in January 1920. The Treaty of Sèvres, concluded in January, was interpreted by Indian Muslims as a severe blow to Turkish interests, for which the pro-Greek policy of the British government was held responsible. Orthodox Muslim leaders like the Ali brothers were provoked and began talking in terms of rebellion and bloodshed. The second factor was the support given to Dyer by a section in the House of Commons and a majority in the House of Lords. Dyer had been censured for the Amritsar killings and the army council in England had forced him to retire on half-pay with no prospects of future employment. This decision had been approved by the Commons by a majority vote but the Lords voted for Dyer by 129 to 86 votes. This at once shocked the Indian leaders and increased racial animosity. The results of the Dyer debates in Parliament showed, said Rabindranath Tagore, 'that no outrage, however monstrous, committed against us by the agents of their government can arouse feelings of indignation in the hearts of those from whom our governors are chosen'.[56] 'This cold-blooded approval of the deed' shocked young Jawaharlal Nehru greatly. It seemed to him 'absolutely immoral, indecent, to use public school language, it was the height of bad form'.[57] The defence of Dyer's conduct by the Lords and the raising of private funds for him in Britain and India by British ladies, took place at a time when the details of the Punjab tragedy were being brought to the notice of Indians by the committees appointed to inquire into the matter; in March the Congress sub-committee published its report and in May came the Hunter Committee report.

Gandhi's reaction was perhaps too hasty. There was no time to be lost. The Muslim agitation on behalf of the Caliphate must be harnessed soon in a national movement, otherwise they might start a separate violent movement and become crushed and disillusioned. Then at the back of his mind might have been the sad experience of the failure of his first civil disobedience movement of April 1919. His firm belief in the ultimate victory of *Satyagraha* may have induced him to try it again, and he may have reckoned that the time was most opportune, for there had emerged a deep nation-wide resentment against the *Raj*. He therefore planned his non-violent non-co-operation movement. He discussed his scheme in the meeting of the All-India Khilafat Committee. The difficulty lay in persuading the Muslims to accept non-violence. For Gandhi there was no compromise on this. The orthodox Muslim leaders of the Khilafat Committee did not grasp this idea but they finally agreed, 'making it clear that they did so as a policy only and not as a creed, for their religion did not prohibit the use of violence in a righteous cause'.[58] The Council of the Muslim League was then persuaded to agree to follow Gandhi's lead.[59] Gandhi, thus backed by the two major Muslim organisations, explained to the people the details of his non-co-operation scheme. Non-co-operation with the government involved:

Firstly, to renounce all honorary posts, titles and member-ship of legislative councils. Secondly, to give up all remuneratory posts under government service. Thirdly, to boycott law courts, schools and colleges. Fourthly, to give up all appointments with the police and military forces. Finally, to refuse to pay taxes to the government.[60]

As the British government in India functioned solely with the co-operation of the Indian people, it would collapse, Gandhi calculated, if the people withdrew their co-operation. The success of Gandhi's non-co-operation thus depended on from which government departments, and to what extent, the Indians withdrew their co-operation. If a majority of Indians left the government services and the army the functioning of the government would be

1*a*. 'An imperialist heart and soul', Lord Curzon (Viceroy 1899–1905) treated the rulers of Indian states as unruly schoolboys who should be disciplined firmly but not unkindly. Here the Nizam of Hyderabad sits between Lord and Lady Curzon

1*b*. The great Delhi Durbar procession, December 1911. For the first time the reigning monarch, King George V, visits his Indian Empire with the Queen

2a. Moplah rebels taken to trial. Gandhi's civil disobedience campaign (1920–2) involved the masses for the first time but they shocked him by resorting to violence. In 1921, Moplah Muslims rose against the *Raj* and killed their Hindu moneylenders

2b. Chauri Chaura victims and the ruined police station in the background. In February 1922, Hindu villagers of Chauri Chaura revolted against the *Raj* and set fire to the village police station. Twenty-one Indian policemen were burnt to death

SITTING TIGHT.

BRITANNIA (to Tiger). "IN CASE YOU'RE UNDER ANY MISAPPREHENSION, I AM NOT LIKE 'THE YOUNG LADY OF RIGA.' I PROPOSE TO RETURN FROM THIS RIDE WITH OUR RELATIVE POSITIONS UNCHANGED."

3a. Cartoon from *Punch*,
14 May 1930

A QUESTION OF CONTROL.

⸺. "WHAT ABOUT CHANGING PLACES?"
⸺ BULL. "WELL, YOU'RE WELCOME TO SEE WHAT YOU CAN DO AT THE WHEEL; ⸺HINK I'D BETTER SIT BESIDE YOU—WITHIN REACH OF THE BRAKE."

3b. Cartoon from *Punch*,
28 January 1931

4*a*. Lord Wavell. Sincere and straightforward, the last but one Viceroy, Lord Wavell (1943–7) failed to impress upon Churchill that power must be transferred to Indian hands without delay

4*b*. Jinnah and Nehru. The lives of 400 million people rested in their hands but Jinnah and Nehru did not understand each other. Strolling together for the last time in Simla, 1946, they were poles apart in everything but their handsome appearance

5*a*. Clement Attlee.
Prime Minister Attlee
courageously resolved in
February 1947 that
Britain must withdraw
from India

5*b*. Lord Mountbatten
and Mahatma Gandhi in
March 1947. The Prince
and the Mahatma shared
detachment and glory in
common

6*a*. Sir Stafford Cripps (*right*) with Jinnah in 1942. Cripps's mission failed to solve the Indian deadlock but it gave a boost to Jinnah's scheme for Pakistan

6*b*. The first Simla Conference (June–July 1945), convened by Wavell, abruptly ended in failure. In the picture are seen the provincial leaders of Congress, Jinnah (sixth from the right) and on his right the Sikh leader Master Tara Singh

7a. The Cabinet Mission at a press conference, 17 May 1946, to explain their constitutional plan. *Centre:* Lord Pethick-Lawrence, Secretary of State for India; *right:* Sir Stafford Cripps; *Left:* A. V. Alexander, First Lord of the Admiralty

7b. The historic meeting of 2 June 1947, when Congress leaders, the Muslim League and the Sikh community accepted the Mountbatten–Menon plan for the division of India

8*a*. The birth of Pakistan, Karachi, 14 August 1947. When it was rumoured that Jinnah might be assassinated Mountbatten offered to drive with him. On arrival at Government House, Jinnah said, with evident emotion, 'Thank God I have brought you back alive'

8*b*. Inauguration of the Indian Dominion, 15 August 1947. Mountbatten swears in Nehru as India's first Prime Minister. On the left of Lady Mountbatten, standing in line, are Vallabhbhai Patel, Deputy Prime Minister, and A. K. Azad

rendered impossible. But if only the students left the government schools and colleges and a handful of politicians left the legislatures, the government would at the worst be inconvenienced or harassed but it could hardly be expected to collapse.

The start of the non-co-operation movement was fixed for 1 August. Once again Gandhi planned his *Satyagraha* and secured the support of the people outside Congress. Why? He was aware that his *Satyagraha* plan would be opposed by a certain section of people in Congress – Mrs Besant, Jinnah and the Maratha group of politicians under Tilak (who died on 1 August). He was then not the undisputed leader of Congress and he knew it would be difficult to control it without solid mass support behind him. But by the end of August Gandhi had secured support for his non-co-operation scheme from the majority of middle-class Muslims. He had by then also captured a majority following in the Punjab, Bombay, the United Provinces, Bihar and Bengal.

Thus, when Congress met at a special session in Calcutta in September to consider Gandhi's scheme it was virtually faced with accomplished facts. Gandhi won. But it was not an easy victory. 884 delegates, mostly from the Central Provinces and Berar, voted against Gandhi's resolution on non-co-operation.[61] Some of the liberals who had their eyes on the Act of 1919 and had hopes of entering the legislatures formed an anti-non-co-operation committee to oppose Gandhi's movement. Gandhi, however, secured final control over Congress at its annual session held at Nagpur in December 1920. A large number of Muslims attended this session and it looked almost like a Muslim session.[62] Gandhi's non-co-operation resolution was passed by an overwhelming majority. Among the few who opposed it was Jinnah who considered non-co-operation unconstitutional. He was shouted down by the Ali brothers, among others. The options before Jinnah were to surrender to

E

Gandhi's leadership and to Gandhian politics which involved suffering, imprisonment and mob-hysteria, or to quit Congress. Temperamentally he was unsuited to the 'new Congress'; 'he felt completely out of his element in the Khadi-clad crowd demanding speeches in Hindustani'.[63] He therefore decided to quit and on that day his fifteen years of close association with Congress came to an end. Jinnah's political life from then until 1934 was that of a leader in search of a party.

With Tilak dead, Mrs Besant and Jinnah cast off, Malaviya and Lajpat Rai subdued, the Nehrus (Motilal and Jawaharlal) and C. R. Das won over, Gandhi became the undisputed leader of Congress and the Indian National Movement from December 1920. In the hour of his glory on 31 December he promised to attain *Swaraj* (self-government) for India within a year.

The non-violent non-co-operation movement which progressed vigorously for the first six months of 1921 was shaken to its foundation by the first blast of violence in August. The Moplah Muslims of Malabar – untouched by the sophistication of non-violence, too ignorant to comprehend the new tides of nationalism and Hindu–Muslim brotherhood, but nonetheless seized with anger and lawlessness – fell back on their traditional and well-cherished hostility against the Hindu moneylending class and butchered as many of them as they could lay their hands on before the army arrived.[64] The Ali brothers – the spearhead of the Khilafat flank in the non-co-operation movement – began to crack under the strain of non-violence. In June Gandhi had forced them to apologise to the Viceroy for one of their violent speeches. They thought they had lost prestige in apologising. Hence in July they made the most fiery of all their speeches against the government. The new Viceroy, Lord Reading, was hoping for a rift between Gandhi and the Ali brothers which he thought would mean the 'collapse of the bridge over the gulf between Hindu and Muslim'.[65] The rift would have come sooner had the Ali brothers not been arrested in September of that year. Gandhi was further disillusioned in November when a crowd, while demonstrating against the arrival of the Prince of Wales in Bombay, grew violent and attacked the police. In the riots that followed 53 died and 400 were wounded. Gandhi's heart was saddened and he declared 'I am bankrupt'.[66] The movement staggered on and Gandhi, deciding that the country as a whole was not ready to be trusted with a non-violent movement, experimented with mass civil disobedience in a small area only. The people of Bardoli, a small subdivision in the Surat district, had satisfied Gandhi of their suitability for such a movement. He therefore sent an ultimatum to the Viceroy on 1 February 1922.[67] He demanded, among other things, the release of political prisoners. If these demands were not conceded within a certain number of days he threatened to start civil disobedience in Bardoli. On 6 February the Viceroy rejected the demands made in Gandhi's ultimatum, thus depriving Gandhi of an opportunity to terminate gracefully his non-co-operation movement which he had been trying to end on a good excuse. On 4 February, two days before the Viceroy's communication, the infuriated mob of Chauri Chaura village, in Gorakhpur district, United Provinces, had murdered twenty-one policemen. This incident was the 'last straw' and Gandhi suspended his non-co-operation movement on 12 February 1922.

The abrupt suspension of *Satyagraha* was a shock to all the prominent Congress leaders who, from behind their prison bars, were watching the progressive involvement of the masses in the National Movement and hoping that the projected civil disobedience in Bardoli would bring the government to its knees. Gandhi did his explaining. To Jawaharlal Nehru he wrote on 19 February:

I assure you that if the thing had not been suspended we would have been leading not a non-violent struggle but

essentially a violent struggle. . . . The cause will prosper by
this retreat. The movement had unconsciously drifted from
the right path. We have come back to our moorings, and
we can again go straight ahead.[68]

Jawaharlal was angry. Even more so was his father Motilal
Nehru, who, when arrested with his son in December 1921,
had proudly said in his farewell address, 'Having served
you to the best of my ability, it is now my high privilege to
serve the motherland by going to gaol with my only son.'[69]

It is, however, doubtful whether the further continuation
of *Satyagraha* would have yielded any immediate results.
Few people had renounced their titles and fewer still their
government posts. The Act of 1919 was not made inopera-
tive. The Liberal Federation had fought the elections and
the central legislature had been inaugurated in February
1921. And above all the Khilafat-plaster on the Hindu–
Muslim differences had begun to wear off after the Moplah
rebellion.

The suspension of the *Satyagraha* campaign, however,
brought an anti-climax in Gandhi's political career. Gandhi
was arrested in March 1922, and sentenced to six years'
imprisonment. His *Satyagraha* had failed to achieve any
tangible results, but he had succeeded in converting the
upper middle-class Indian National Movement into a mass
movement.

OPPORTUNITIES GAINED AND LOST, 1922–8

With Gandhi in gaol and Congress divided on its future
course of action, the frustrated people were left on their own
with their suppressed feeling of violence which soon found
expression in Hindu–Muslim riots. In this they were
encouraged by both government officials and the upper
class Hindu–Muslim reactionaries, who formed the second
line of leadership, and whose local influence and power had
been temporarily eclipsed during the non-co-operation
movement.[70] There took place between 1923 and 1928

many more communal riots than ever before or after in the history of India.* It may seem strange that the communal riots should have followed immediately after the heyday of Hindu–Muslim unity. But some of the major factors which caused the riots were themselves the outcome of the short-lived alliance between the Khilafat movement and Congress.

The framework in which these communal riots took place was provided by the religious neutrality which the British government had faithfully followed since the mutiny of 1857. The negative aspect of the policy was not to interfere in the religious and social life of the people. But its positive aspect was to protect people of various religious denominations in the observance of their religious ceremonies and rites no matter how meaningless, superstitious or non-essential they might be. In the course of time the observance of these rituals and rites assumed the status of an 'absolute right' with each community. The 'rights' of one community clashed with the other. The Muslims, for example, at prayer time (*namaz*) demanded their right to have absolute silence in the vicinity of the mosque. The Hindus pray in their temples (*arti*) to the sound of bells and gongs, and their religious processions, unlike those of the Muslims, are always accompanied by musical bands. In many cities and towns of India a mosque stands face to face with a temple. Hence arose the conflict between *namaz* and *arti*, between solemnity and music. Then there was the 'right' of the Muslims to sacrifice the cow which is sacred to the Hindus.

In the days of communal harmony conflicts were avoided and ignored by both communities in towns and cities; villages, where most of the Hindus and Muslims of India lived, were rarely affected by communal riots. But in times of communal tension these 'absolute rights' were strictly observed more for self-assertion against each other than for

* Only 16 communal riots took place between 1900 and 1922 but 72 between 1923 and 1926. The communal riots that occurred during and after the Partition were more in the nature of a civil war.

soul-satisfaction. Thus, in peacetime, the Hindu religious procession while passing a mosque where Muslims were praying would normally stop playing music as a mark of respect for their Muslim brothers. Similarly, a Muslim butcher would take the precaution of wrapping and covering beef while in transit or on sale. But when the harmony was disturbed their 'rights' were flaunted and the Hindu band played louder when passing a mosque and the Muslim butcher conveyed uncovered the whole carcass of the mother-cow from the slaughter house to the shop.

In spite of these religious conflicts the average Hindus and Muslims, if left on their own, would have lived in harmony. But they were not. Since the introduction of the communal electorates in 1909 there had rapidly emerged a class of communal politicians in both communities. These men were not nationalists. They were orthodox sectarians; each one of them sought political and economic power for himself. Now that the government allotted seats in the legislatures and posts in the services on a communal basis and not on grounds of merit, it was in their interests to separate one community from the other and, if necessary, to create sub-divisions within a single community. They interpreted religious scriptures and history to revive fanaticism and vegeance. They whipped up dying prejudices into new life and choked tolerance to death. The average Muslim was told that the Hindus were *Kafirs* and it was holy to loot them, to convert them, to disgrace their women and to desecrate their temples.[71] Likewise the Hindu was told of the massacres and the atrocities committed by the Muslim rulers of the past and incited to avenge the wrongs done to his ancestors.

Communalism grows stronger in a minority community. The Muslim community in India on the whole was more communally minded, more conscious of its separate identity and for that reason more compact, than the Hindu community. The same principle operating in the provinces had made the Hindus in the Punjab, Sind, the North-West Frontier Province, and Bengal, where they were in a minority, more communally minded than the Hindus living in the Hindu-majority provinces. Similarly the Muslim minorities in the United Provinces, Bihar, Bombay, the Central Provinces and Madras were more communally conscious than the Muslims living in Muslim-majority provinces. Thus the Hindu politicians from Hindu-majority provinces and the Muslim politicians from the Muslim-majority provinces were liberal-minded and least affected by communal considerations. It is, therefore, no strange coincidence that most of the leaders of the communal Muslim League hailed from the United Provinces and Bombay, and the leaders of the Hindu *Mahasabha* from the Punjab and Bengal. The top men of Congress were Hindus and most of them – Gokhale, Tilak, Gandhi, the Nehrus, Patel, Rajendra Prasad – came from Hindu-majority provinces. They had, thus, no experience or understanding of the fears and prejudices, aspirations and designs, of a minority group. These men dismissed communalism as an archaic and reactionary force. They considered it disgraceful even to stoop down from their high pedestal to look at the dirty stream of communalism and trace its sources. They ignored it and expected it to dry up in the hot winds of nationalism.

Their disbelief in the seriousness of communalism was partly responsible for the failure to ease communal tensions through All-Party and Unity conferences which were held during 1924 and 1928. They were shocked by the frequency of communal riots, but not knowing their sources they put the whole blame on the British policy of divide and rule. Communalism, they thought, was the creation of the British and it would disappear soon after the British left India. But by the time the British came to leave the communal stream had widened into a mighty river setting the separate boundaries of India and Pakistan.

The religious neutrality of the government, the introduction of separate electorates, the growth of communalist politicians, and the indifference of secularist Congress towards communalism – these among others were the general factors which operated over a long period of modern Indian history, in causing the rise and growth of Hindu–Muslim problems. The specific factors which caused communal tension and riots in the period between 1923 and 1928 had emerged during the Khilafat agitation from 1914 to March 1924, when the Turkish leader Kemal Pasha abolished the Caliphate. The Khilafat agitation had brought too much religion into political life and too many orthodox Muslim religious leaders into the front line. The utterances and injunctions of the Muslim priests,* the pan-Islamism of the Muslim leaders, and the general talk of Muslim unity and strength (*Tanzim*),† had aroused suspicions and fears among the orthodox sections of the Hindu community. The Muslims professed greater affinity with the Afghans and the Turks, whom they may not have met, than with their Hindu countrymen. The Hindu orthodox posed the question: What if they were trying to conquer India with the aid of Afghanistan and Turkey and re-establish autocratic Muslim rule in India? The Hindu nationalist noticed that political consciousness among the Muslims was not developed, as evinced by the very little support they gave to the non-co-operation movement in the Punjab, and the North-West Frontier Province where they constituted nearly 90 per cent of the population.[72] Also, that the Muslims generously subscribed to Khilafat and

* In November 1920 the Muslim priests passed a decree (*Fatwa*) declaring India to be a place of war (*Dar-ul-Harab*). In view of the anti-Muslim policy of the government, the decree declared, it was right for Muslims to leave India for a Muslim country. In consequence the exodus (*Hijrah*) of about 20,000 Muslims began. They marched to the gates of Afghanistan but were refused entry.

† The Muslims had always believed in increasing their number by converting the Hindu untouchables to Islam. Their population had increased more rapidly than that of the Hindus since the turn of the last century.

Angora funds – which were raised to help the Caliphate – but very little to the Tilak Swaraj fund which was raised to help the freedom movement in India.

The Hindu communalists reacted for the first time on a large scale. As a counter to the Muslim conversion and unity movement, the Arya Samaj started the *Shuddhi* (reconversion to Hinduism through purification) ceremony and *Sangthan* (Hindu unity) movement. Hinduism, which did not take converts to its fold, officially sanctioned for the first time in 1924 reconversion to Hinduism of those Hindus who had been converted to Islam. This movement must have alarmed the Muslims because most of the Indian Muslims were originally Hindus. The Arya Samaj with its anti-Muslim bias now became more open in its attacks on Islam.* There was a counter-reaction among the Muslims. Riots broke out. Shraddhanand, whom the Muslims had elevated in 1919 to the pulpit of the Delhi mosque, was in December 1926 murdered by a Muslim.

While social life was surcharged with communal tension and violence, Indian politics were staggering through a phase of dissension and division. Soon after the suspension of the non-co-operation movement in February 1922 Congress was divided on its future course of action. A group of Congressmen led by C. R. Das and Motilal Nehru were of the opinion that Congress should contest elections to the legislatures and put their demands to the government through their elected members. If the government did not concede those demands then the Congress members should adopt a policy of uniform, continuous and consistent obstruction within the Councils, with a view to making government through Councils impossible. The other group, led by C. Rajagopalachari, was planning to resume shortly

* Mahashe Rajpal, an Arya Samajist, published in 1927 a brochure in Urdu, *Rangila Rasul*, which contained attacks on the life of the Prophet. The author was murdered by a Muslim. The orthodox Muslims published a pamphlet which attacked Dayanand, the founder of Arya Samaj.

a civil disobedience movement and was opposed to co-operation with the government, even with a view to 'obstruct from within'. The matter was formally debated at the annual session of Congress held at Gaya (Bihar) in 1922. Those who stood for Council entry lost by 1740 to 890 votes.[73] In consequence Das and Motilal Nehru started a new party, the Swaraj Party. The party contested the general elections in November 1923, and won 42 out of 101 elective seats in the central legislature. It did very well in the provincial elections except in Madras and the Punjab. The Swarajists thus defeated the Liberals who had seceded from Congress in 1918 and had been elected to the legis-latures in the first election held in 1920 under the Act of 1919. With the support of the independent members led by Jinnah, the Swarajists commanded an absolute majority in the central legislature. As their demands were not accepted by the government they launched their pro-gramme of defeating every government motion that was introduced in the House. The government, however, was embarrassed but not paralysed because under the Act of 1919 the Governor-General had sufficient power to run the government without the co-operation of the legislature.

Though Gandhi, who was prematurely released from prison in 1924 on grounds of ill-health, was opposed to 'Council-entry', he was more concerned about the division that had taken place in Congress. In order to bring back the Swarajists to the Congress fold he was anxious for a compromise which was accordingly made at the annual session of Congress in 1924.[74] It was agreed that the work in the central and provincial legislatures should be carried on by the Swaraj Party on behalf of Congress and 'as an integral part of the Congress organisation'.

The 'obstructive co-operation' of the Swaraj Party with the government was neither fully obstructive nor co-operative. By refusing to accept offices in the government the Swarajists had denied themselves the means of applying government machinery to public service. Their merely vocal opposition to the government, on the other hand, had yielded no results. This caused a sense of frustration among them and some of the Swarajists, realising the futility of their negative role, decided in 1925 to accept offices in the provincial government. Motilal Nehru, who after the death of C. R. Das in June 1925 had become the president of the party, expelled these members from the Swaraj Party. The party, therefore, was weakened due to the split, and in the general election of 1926 it fared badly. The Swarajist interlude virtually came to an end in March 1926, when in protest against the government's failure to respond to their demand for responsible self-government, the Swarajists walked out of the legislatures.

The non-co-operation of Congress with the government in working out the Act of 1919 had enabled the communal organisations to enter legislatures and accept government offices. The 'transferred subjects' of the provincial governments were virtually administered from 1920 to 1937 by Indians who did not belong to the largest and the most representative political party of India – Congress. It is hard to speculate as to what might have happened if Congress had co-operated with the government from the beginning. This co-operation might have prevented the growth of Hindu communal parties. Unlike Muslim politics which had been communalist since birth, Hindu politics had remained submerged in the secular Congress until 1922. The growth of Hindu communalism from 1923 to 1927 aroused more fears among the communal-minded Muslim politicians and stiffened their attitude towards the Hindus and Congress. The Muslims who in 1919 rose in defence of Islam against the Cross were in 1927 talking of organising themselves 'in defence of Islam against the Hindus'.[75]

Muslim politics in these years was at a cross-roads. The All-India Khilafat Committee lost its purpose in 1924 when the Caliphate was abolished. It continued for some years and then receded into oblivion. Some of its Muslim members joined Congress and came to be called the Nationalist Muslims. Some joined the Muslim League, and the rest drifted towards more orthodox organisations. The Muslim League, which had since 1919 been overshadowed by the Khilafat Committee, was revived in 1924, but it was too weak to function as an effective organisation. Over a dozen Muslim organisations, national and provincial, had sprung up. Hence, to ascertain Muslim opinion on national issues, it was necessary to hold an All-Parties Muslim Conference. Jinnah, the ablest among the Muslim leaders, had drifted away from Congress since 1920 but he was still a nationalist. He had a long and close association with, and a great hold over, the Hindu community of Bombay. His young second wife, Ruttenbai Jinnah, was a Parsi and a staunch nationalist. These personal factors in his life might have had some influence on his political views. In 1927 Jinnah was hoping to start 'a new non-Congress non-Communal independent party'.[76] He did not succeed. He did, however, try to solve the Hindu–Muslim problem by persuading the Muslim leaders in March 1927 to give up the communal electorates – the bone of discord between the two communities – and accept joint electorates on condition that Congress agreed to give one-third of the seats in the central legislature to the Muslims. Sind was separated from Bombay and reforms were introduced in the North-West Frontier Province.[77] This, indeed, was the most generous offer made by the Muslim leaders. But it was made at a time when there appeared no immediate prospect of a new set of reforms being introduced by the British government. Congress accepted Jinnah's offer. But the more communalist of the Muslim leaders started withdrawing when in November of the same year the British government appointed a statutory commission under Sir John Simon to inquire into the working of the Act of 1919 and recommend further reforms.

The appointment of a statutory commission was not due until 1929. But the Tory government expedited the date to forestall the possible appointment of a commission by a Labour government which might come into power after the 1929 elections.[78] The Conservatives feared that such a commission might suggest radical changes, as the Labour party was committed to granting self-government to India. The news that all the members of the commission were British, and it had no Indian member, was taken by the Indian leaders as a national insult. It was implied that Britain was going to decide the fate of a country over the heads of its representatives. All parties and all Indian leaders, except some liberals and Muslims,* decided to boycott the commission which arrived in India in February 1928.

Once again political life in India rose to a crescendo. The negative aspect of the political fervour was a complete boycott of, and demonstration against, the commission wherever it went in India. On the positive side all parties in India agreed, at the instance of Congress, to draft their own constitution for India. In consequence a committee was appointed under Motilal Nehru in May 1928. The Nehru committee, as it is called, submitted its report in August. It was an able report, drawing on both the American and British constitutions, and demonstrating the maturity of the Indian politicians. Most of its recommendations found their way into the constitution of independent India.† Two recommendations turned out to be controversial. First: the committee dispensed with the communal

* The Muslim League split into two sections: one under Sir Muhammad Shaffi stood for co-operating with the commission and the other under Jinnah for its boycott.

† Among its important recommendations were: (1) a declaration of rights, (2) a parliamentary system of government, (3) a bicameral legislature, (4) adult franchise, (5) allocation of subjects between the centre and the provinces, (6) redistribution of provincial boundaries on a linguistic basis and, (7) an independent judiciary with a supreme court as its head. *All Parties Conference* (1928) Nehru Report, 1–13, 100–23.

electorate and offered joint electorates for elections to both the Indian Parliament and the provincial legislatures, providing no reservation of seats for any community in Parliament. Secondly: the committee recommended that India be immediately made a self-governing Dominion within the Commonwealth. Under the pressure of Hindu communalism, which had gathered strength in recent years, the Nehru Committee ignored the demands of the Muslims. And to reconcile the liberals the Committee recommended Dominion status and not complete independence for India.

In December 1928, leaders of all parties met in an All-India Convention and subsequently in the separate sessions of Congress and the Muslim League, all held in Calcutta, to consider and approve the Nehru Report. Jinnah attacked the report. The Muslims had gone back on their offer of the previous year and insisted on the continuation of the communal electorate. The report not only rejected the communal electorate but ignored some of the other demands which the Muslims had made in return for their acceptance of the joint electorate. Jinnah demanded, among other things, that the Muslims should have one-third of the seats in the future Parliament of India. He was then sincere in his belief that if the Muslim demands were conceded they would be reconciled to the Hindus and both the communities would march together in future.[79] But the Convention on the whole was in a secular mood and it seemed unfashionable to pursue a communal point. The communal-minded Hindu members of Congress, M. R. Jayakar and M. M. Malaviya, opposed Jinnah's amendment. The Congress secularists, the Nehrus, were indifferent. Jinnah lost. He left Calcutta broken-hearted, and with tears in his eyes he said to a friend, 'This is the parting of the ways'.[80]

The Calcutta Convention marked the temporary exit of Jinnah from Indian politics; when he re-entered in 1934 he was no longer a nationalist or an ambassador of Hindu-

Muslim unity. It also witnessed the bold entry of Jawaharlal Nehru into Congress politics. After a year's tour in Europe Jawaharlal had returned to India in 1927 as a Socialist and a staunch anti-imperialist. While in Europe he had attended the Congress of oppressed nationalities in Brussels and had gone to Moscow in November to witness the tenth anniversary celebrations of the U.S.S.R. With Subhas Chandra Bose (1897–1945) Jawaharlal represented the left wing of the Congress party which then aspired for nothing short of complete independence for India. In the Convention and in the Congress session he attacked his father's report for its compromise on Dominion status for India. If in 1947, as India's first Prime Minister and the keenest supporter of India's membership of the British Commonwealth, Jawaharlal had looked back over the events of 1928 he might have been amused and perhaps a little embarrassed at the somewhat academic opposition he offered to the Nehru Report. But then in 1928 there was no uniform definition of the Commonwealth or the Dominion status which was often regarded by Indian leaders as identical with semi-independence. Jawaharlal's strong opposition, however, alarmed Gandhi who hastened to find a way out of the impasse. Gandhi, after seven years of aloofness, had been invited by Motilal Nehru, the Congress president for 1928, to attend its Calcutta session. He effected his re-entry into Congress politics by putting forward a compromise solution. If the government did not accept the Nehru Report within a year, i.e. by December 1929, Congress would stand for complete independence and start *Satyagraha* to achieve it.[81] Gandhi's amendment was accepted.

[1] Khaliquzzaman, *Pathway to Pakistan* (1961), p. 137.

[2] J. Nehru, *Autobiography* (1936), p. 27.

[3] Ikram, *Modern Muslim India* (1965), p. 118.

[4] Gokhale Papers, file 579, part ii, Ameer Ali to Wedderburn, 25 Oct. 1910.

[5] Lal Bahadur, *The Muslim League* (1954), p. 86.

[6] Gokhale Papers, file 203, part ii, Gokhale to Wedderburn, 25 Jan. 1912.

[7] Ikram, p. 146.

[8] Ibid., p. 137.

[9] Ibid.

[10] Nehru, *Autobiography*, p. 119.

[11] Khaliquzzaman, p. 28.

[12] Ibid., pp. 32–3.

[13] Ibid., p. 33.

[14] Gandhi, *His Own Story* (1930–1), pp. 69–70.

[15] Ibid., p. 89.

[16] Ibid., p. 90.

[17] Ibid., p. 98.

[18] Radhakrishnan (ed.), *Mahatma Gandhi* (1939), pp. 277–8.

[19] Rajendra Prasad, *Autobiography* (1957), p. 88.

[20] Gandhi, p. 262.

[21] Duncan, *Selected Writings of Mahatma Gandhi* (1951), p. 59.

[22] Prasad, p. 92.

[23] Dwarkadas, *India's Fight for Freedom* (1966), pp. 90–1.

[24] Panjabi, *The Indomitable Sardar* (1962), p. 77.

[25] Gandhi, p. 277.

[26] Gandhi to Viceroy, 29 April 1918. Quoted in Nanda, *The Nehrus* (1962), p. 155.

[27] Gandhi, p. 282.

[28] Report of the 23rd Indian National Congress, 1908, p. 17.

[29] Gokhale Papers, file 119, part i, Besant to Gokhale, 15 Nov. 1914.

[30] Hector Bolitho, *Jinnah* (1954), p. 55.

[31] Jayakar, *Story of my life* (1958), vol. i, p. 142.

[32] Mukherji (ed.), *Indian Constitutional Documents* (1918), 765.

[33] Jayakar, vol. i, p. 161.

[34] Dwarkadas, p. 27.

[35] Quoted in Nanda, p. 131.

[36] Quoted in Nanda, p. 142.

[37] S. R. Mehrotra, *India and the Commonwealth* (1965), pp. 99–100.

[38] *Report on Indian Constitutional Reforms*, Cd. 9109 (1918), para. 6.

[39] Jayakar, vol. i, p. 214.

[40] Montagu, *Indian Diary* (1930), p. 56.

[41] Report of the Indian Sedition Committee (1918).

[42] K. Singh, *A History of the Sikhs* (1963–6), vol. ii, p. 177.

[43] Dwarkadas, p. 73.

[44] Jayakar, vol. i, p. 272.

[45] Quoted in Nanda, p. 157.

[46] Dwarkadas, p. 99.
[47] Gandhi, p. 298.
[48] Ibid., p. 299.
[49] Dwarkadas, p. 109.
[50] Gandhi, p. 310.
[51] Nehru, *Autobiography*, p. 70.
[52] Nanda, p. 166.
[53] Dwarkadas, p. 137.
[54] 9 & 10 Geo. V, c. 101.
[55] Report of the Thirty-Fourth Session of the Indian National Congress (1919), Resolution xiv, p. 176.
[56] Quoted in Dwarkadas, pp. 118–19.
[57] Quoted in Nanda, p. 175.
[58] Nehru, *Autobiography*, p. 46.
[59] Ibid., pp. 46–7.
[60] Dwarkadas, p. 149.
[61] Ibid., p. 154.
[62] Khaliquzzaman, p. 57.
[63] Nehru, *Autobiography*, pp. 65–6.
[64] *East India (Moplah Rebellion)*, Cmd. 1552 (1921), 39–40.
[65] Quoted in Nanda, p. 193.
[66] Dwarkadas, p. 187.
[67] Jayakar, vol. i, pp. 546–8.
[68] Nehru, *Bunch of Old Letters* (1958), pp. 23–4.
[69] Ibid., p. 196.
[70] Nehru, *Autobiography*, p. 138.
[71] Joshi (ed.), *Lala Lajpat Rai: Writings and Speeches* (1966), vol. ii, p. 192.
[72] Joshi, vol. ii, p. 92.
[73] Nanda, p. 205.
[74] Congress Report, 39th Annual Session (1924), Resolution 2, pp. 38–41.
[75] S. Ali to Gandhi, 4 Mar. 1927. Quoted in Nanda, p. 271.
[76] Dwarkadas, p. 324.
[77] Ibid., p. 325.
[78] Gopal, *Lord Irwin* (1957), p. 19.
[79] Dwarkadas, p. 341.
[80] Ikram, p. 95.
[81] Sitaramayya, vol. i, p. 330.

5 Democracy Divides, 1929–1939

THE ball was now in the British court. But the British government, whether Labour, Liberal or Conservative, was then not prepared to grant self-government to India, which would have virtually meant the liquidation of the empire. The Labour party, however, when not in power, had always sympathised with Indian aspirations. Hence, when it came into power in June 1929 under Ramsay Mac-Donald, Congressmen looked hopefully towards London. Lord Irwin, the Viceroy (1926–31) took the initiative and visited London for consultations with the Labour ministers. The hands of the Labour government were not free for it depended for its survival on the support of sixty Liberal members, who were over-cautious. Besides, the recommendations of the Simon Commission were not yet published. It would be irregular to ignore the commission. But Irwin impressed upon the hesitant Labour ministers the gravity of the Indian situation and the urgency for the Indian government to make the next move. He succeeded in getting Cabinet approval for a scheme which he announced soon after his return to India in October:

I am authorised on behalf of His Majesty's Government to state clearly that, in their judgement, it is implicit in the declaration of 1917 that the natural issue of India's constitutional progress, as then contemplated, is the attainment of Dominion Status.[1]

With a view to discussing the next constitutional advancement, Irwin stated, there would be held a Round Table

Conference of representatives of British India and the Indian states with the British government.

The declaration was a reaffirmation that the British government did not want to go back on its declared policy of eventually granting self-government to India. But when? Was the proposed Round Table Conference actually to draft the Dominion status constitution for India? The Congress leaders welcomed Irwin's declaration in their Delhi manifesto of 4 November on the condition that the proposed conference 'is to meet not to discuss when Dominion Status is to be established but to frame a scheme of Dominion Constitution for India.'[2] Irwin could not give any assurance on this point. The adverse criticism of Irwin's hasty declaration in Britain by both Liberals and Conservatives convinced Congress that the British government did not mean business.[3] In Congress, the leftists led by Jawaharlal Nehru exerted pressure on Gandhi, who finally rejected Irwin's proposal on 23 December.

1929 was the year of glory for Jawaharlal Nehru. Only forty, he was in that year president of the All-India Trade Union Congress. And on Gandhi's proposal he was elected to succeed his father as president of Congress, a rare event in the history of that movement. Jawaharlal owed his early political success partly to his father and partly to Gandhi, though he had very little in common with either. The father was practical, confident, and optimistic; the son was academic, introspective and diffident.[4] They had, however, one thing in common, a quick temper. Gandhi and Jawaharlal were poles apart in appearance and background, but both of them were endowed with a great measure of vision. They both played big games for high stakes. They were unsuited to strike small bargains in politics, which for them was not a game for compromises. They believed in the absoluteness of the truth – truth is truth because it is truth, not because it is accepted by people as truth. Theirs was, thus, a dictatorship of righteousness.

Many lone voices were raised in pain and anger when the Mahatma in 1920 commenced his march on the 'path of truth' and many more were to be raised when Nehru began his in 1929. These two men, however, set high political standards and, perhaps for the first time, made the age-old game of power look moral, decent and self-elevating in India. But for many Congressmen the standards were too high to attain. Consequently a certain measure of hypocrisy crept into the rank and file of Congress. There emerged many little Gandhis without Gandhi's 'soul-force' and little Nehrus without his sincerity and convictions. When Gandhi noticed it in 1934 he decided to resign from Congress. He wrote to Sardar Vallabhbhai Patel: 'When I leave Congress, there will be an end of the hypocrisy in it.'[5]

The one year of grace given by Congress to the government expired at midnight on 31 December 1929. And at that very hour Congress, at its annual session held at Lahore under the presidentship of Jawaharlal Nehru, declared its goal to be the achievement of complete independence for India.[6] It was resolved that the proposed Round Table Conferences should be boycotted, that Congressmen should walk out of the central and provincial legislatures, and a civil disobedience movement be launched at a proper time in the near future. United and uncompromising, Congress leaped forward leaving behind the Muslim community divided among itself – one section wanting to go all the way with Congress, the other in favour of parting ways with Congress, and the third willing to strike a compromise.

Congress celebrated 'Independence Day' all over India on 26 January 1930* Gandhi, authorised by Congress, commenced the civil disobedience movement on 11 March

* 26 January became a sacred day for Congress. The Constitution of Independent India was inaugurated on that day in 1950 and since then 26 January is celebrated each year as Republic Day.

by starting what is commonly called his 'Dandi Salt March'. On that day he set out on foot from Ahmedabad on a long journey to Dandi, on the coast, for the purpose of breaking the salt-tax law. The long march to Dandi was aimed to secure full publicity, and 'as people followed the fortunes of this marching column of pilgrims from day to day, the temperature of the country went up'.[7] Gandhi reached Dandi and on 6 April broke the law by making salt from sea water on the beach. He declared: 'At present Indian self-respect is symbolised, as it were, in a handful of salt in the Satyagrahi's hand. Let the fist be broken, but let there be no surrender of the salt.'[8] In a few days a nation-wide attack on the salt laws was started. The government, hoping to minimise the impact of the Dandi march on the people by not arresting Gandhi, soon changed its tactics and ordered the arrest of the lawbreakers.[9] Gandhi was detained in May and in the next five months over 60,000 Indians courted imprisonment for non-violently defying the salt law, and picketing liquor and foreign cloth shops. For the first time Indian women took part in the movement and many went to prison.

Further to outmanoeuvre Congress the government, with the readily available co-operation of the Liberals, Hindu communalists, Muslim leaders and Indian princes, went ahead with its plan for a Round Table Conference. Fifty-eight delegates from British India, representing all parties except Congress, and sixteen from the Indian states, met in London at the first conference held from November 1930 to January 1931. It was a modest success. The idea of a self-governing federal British India was mooted and the Indian princes agreed to join it. The British government conceded full provincial autonomy and the gradual introduction of responsible government at the centre. Encouraged by the Labour government the Hindu and Muslim delegates had nearly reached agreement on the communal problem – the Muslims accepting joint electorates provided that one-third of the seats were reserved for them in the central legislature and Sind was made a separate province. But the agreement was foiled by some Hindu communalists at the conference and Muslim reactionaries in India, encouraged respectively by some members of the Conservative party in Britain and government officials in India.[10]

In January 1931 the delegates returned to India with hopes for the future. It was then generally believed that the British government would transfer full power to Indian hands in less than a decade. The Indian government made the political atmosphere more congenial by releasing the Congress leaders, including Gandhi, in January. Gandhi declared that he was prepared 'to study the whole situation' with 'an absolutely open' and unbiased mind. In this, he was perhaps influenced by the positive gains India had made at the Round Table Conference.

The Gandhi–Irwin negotiations started on 17 February and culminated on 4 March in an agreement called the Gandhi–Irwin Pact.[11] Gandhi agreed to discontinue the civil disobedience movement and to support Congress participation in the second Round Table Conference. The Viceroy agreed to release the Civil disobedience prisoners, to allow people living on the coast to manufacture salt and to recognise the picketing of foreign cloth shops. The Pact shocked Jawaharlal Nehru. The agreement did not touch the 'vital question' of India's independence. It did not even provide for the grant of Dominion status in the immediate future. For Nehru the world ended 'not with a bang, but a whimper'.[12]

Gandhi, the poor negotiator, got less in 1931 than Irwin was prepared to give in 1929. He must soon have noticed the unfavourable reaction of Patel and Nehru to the Pact and might have realised that after all it was a mistake to make the deal and discontinue civil disobedience. He might have wavered between a serious participation in the second Round Table Conference and the resumption of the civil disobedience movement on some excuse or other. This might explain why Gandhi – the sole representative of Congress* at the second Round Table Conference held in London from September to December 1931 – was vague in his stand and indifferent towards the outcome of the conference. He wanted 'to break away from the conference' on some 'decent excuse'. He was therefore non-accommodating in his statements. He declared that Congress alone represented all classes and all the people of India and that the other delegates represented no vital interests in India. He made no serious attempt to come to an agreement with the Muslim delegates on the communal problem. Dr B. R. Ambedkar (1893–1956), attending the conference on behalf of the Hindu Untouchables, pressed his demand for a separate electorate for those he represented. This made the communal problem more complicated. The representatives of minority communities finally agreed to leave the communal problem with the Prime Minister, Ramsay MacDonald, for his decision.†

Gandhi returned to India in December and the civil

* The government was ready to send twenty delegates from Congress. But Congress decided to send only one delegate, Gandhi, because there were 150 applications from the Congressmen and to choose twenty out of them would have displeased the remaining 130.

† The Prime Minister announced his "communal award' on 17 August 1932. Under this the Muslims were to continue to have separate electorates and in addition to have a certain percentage of seats reserved in central and provincial legislatures. The award conceded for the first time separate electorates for the untouchables – the depressed classes as they were called. Gandhi vehemently opposed this and started his 'fast unto death' on 20 September. The Prime Minister declined to withdraw the separate electorate given to the depressed classes. The Indian leaders, however, put pressure on Ambedkar who finally agreed on 26 September, in what is called the Poona Pact, to withdraw his claim for separate electorates. In return he obtained doubled representation for the depressed classes in the provincial legislatures. The communal award had given a total of 71 seats to the depressed classes; the Poona Pact gave them 148. The Prime Minister accepted the Poona Pact and to that extent his communal award was amended.

disobedience movement was resumed in January 1932. But this time the government, under the new Viceroy Lord Willingdon (1931–6), took sterner measures against Congress. All prominent Congress leaders were at once arrested; Congress was outlawed; the buildings, property, automobiles and bank accounts of individuals and organisations participating in the movement, were seized; public gatherings and processions were forbidden; and newspapers were fully controlled.[13] The fear that their property would be confiscated dismayed the middle-class agitators who soon withdrew their support from the civil disobedience movement. The movement lost its vigour, began to decline, and collapsed long before it was officially discontinued by Congress in May 1934.

It took eight years to produce the Government of India Act of 1935, the longest Act on the Statute book.* It was essentially an Act of compromise between various rival claims – between communalism and nationalism, between Tory and Labour, between British and Indian economic interests, between British India and the Indian states. None of the claims was overpowering. Congress defiance had been suppressed; Muslim opinion was divided; there was a National [essentially Conservative] Government under a former Labour Prime Minister; the Indian princes were not especially concerned about their future; the British economy, which was then going through an acute crisis, had for the moment lost its grip on the Indian economy and it was still an open question whether the pound and the rupee would sink together. Thus the British government, being not so hard-pressed as in 1919, occupied a position of strength from which it could dictate the future of India. It was in a position to grant immediate Dominion

* From the appointment of the Simon Commission in 1927, through the three Round Table Conferences, 1930–2, the White Paper 1933, the Report of the Joint Select Committee of the British Parliament 1934, to the final document, August 1935.

status to India and persuade the 600 Hindu and Muslim princes to merge in the Indian union. Muslim separatism was not so formidable and sharp in 1935 as it was to be four years later. No Muslim politician then contemplated the possibility of the division of India.[14] Jinnah had given up politics in 1932 and settled in London to practise law before the Privy Council. A union of Congress and Muslim politics, which the British government could then establish on its own initiative, would have effectively induced the princes to join British India in a Federation or Union.[15] Of all the great number of Indian states only half a dozen possessed territory and population enough to be constituted each into a separate administrative or federal unit.[16] The rest were bound to merge with each other or with adjoining provinces to form administrative units. Thus the problem of the Indian states was not as great as their number might suggest.

It was, therefore, an opportune time for the British government, on their own initiative, to create a united and free India. But the government possessed neither the determination nor the sense of urgency to do so. When it had both in 1946, Indian conditions had changed. In 1935 the British government and members of Parliament, whether Conservative, Liberal or Labour, were prepared neither to grant full responsible government to India nor to indicate a future date when it could be granted. Within this framework of their policy they therefore took all possible rival claims into consideration, offset one against the other, and produced a compromise scheme, hedged with too many 'safeguards', checks and balances, which satisfied no political party, not even the liberals in India.

However, had the Act been passed gracefully and earlier than it was, it might have been given a trial in India before the Second World War broke out. As it happened, the most important part of the Act, the Federal part, was never implemented owing to the outbreak of the war. It has been

suggested by some politicians who played an important
role in the passing of the Act, that had its Federal provisions
been implemented before the war there would have been no
partition of India.[17] The blame for the delay has been
rightly put on the obstructionist tactics of the diehard
imperialists who were not prepared to concede even the
little authority which the Bill intended to transfer to
Indians. Winston Churchill was opposed to the transfer of
any measure of power to Indian hands, for he believed that
'we [the British] are there [in India] for ever'.[18] If Churchill
delayed it, the two Viceroys, Willingdon from 1931 to
1936 and Lord Linlithgow from 1936 to 1943, failed to
implement it within the three years they had together at
their disposal before the war. Halifax reasoned that whereas
Willingdon 'liked the Princes and really disliked the British
Indian leaders', Linlithgow 'had not much use for the
Princes and did not really get on human terms with anybody'.[19] These personal factors may not be held entirely
responsible for the non-implementation of the full Act.*
But it is certain that the speeches made against the Bill by
some British politicians, and the anti-Congress policy
followed by Willingdon, shook the Congress's faith in
British intentions. When the Bill was being piloted through
the House of Commons during the winter of 1934–5,
Jawaharlal Nehru, who was then in jail, wrote in his autobiography: 'It is an illusion to imagine that a dominant
imperialist Power will give up its superior position and
privileges unless effective pressure amounting to coercion is
exercised.'[20] Congress had lost interest in the Act before it
was passed. It was thinking in terms of yet another long and
hard struggle against the British before its demands were
conceded.

It was in this hostile atmosphere that the 1935 Act was

---

* Some scholars are of the opinion that the Act was unworkable, and
Willingdon and Linlithgow would have achieved nothing even if they
had put forth their best efforts. *P.I.S.P.*, Moore.

born.[21] It provided for a Federation of India consisting of
the British Indian provinces and the Indian states. The
Federal Legislature was to consist of two houses – the
Federal Assembly and the Council of State. The Indian
states, with their population of only 24 per cent of the total
population of India, were to have 40 per cent of the seats
in the Council and a little over one-third of the seats in the
Assembly. The representatives from the Indian states were
to be appointed by the princes and not elected by their
people. The princes were thus left to enjoy their autocratic
powers except in matters of defence, communication and
foreign affairs, which were to be controlled by the Federal
executive. The Federal executive was not made responsible
to the Federal legislature. It was to be run by the Governor-
General with his Councillors and Indian ministers whose
advice he was not bound to accept. This part of the Act,
which provided no responsible government at the centre,
was to come into force only when one half of the states,
reckoned by population, had voluntarily joined the Federation.

The Act introduced a greater measure of autonomy in
the provincial administration. Most of the British Indian
provinces were to have a bicameral legislature of directly
elected representatives of the people. The British Governor
was to remain as the head of the executive with overriding
and emergency powers, but the administration was to be
carried on by Indian ministers responsible to the legislature.

The provincial part of the constitution was implemented
in 1937. The Federal part, having initially failed to get
sufficient response from the princes and later being opposed
by the Muslim League, was never implemented. The four
big Indian states (Hyderabad, Baroda, Mysore, Kashmir)
had never shown enthusiasm for the Federation. Encouraged by the British officers in the political departments,
they hoped to retain their independent existence in the
case of the British leaving India.[22] They had, however,

formed no strong convictions. Theirs was, on the whole, a policy of 'wait and see'. Among the rulers of petty states there was apparent enthusiasm in the beginning, at the first Round Table Conference, to join the Federation. But this was generated as much by misunderstanding on their part as by insincerity. Some rulers thought that by joining the Federation 'they would free themselves from the odious supervision of the Viceroy's Political Department.'[23] Some might have reasoned that as there was no future for them in any event why not give in gracefully on the spot and be left with some powers and privileges. Whatever might have been the reason for their initial enthusiasm it soon subsided when they found that after all India was not going to have Dominion status in the near future. The very provisions of the 1935 Act might have strengthened them in their belief that the British government was committed to preserving their own position and power no matter how feudal and medieval they appeared in the eyes of a socialist Nehru.

Nehru's reaction to the Act was sharp and quick. He called it 'a charter of slavery' which deserved to be rejected 'in its entirety'.[24] He did not believe in the existence of an intense communal problem, which the British had hitherto used as an excuse for not conceding independence to India. The problem, as he saw it, was a creation of the British and a handful of upper-class politicians both Hindu and Muslim, 'who wrangled endlessly over the distribution of seats in legislatures and jobs under government, which in any case could benefit only a tiny minority'. He had come in close contact with the masses in recent years. He believed that they needed protection from the exploitation of the feudal landlords and greedy moneylenders, rather than the protection of their temples and mosques, of their so-called separate cultural identities. The essential fight was not between Hindus and Muslims but between the classes – between the poor peasants and the rich landlords, between the labourers and the capitalists. Thus for Nehru the solution of the Indian problem lay in the replacement of Imperialism by Socialism; in the drafting of a constitution for free India by a constituent assembly elected on adult franchise.[25]

Nehru's views and aspirations were not shared unanimously by Congress. Next to Gandhi he was, indeed, the most popular leader in India. He was the ideal hero of youth and the chief spokesman of the leftists in Congress. He commanded majority support in the country and perhaps in the general body of Congress itself. But the High Command of Congress, the Working Committee, consisted of the Old Guard – the rightists – who were neither socialists nor fully fledged secularists. They had the blessing of Gandhi and they controlled the policy of Congress. Their leader was Vallabhbhai Patel, Nehru's unsuccessful rival for the Congress presidency in 1929, 1937 and 1946 and for the Prime Ministership in 1947. Gandhi and the Old Guard were willing to explore the possibility of working the Constitution of 1935.[26] They prevailed upon Nehru, though in gradual stages. Congress first decided to reject the constitution but to fight the elections to the provincial legislatures. After the elections it decided to accept office provided an assurance was given by the government that the Governors would not interfere with the administration. After the Viceroy gave such an assurance in June 1937 Congress formed ministries in July in six of the eleven provinces of British India.

In order to keep the Left and Right together as well as to capture votes Gandhi got Nehru elected to the Congress presidency for 1936. Nehru was to make election tours all over the country and the Old Guard – Patel, Rajendra Prasad and Azad were to run the Parliamentary Board which Congress set up.

Though the greatest check on Nehru's socialistic aspirations was the Old Guard in Congress itself, the feudal and reactionary forces in the country were, all the same, alarmed. The provincial governments, particularly of

the United Provinces, were anti-Congress and they encouraged the landlords to join hands against Congress.*
Nehru took up this challenge and declared:

The real contest is between the two forces – the Congress as representing the will to freedom of the nation, and the British Government of India, and its supporters who oppose this urge to try to suppress it. . . . For the Government, there is only one principal opponent – the Congress.[27]

Nehru began his election tour in May 1936, and during the eight months preceding the elections he covered some 50,000 miles, using every conceivable means of transport, and addressing a total of ten million people. In his own words he carried the message of Congress 'not only to the thirty million and odd voters but to the hundreds of millions of non-voters also'.

Nehru's labours were rewarding for both himself and the Congress. He obtained a remarkable hold on the popular imagination and in fact became Gandhi's successor as the leader of Congress. Congress, much to the surprise of the government, won the elections. It secured a clear majority in six (Bihar, Bombay, Central Provinces, Madras, United Provinces, Orissa) of the eleven provinces of British India.[28] In the legislature of three (North-West Frontier Province, Bengal, Assam) of the remaining five provinces, Congress became the largest single party. It won not only in all the Hindu-majority provinces but also in two of the four Muslim-majority provinces. Communalism could not make any headway even in the remaining two Muslim provinces, the Punjab and Sind. In the Punjab the Unionist Party, supported by Hindus, Sikhs and Muslims, won the election. And in Sind the Muslims, divided into four parties, won only 35 of the total of 60 seats. Nehru could very well

* In September 1936 Nehru came across a copy of a circular letter from a high official in the United Provinces addressed to all district officers. It advised them that it was essential in the interests of landlords that a crushing defeat be inflicted on Congress. *P.I.S.P.*, Nanda.

regard it as the victory of Congress over the combined
forces of imperialism, feudalism and communalism. The
government officials were entirely frustrated in their expecta-
tions that Congress would lose all rounds. The parties of
the landlords (in particular the Agriculturalists Party in
the United Provinces and the Justice Party in Madras) were
uprooted all over the country. And, above all, the communal parties, including the Muslim League, lost miserably
in all provinces of India. This strengthened Nehru in his
belief that the only way to counteract communalism was
by direct appeal to the masses. He reckoned that communalism was nearly dead and whatever was left of it
could be neutralised by further mass contact. Raised to this
high position he felt no need to placate Jinnah and the
League.

The election results were a great disappointment for
Jinnah. He had parted company with his nationalist wife
and then with Congress in 1928. He had become gradually
disillusioned by Muslim politics and, finding Hindus
'incorrigible' and Muslims 'spineless', finally abandoned
his political ambitions in 1932 and settled down in London
with his daughter and sister. It was while he was endeavouring to compromise with a peaceful though unglamorous
professional life that his dying political ambitions were
suddenly aroused by a combination of a thought, a prospect,
and a promise. The inspiration and thought came from a
study of the life of Kemal Atatürk. H. C. Armstrong's
work, *Grey Wolf, an Intimate Study of a Dictator*, became his
Koran and his young daughter often teased him by calling
him 'Grey wolf'. The prospect was provided by the new
constitution which conceded all the Muslim demands – the
creation of Sind as a separate Muslim province, the reservation of seats for Muslims in the central and provincial
legislatures and the continuation of separate electorates. If
the Muslims of India united and promised to follow him,
he may have thought, he would go back and achieve his

unfulfilled ambition to lead. The promise was made to him in London by Liaquat Ali Khan (1896–1951), a landlord politician from the United Provinces who became the first Prime Minister of Pakistan, and Dr Muhammad Iqbal (1877–1938), a poet-politician from the Punjab who had for the first time in 1930 conceived of a separate Muslim state consisting of the Muslim provinces of the Punjab, North-West Frontier Province, Sind and Baluchistan. Jinnah returned to India in 1935. But he returned in the new robe of a Muslim politician, having abandoned the role of a national politician and the ambassador of Hindu-Muslim unity.

Jinnah was elected the permanent president of the Muslim League and he threw his heart and soul into reviving that dormant body and bringing within its fold all Muslim parties and provincial leaders. The task was not easy and the time before the election was short. The Punjab and Bengal, the key Muslim provinces, were difficult to win over. Fazl-i-Hussain (1877–1936) in the Punjab and A. K. Fazl-ul-Haq in Bengal were less communal and very well secured in the enjoyment of political powers in their respective provinces. They would not accept the dictatorship of Jinnah and surrender their powers and influence to the League which then had an uncertain future. Jinnah had very little time to overpower these formidable rivals. The election results were a great set-back for the League. Of the total 482 seats allotted to the Muslims, the League won only 109, which meant it had secured only 4.8 per cent of the total Muslim vote. The League was virtually rejected by the Muslims of the four Muslim-majority provinces. It did, however, find some support in the minority-conscious communal-minded Muslims of the Hindu-majority provinces of United Provinces and Bombay.* Jinnah was frustrated. He had agreed to work the 1935 Act on the

* Of the 29 seats reserved for Muslims in Bombay, the League won 20 and of the 64 in the United Provinces it secured 27.

assumption that the League would dominate at least the four Muslim provinces. His high hopes were now reduced to entering some sort of agreement with Congress in order to form a Congress–League coalition ministry in the United Provinces and Bombay.

It is understandable why Jinnah expected that Congress would include some Muslim Leaguers in the ministries. First: the Muslim élite, including Jinnah, had not really accepted the full implications of democracy and the parliamentary form of government. Since 1909 they had shared political and administrative powers in Hindu-majority provinces through separate electorates and weightage. They expected to share those powers even in a parliamentary form of democracy which the 1935 Act introduced for the first time in the provinces. In the United Provinces, for example, out of a total number of 228 seats in the Legislative Assembly, the Muslim League, having got only 27 seats against Congress's 133, expected to have one-third of the total strength of the Cabinet. It was an undemocratic demand in a democratic situation. But what if it were not conceded? Was the power-conscious, communally-minded Muslim élite in a Hindu province to remain powerless for ever? Second: during the election Jinnah and his League did not manifest an uncompromisingly anti-Congress or anti-National outlook. He was quite willing to co-operate with Congress on a national programme.[29] The idea of a separate Muslim state had not yet made an impact on his mind and he still believed that the solution to the Indian problem lay in Hindu–Muslim unity.

Nehru and Congress had their justification too for the stand they took towards Jinnah and the League after the election. First, Nehru sincerely believed that communalism – the evil spell cast on India by the British – had been for the first time beaten and defeated at the polls. Any alliance with the League would revive and prolong its evil life. From this followed the second argument. Why should Congress

F

form coalition ministries in provinces where it had secured an absolute majority? Congress would have Muslims in the ministries but they would be Congress Muslims, not League Muslims. Further, Congress feared that the introduction of League members into the cabinets would destroy their cohesion. For example, in the United Provinces the League leaders, being landlords themselves, would be opposed to the abolition of landlordism to which policy Nehru's Congress was committed.[30] Third: the Muslim League soon after the election seemed to be disintegrating. For example, in the United Provinces the Ulema party of the Muslims which had joined the League before the election left it and joined Congress in May 1937.

From this lofty stand Congress dictated its terms to the League. The members of the League in the legislatures should join Congress and in future vacancies no candidate should be put up by the League.[31] Virtually, it amounted to asking the League to disband itself. Having no faith in the future of the League, some provincial leaders of the League – for example Khaliquzzaman in the United Provinces – were willing to accept the Congress terms and take office. But Jinnah intervened just in time and exerted all his pressure on his wavering colleagues to dissuade them from signing the League's 'death warrant'. The negotiations between the League and Congress failed and they parted on a note of challenge. Congress determined to put the last nail in the League's coffin by direct contact with the Muslim masses. Jinnah resolved to play on all the communal chords in order to unite the Muslims under the League's banner.

Some politicians and very many scholars have claimed that had Nehru accepted the League's co-operation in the summer of 1937, India would have remained undivided.* This could be accepted provided it were also proved that Nehru, or for that matter anybody in Congress, had in 1937

* Abdul Kalam Azad in *India wins Freedom* (1959).

reasons to anticipate that the rejection of the League's co-operation would lead to the division of the country. The fact of the matter is that in the political atmosphere of mid-1937 nobody, not even Jinnah, could foresee the future of the country a decade ahead. Wisdom dawns on even short-sighted individuals ten or thirty years after history has taken its toll. It may, however, be said that Nehru put too high a value on the Congress victory at the polls. He interpreted this victory as a deliberate rejection of communalism by the masses. In this he saw too much where very little existed. In fact communalism with all its political ramifications had not till then filtered down to the masses. When after the election Jinnah and the League started doling it out to the masses they did respond. Nehru did not realise that the illiterate and ignorant masses would more faithfully respond to the cries of 'religion in danger' than to the slogans of socialism. Jinnah did not like the masses but he knew their weaknesses and used them unscrupulously. Nehru romantically adored the people and fashioned them in his own image. In this sense Jinnah was close to the people he commanded; Nehru was far removed from the masses who followed him. In the game of politics which followed Jinnah was to win and Nehru to be disillusioned.

Jinnah planned his strategy carefully, executed it ruth-lessly, and achieved in a short period between August, 1937 and December 1939 what had been denied him at the poll in 1937. His aim was to unite all Muslims and various Muslim parties under the Muslim League of which he was the sole leader. This he was to achieve by propaganda methods similar to those which the Germans had recently utilised in Czechoslovakia. He was soon to demand that the League must be recognised by both Congress and the Government as the sole representative of the Muslims of India, and no other party should be allowed to speak for the Muslims. In other words Congress was to be denied the status of an all-representative organisation. In essence it meant that Indian politics were to be divided on communal lines, the League representing the Muslims and Congress the Hindus. Acceptance of this demand would mean the death of the secular Congress which had hitherto claimed to represent all Indians irrespective of their religion, class, trade or profession.

Jinnah reorganised the Muslim League and branches were opened even in the remotest villages.[32] Paid workers were employed and speakers were trained to carry the message of Muslim unity. The membership fee was reduced to a minimum (2 annas) which even a poor Muslim could afford. But the main part of his strategy was communal propaganda. The alarm was raised – Islam is in danger. In the name of Allah and the Holy Koran leaflets and appeals were issued asking the Muslim masses to unite in defence of their faith. No means was considered bad if it could arouse religious and communal passions. The Muslims were told that Congress was a Hindu organisation and the Congress ministries in the provinces were trying to establish a Hindu *Raj*. The Congress flag, which Jinnah himself had saluted for a number of years, the Congress National Anthem, the Congress language policy – all these were now condemned as symbols of Hindu *Raj*. League committees published reports describing in detail the atrocities alleged to have been committed on Muslims by the Congress ministries in the Hindu-majority provinces.

The results were gratifying for Jinnah. The Muslims rallied to the support of the League. In a by-election held in the United Provinces, the League candidate defeated the Congress candidate. Communal riots broke out in Allahabad, Nehru's home town. Muslim parties started merging in the League. The Muslim leaders of the Punjab and Bengal (Sir Sikandar Hayat Khan of Punjab and Fazl-ul-Haq) at last joined the League in October 1937, though reluctantly. The political stature of Jinnah was raised enormously. The Congress High Command was nonplussed. Gandhi, Rajendra Prasad, S. C. Bose, Nehru – all rushed to Jinnah for negotiations which he shrewdly avoided. He had nothing to negotiate for. He needed no explanations and he wanted to give none. His sole concern in those three crucial years was to strengthen his own position in the League and that of the League in the Muslim community.

While Jinnah was gathering strength on the domestic front, Nehru's eyes were fixed on the gathering storm in Europe and the Far East. He paid two visits to Europe in 1938 and 1939 and he was in China when the war broke out. He interpreted the war as being between democracy and fascism, and his sympathies were on the side of democracy and with the Allies. He hurried back to India to give a lead to Congress. He wanted India 'to play her full part and throw all her resources into the struggle for a new order'.

On 3 September 1939, the Viceroy, Linlithgow (1936–43), announced that India also was at war with Germany. He made this declaration of war without consulting Congress which then was in partnership with the government. Congress felt slighted and its sympathy for Britain began to decline. After much deliberation in its working committee Congress offered in September to support the British in their war against fascism provided that the British government declared what their aims were in the war, that they gave an assurance that independence would be granted to India soon after the war, and an Indian Constituent Assembly elected to frame her constitution, and that during the war Indians would be included in the central government to share responsiblity and power.[33] In essence Congress demanded that if Britain was fighting the war for democracy and freedom, it must concede to India the right of self-determination.

Linlithgow lacked imagination and initiative. He resorted to the old policy of setting communal and special interests against Congress. To his great satisfaction he had watched the rise of Muslim communalism. Then there were other communities – the Untouchables, the Parsis, the Hindu Mahasabha – whose leaders rejected the Congress claim to be representative of all interests. In the same list were included the special interests of the princes and the European business community. The Viceroy believed that Britain's hold on India was safe so long as the discords between the communities and classes remained. The Congress demand was, therefore, not taken seriously. In the statement the Viceroy made on 17 October, he explained nothing and gave no assurances to Congress.[34]

Congress viewed the situation as a national crisis. On 18 October Nehru begged Jinnah to join Congress in protesting against the government's policy. He appealed to Jinnah's patriotism – 'our dignity and self-respect as Indians has been insulted'.[35] Jinnah listened but did not respond. Congress went ahead on its own and on 23 October condemned the Viceroy's statement and called upon the Congress ministries to resign. By the end of the month the Congress governments in the provinces came to an end and Governor's rule began.

The resignation of the Congress ministries further tipped the scale in favour of Jinnah. The waverers among the Muslims began joining the League. The Viceroy leaned more on the support of the Muslim League. Jinnah celebrated his victory by fixing 22 December 1939 as 'Deliverance Day' to be celebrated by Muslims as a day of thanksgiving to mark their deliverance from the 'tyranny, oppression and injustice' of the Congress *Raj* in the provinces.[36]

The breach between Congress and the League could not have been more complete.

[1] *The Times*, 1 Nov. 1929.

[2] Ibid., 4 Nov. 1929.

[3] Lord Halifax, *Fulness of Days* (1957), p. 120.

[4] Nanda, p. 118.

[5] Quoted in Dwarkadas, pp. 443-4.

[6] *Indian Quarterly Register*, vol. ii (1929), p. 300.

[7] Nehru, *Autobiography*, p. 210.

[8] Quoted in Nanda, p. 328.

[9] Gopal, *Lord Irwin*, p. 70.

[10] See Setalvad, *Recollections and Reflections* (1946).

[11] Gopal, *Lord Irwin*, pp. 106-7.

[12] Nehru, *Autobiography*, p. 259.

[13] Ibid., p. 327.

[14] Templewood, *Nine Troubled Years* (1954), p. 52.

[15] *P.I.S.P.*, R. J. Moore.

[16] *P.I.S.P.*, Sir Francis Wylie.

[17] Lord Templewood in *Nine Troubled Years* and Lord Halifax in *Fulness of Days*. Templewood was Secretary of State for India as Sir S. Hoare (1931-7) and Halifax was Viceroy as Irwin (1926-31).

[18] Parl. Debates, H.C., vol. 297 (1935), cols. 1650-63.

[19] Quoted in P.I.S.P., Moore.

[20] Nehru, *Autobiography*, p. 544.

[21] 26 Geo. V, c. 2.

[22] *P.I.S.P.*, Wylie.

[23] Ibid.

[24] Nehru, *India and the World* (1936), p. 86.

[25] *P.I.S.P.*, Nanda.

[26] *P.I.S.P.*, B. Shiva Rao.

[27] Quoted in *P.I.S.P.*, Nanda.

[28] *Return showing the Results of Elections in India*, 1937. Cmd. 5589.

[29] Jinnah's public speech on 7 January 1937. Quoted in *P.I.S.P.*, Zaidi.

[30] *P.I.S.P.*, Nanda.

[31] Khaliquzzaman, p. 162.

[32] *P.I.S.P.*, Raja of Mahmudabad.

[33] Parl. Papers, x (1939-40), Cmd. 6196, pp. 39-40.

[34] *P.I.S.P.*, Nanda.

[35] Ibid.

[36] Jamil-ud-Din Ahmad, *Speeches and Writings of Jinnah* (1960-4), vol. i, p. 98.

6 When Men Made History, 1940–1947

DURING this crucial period in world history the course of events in Europe and India was shaped more by individual statesmen, politicians and administrators than by historical forces. The Second World War was not inevitable, nor was the partition of India. It may be said that the former was caused by Hitler and the latter by Jinnah. However, Jinnah's determination and strategy alone would not have succeeded in creating Pakistan. His cause was promoted more by the shortsightedness and failings of his adversaries than by the active support of his followers. The men responsible, in varying measure, for the withdrawal of British power from India and its partition were, from the British side, the last three Viceroys – Linlithgow, Wavell and Mountbatten; two Prime Ministers – Churchill and Attlee; a Cabinet Minister – Sir Stafford Cripps; from Congress, Nehru, Gandhi, Patel, and Azad; and Jinnah from the Muslim League. These were the leading players in the last act of the Anglo-Indian drama. On them rested the destiny of the Indian sub-continent. What they said or did was to affect the lives of 400 million people. By their vision or shortsightedness, love or hatred, humility or arrogance, sense of national interest or lust for power, good health or illness, a nation was to rise or sink. India's fate rested in such very few and different hands.

GOALS VAGUELY DEFINED, 1940–43

The middle-class Muslims of the United provinces were the first to react against democracy as introduced by the

1935 Act and worked out in the provinces by the Congress ministries between 1937 and 1939. This class 'consisted of big and small landlords, and lawyers, doctors, government servants, who belonged to the families of these landlords'. They were more interested in obtaining a share of power than in maintaining the cultural entity of Islam. Congress refused in 1937 to share power with this class. Consequently its members turned against Congress. They exploited, for political ends, the frustration and despair of the poorer classes of Muslims – the weavers, embroiderers, tin- silver- and gold-smiths, workers in ceramics, shoemakers and landless labourers.[1] Jinnah's cry of 'Islam in danger' was carried by the middle class to the lower classes whose response to this religious appeal was quick and blind. The poor, pious and ignorant Muslim believed in every rumour that was fabricated by the middle-class Muslim. He was, for instance, told that in the Congress scheme of education all schools would be turned into Hindu temples and all girls would be forced to learn dancing.

By playing constantly on their religious emotions, Jinnah succeeded in obtaining the support of a large section of the Muslims. But he had no plan for the future. He had brought himself and the League into the political arena by pulling and hanging on to the tail of Congress. But now in 1940 it was not enough that the League was anti-Congress, anti-national and anti-democratic. It must have a positive plan. Jinnah had to think of doing something spectacular.

The thinking was done for him by some United Provinces Muslims. They had been in search of an ideology since 1938. Two Muslims, Siddiqi and Khaliquzzaman, met Lord Zetland, the Secretary of State for India, in London on 20 March 1939 and told him that the Muslims were against a strong federal government for India as laid down in the 1935 Act. When asked whether they had any alternative suggestion they vaguely proposed that India should have 'three or four federations of provinces and states which would be co-ordinated by a small central body of some kind or another'.[2] Zetland soon informed Linlithgow of this meeting and commented that what the Muslims wanted was autonomous Muslim and Hindu federations with a weak centre where they could share power equally with the Hindus.

The scheme for a weak union of autonomous states gained wide support among the Muslim élite soon after the resignation of the Congress ministries in October 1939. But this scheme had an obvious drawback for the politically ambitious leader of the minority party, Jinnah. He could not reasonably aspire to the Prime Ministership of an Indian union. Was he then to be second man in a union cabinet headed by Nehru or Gandhi, or to be the chief minister of a Muslim-majority province? His political stature in 1940, however, had not reached its fullest size. He still aspired to be treated as Gandhi's equal. He still did not hold effective control over the Muslim provinces. In fact he was opposed by the Muslim premiers of the Punjab (Sikandar Hayat Khan), Sind (Allah Baksh) and Bengal (Fazl-ul-Haq).* These provincial Muslim leaders could not be coerced into accepting Jinnah's undisputed leadership so long as political activities and negotiations were carried on within the framework of an Indian union. Thus Jinnah's problems were: how to raise his political stature, to strengthen his bargaining position, to tighten his grip on the Muslim middle classes and above all, to outmanoeuvre the Muslim leaders of the Muslim provinces. With these problems in mind Jinnah did some serious thinking and reading. In February 1940 he had no scheme but only a mounting fear; fear that the government, under the pressure of the war, might ignore the minority party and enter into an agreement with Congress. He was thus earnestly asking the Viceroy to treat the Muslims not as a minority but as a separate nation, to

* The Sind leader, Allah Baksh, was a nationalist and a most formidable rival to Jinnah for the all-India leadership of the Muslims.

abandon the 1935 Act, and the idea of Dominion status, to abstain from reaching any agreement with Congress without the League's consent, and to maintain the *status quo*. He was virtually asking Linlithgow to do nothing and keep Congress out until he had found a solution to his problems. But the Viceroy warned Jinnah that Parliament and public opinion in Britain would not acquiesce in the maintenance of a *status quo* which amounted to a deadlock.[3] Jinnah was therefore under mounting pressure to find a plan at once.

He glanced over the history of the Balkan states and the separation of Portugal from Spain, hurriedly conceived a plan and got it approved by the League on 24 March 1940.[4] On that day the Muslim League in its assembly at Lahore demanded that the Muslim-majority areas in the north-western and eastern zones of India should be grouped to constitute 'independent states'.[5] The Lahore resolution, which was soon baptised by the Indian press as the 'Pakistan resolution', was as vague in its wording as it was insincere in its demands. The demand was for two independent Muslim states, one in the eastern and the other in the western zone of India. The phrase 'independent states' leads to the inference that Jinnah could not then conceive of a single Pakistan consisting of two zones separated by over a thousand miles. Perhaps the vagueness was deliberate. It was not a serious demand, for no one, not even Jinnah, then believed that it was obtainable. The Lahore resolution was intended to solve Jinnah's immediate problems. It gave him a definite stand from which he could bargain with the government and Congress. It was designed to catch the fancy of the Muslim middle class and the Muslim civil servants who could share the political, economic and administrative powers of a Muslim state without any competition from Hindus. At the same time it was to break the resistance to Jinnah of the provincial Muslim leaders. They would have to think hard before adopting any definite line of policy. Supposing a Muslim state did come into existence, Jinnah would certainly be the head of its government. What would then be their fate if they persisted in their opposition to him? But supposing they surrendered to Jinnah and the fantasy of a separate Muslim state did not come true. They would then lose the support of the non-Muslims and Congress on whose co-operation their power rested. The Muslim leaders from now on kept a careful watch on the fortunes of both Jinnah and Congress. As subsequent events showed they opposed the idea of Pakistan when Jinnah's fortunes were low and rallied to his support when they were in the ascendant.

Having thus defined the League's maximum demand Jinnah, on his part, was willing, at least during the early forties, to accept the minimum – a union or federal constitution for India – provided he was treated equally with Gandhi and the central powers were divided between the League and Congress. His hopes were pinned less on the response of Congress than on that of the government. That response was more than Jinnah expected. In fact, in less than two years the spokesman of the British government gave an air of feasibility to the demand for Pakistan which, when first made in March 1940, was no more than a 'political phantom'.

The basic hostility of the British administrators in India towards Congress often determined their policy towards the Muslim League. Congress had for long challenged their rule in India, their pride and prejudices, their position and privileges, and their moral and racial superiority. It had boycotted their Prince of Wales and defied their laws and regulations. Congress was thus treated as their greatest enemy. It was sometimes ignored, sometimes suppressed, and sometimes believed to be dead. But never did a British official in India imagine what he himself would have done if he were in a Congressman's shoes, and understood and sympathised with the cause for which Congress was fighting.

The British official had more personal bitterness towards Congress than the Congressman had towards the British *Raj*. The greatest enemies of the British *Raj*, Gandhi and Nehru, were the best friends of the British. The British appraisal of Congress, therefore, was biased and unrealistic. Even as late as the 1940s a senior British civil servant in India considered Congress as a force of 'disorder and in-discipline' and a 'movement of Hindu hooliganism', and hoped that in a few years India would reject Congress and turn to 'something a little more reasonable'.[6] An enemy of Congress was a friend of the government. 'The Muslim League, though they do not like us, like the Congress still less' – this was a good enough reason for supporting the League.[7]

Linlithgow, who was still at the head of the administration in the first crucial years of the 1940s, was more than anti-Congress. He lacked 'constructive talent', 'political imagin-ation' and sensitiveness. He 'esteemed the advantage to Britain of her Indian empire' and was reluctant to hasten democratic change. He was a good fair-weather Viceroy, but his reaction to a crisis was to batten down hatches and try to ride out the storm. He had let the Congress ministries resign in 1939 and fallen back on the policy of 'lie back, wait and see'. In the early months of 1940 he advised the London government not to run after Congress and refrain from any action.[8] It was the time when the war was entering into an uneasy phase and the London government was anxious to secure the co-operation of Congress, the biggest party in India, with the Indian government. On 23 Feb-ruary 1940 the Congress working committee resolved to start the civil disobedience movement. Linlithgow's anxieties were aroused but instead of negotiating with Congress he schemed to checkmate it.

He met Jinnah on 13 March, listened to his offer of partnership with the government, and his idea for separate Muslim states. Less than twelve days after their meeting

Jinnah and his League came out with such a demand. On
19 April the Viceroy assured Jinnah that no constitution
for India would be enforced by the British government
without the approval and consent of the Muslims of India.[9]
The deadlock was complete and Linlithgow could safely
'lie back'.

But he could not postpone action for long. In the summer
of 1940 the war took a bad turn for the Allies. In May
Winston Churchill replaced Neville Chamberlain as Prime
Minister and Zetland was replaced by L. S. Amery as
Secretary of State for India. In the same month Germany
invaded Holland and Belgium and the British army was
evacuated from Dunkirk. In June Italy declared war on the
Allies and France surrendered. The new Secretary of State
wanted the Viceroy to secure the active and conscious
co-operation of the Indian parties in the Allies' effort to
crush Hitlerism. It was the most opportune time for Britain
to take a bold initiative in the solution of the Indian deadlock.

The situation demanded that the government should for
the first time make a fair appraisal of the Congress stand.
The sympathy of Congress lay with the Allies. It was
willing to support Britain in the war provided two main
conditions were fulfilled. First, the British government
should give a definite and solemn assurance that India
would be made independent immediately after the war
and would be allowed to frame its own constitution through
a democratically elected constituent assembly. Secondly,
Congress should be allowed to form a 'national government'
at the centre with other parties during the continuation of
the war. Congress was in a distrustful mood. The past
experiences of its leaders had made them believe that the
British government did not intend ever to transfer power to
Indian hands but was perpetually occupied in out-
manoeuvring the national movement of Congress by setting
against it the communal forces of the Muslim League,

which was entirely their own creation. Congress had noticed with grief that whereas it had taken decades of hard struggle and suffering on its own part to get one of its demands accepted by the British government, the Muslim League's demands were incorporated *in toto* in British policy even before they were made. The Congressmen believed that the Muslim League movement thrived on the support of the British. It had neither body nor soul and would evaporate as soon as the British left India. They had therefore maintained an attitude of indifference towards the League. Jinnah's 'Pakistan resolution' of March 1940 was not taken seriously. Gandhi called Jinnah's two-nation theory 'an untruth'; Nehru and Azad described it as 'meaningless and absurd'. Even the Muslim leaders, some of whom later became Jinnah's lieutenants, branded his Pakistan plan as a 'castle in the air'.

The initiative therefore lay clearly with the British government. By giving a definite assurance to Congress that India would be free after the war they would have brought both Congress and the League into the war-time government and helped both the parties to evolve a lasting pattern of mutual co-operation. History might then have taken a different course. But this was not to be. When Linlithgow was galvanised into action he went as far as conceding Dominion status to India within a year after the war. But even this was considered by Churchill as giving too much. Amery's draft statement of British policy, which incorporated Linlithgow's suggestions, was substantially modified by the Prime Minister to become 'a much more long-winded and imprecise document'. In this form the document appeared as the Linlithgow Offer of 8 August 1940.

The August offer made no precise promise and gave no definite assurance. It stated that Dominion status for India was the objective of the British government, but neither the date nor the method of introducing it was indicated. It stated that 'with the least possible delay' following the war the British government would set up a representative body to devise India's constitution. The Viceroy, in the meantime, was to invite a certain number of representative Indians to join his Executive Council and a War Advisory Council. An assurance, however, was given to the Muslim League that the British government would not contemplate transferring power to any system of government in India, the authority of which was denied 'by large and powerful elements in India's national life'.

Thus the August declaration of British policy, while conceding none of the demands of Congress, put flesh and blood on Jinnah's chimera of Pakistan. Congress distrust of the British increased and it became convinced that the British 'had no intention to recognise India's independence, and would, if they could, continue to hold this country indefinitely in bondage for British exploitation.' Congress rejected the August offer and authorised Gandhi to start the civil disobedience movement.* Gandhi resisted Congress pressure as long as he could and then finally started a relatively milder form of *Satyagraha* – the individual civil disobedience movement – in October 1940. Nearly 30,000 Congressmen courted imprisonment during the years 1940-1.[10]

Jinnah was gratified and his ambitions sharpened. He offered to join the Executive Council provided the League was given as many seats in the council as Congress and also that Congress, should it change its mind, would not be allowed to come into the council without the consent of the League. The Viceroy was not prepared to go so far as to give the League a veto on the entry of Congress.[11] Hence the League also rejected the August offer. In spite of Jinnah's rejection of the August offer, some of the League leaders

* Linlithgow was prepared to fight the Congress defiance. Strangely enough the very day he made his August offer he had intimated to the provincial Governors his declared determination to crush the Congress organisation as a whole.

including the three Muslim premiers, joined the Viceroy's
Executive Council and the National Defence Council in
August 1941 when the Viceroy decided to go ahead without
Congress and the League. Jinnah, however, exerted pressure
and the premiers of the Punjab and Bengal resigned from
the councils, but the latter at the same time also resigned
from the League in protest against Jinnah's 'arrogant and
dictatorial conduct'.

The stalemate reached once again in August 1940 continued throughout 1941. Congress distrust of Churchill's
administration was further strengthened when he declared
in September 1941 that the Atlantic Charter (which was
born of a meeting between Franklin D. Roosevelt and
himself in the previous month and which promised the right
of self-determination to all peoples) did not apply to India.
Churchill's negative attitude towards the Indian problem
was, however, disturbed when, in December 1941, Japan
struck at Pearl Harbor and the war began in the Pacific. In
February 1942 Singapore fell to the Japanese, and Rangoon
a month later. The war had now moved to India's doorstep.
Churchill and Roosevelt turned their attention to India.
The Congress prisoners were released soon after the Pearl
Harbor disaster. The fall of Rangoon prompted Churchill to
despatch to India in March 1942 a Cabinet Minister, Sir
Stafford Cripps. Roosevelt sent his personal envoy, Colonel
Johnson, to Delhi in April. Generalisimo Chiang Kai-shek had
already visited India in February 1942, conferred with
Indian leaders and urged the British government to give
'real political power' to the Indian people. The Indian
political deadlock suddenly became a matter of concern to
the U.S.A. and China. It became necessary for Churchill to
show the Allies that Britain was endeavouring to find a
solution to the Indian problem. But Churchill was not disposed to sanction the obvious solution.

Cripps, a radical, and an old friend of Congress, was
sent to India with limited authority. His mission first

aroused hopes in the Congress circle and suspicions among the Muslim Leaguers, but turned out to be disappointing to the former and stimulating to the latter. Many factors combined to make his mission a failure. The plan he was sent with was difficult for Congress to accept. It offered that, immediately the war was over, Britain would set up in India an elected, constitution-making body which would frame a Dominion Constitution for the Indian union. But if any province did not want to join the union (meaning thereby all or any of the Muslim provinces) it could frame its own constitution and exist as an independent Dominion. Thus, by implication, the Cripps proposals offered a separate Pakistan if the Muslim provinces did not wish to remain in the Indian union. The same option was vaguely allowed to the Indian states. The other principal part of the plan related to the formation of an immediate interim government. The representatives of the main parties were to join the government but they were to function under the supervision and control of the Viceroy as his councillors and not as members of a national government, free from the control and interference of the Viceroy, as the Congress demanded. Though opposed to the long-term proposals, Congress was willing to accept the interim suggestions provided all responsibility for defence was given to an Indian member of the council. The British government was reluctant to concede this. There was a growing pro-Japanese feeling among Indians. Perhaps Nehru rightly interpreted it as not so much pro-Japanese as anti-British. However, the government feared that, given power over defence, the Indians might seek a separate peace with Japan.[12] This fear was in some measure shared by Roosevelt and his envoy Colonel Johnson.

The Congress stand on the defence question might have weakened if Cripps had persisted in his negotiations with single-minded strength. He might have done so if he had been supported by the Viceroy, his councillors and the

British Cabinet. But the Viceroy and his council, having no foreknowledge of Cripps's plan, were hostile to his mission from the very beginning. Colonel Johnson's intervention in the negotiations and Cripps's intimate concern for Congress further incensed the feelings of the Indian government. When the negotiations had reached a point where, by giving solemn assurances, Cripps might have won over the Congress to his plan, he received on 7 April a 'mysterious' cable from London which caused a definite change in his attitude.[13] He made no further efforts to continue negotiations when Congress formally rejected his proposals on the 12 April, but left for England the following day.

It is unfortunate that Cripps's proposals should have incorporated the 'Pakistan option' at a time when nobody not even Jinnah, considered it a possibility. Four years later, in 1946, a Labour government and a Labour Cabinet mission to India boldly rejected the idea of Pakistan and put forward their scheme for a United India which, even though it came when Pakistan had become feasible, was nearly accepted by Jinnah. If Churchill's government had shown imagination and boldly put forward a similar scheme in 1940 or 1942 the course of subsequent history might have been changed. Admitting that Churchill could not conceive of an independent India and also that Britain's ability to hold India was not seriously doubted in the early 1940s, the fact remains that the inclusion of the 'Pakistan option' in the 1942 offer was not warranted by Indian conditions. Jinnah was less serious about his demand for Pakistan in the years 1940-42 than Congress was in its demand for Dominion status in 1928. But whereas the Congress demand was half-heartedly considered nearly fifteen years after it was made, Jinnah's demand was willingly conceded less than two years after its pronouncement. Yet it is doubtful whether even Churchill, had he been serious about transferring power to India, would have preferred division to the unity of the sub-continent. From that which was offered in 1942 it may be inferred that the Conservative-dominated government was not sincere about its long-term proposals and the 'Pakistan option' was included more to stress the 'complexity' of the Indian problem than to solve it. In effect, the offer added strength to the Pakistan demand.

Though Congress was united in its rejection of the Cripps offer, it was indecisive in its policy towards Jinnah and his League. Two main options were before Congress: either to treat the Muslim League as its enemy and vigorously to combat the growth of its power and influence, or to consider the League as the second most important party in the dispute and make sincere efforts to reach an agreement with it. Congress vacillated between these two options, sometimes patronising and sometimes showing indifference, but never, until it was too late, evolving a definite policy towards the League. If Congress had accepted the first option it would have worked vigilantly to keep the Muslim-majority provinces outside the growing influence of Jinnah and the League. With that end in view it might have felt inclined to accept Cripps's offer, for until then the Pakistan provinces were more under the influence of Congress than of the League. The acceptance of the Cripps offer would have enabled Congress shortly to form a Congress ministry in the North-West Frontier Province, to support the anti-Jinnah Allah Baksh ministry in Sind and the Fazl-ul-Haq ministry in Bengal, and to strengthen the non-League Unionist ministry in the Punjab. Congress, by pursuing this line of action, might have succeeded in neutralising the 'Pakistan option' in the 1942 offer. On the other hand, had Congress decided to reach an agreement with the League, it would have backed up Rajagopalachari's formula of April 1942,* or any such scheme which conceded some of Jinnah's

* Rajagopalachari, realising that the British would not leave India until an agreement was reached between Congress and the League, urged Congress to accept Pakistan in theory. Congress rejected his resolution and he temporarily resigned from the party on 15 July 1942.

demands and at the same time preserved the unity of India.

The failure of the Cripps Mission further sharpened Congress hostility towards the British. The approach of Japan to India's eastern frontiers aroused among Congress-men mixed feeling of fear and hope. There was fear that India might meet the fate of Malaya and Burma and that Japan might turn out to be a new imperialist. Nehru's anti-British attitude did not condone Japan's aggression. He assured President Roosevelt:

Though the way of our choice may be closed to us, and we are unable to associate ourselves with the activities of the British authorities in India, still we shall do our utmost not to submit to Japanese or any other aggression and invasion. We, who have struggled for so long for freedom and against an old aggression, would prefer to perish rather than submit to a new invader.[14]

Underneath the fear was the hope that Japan might liberate India. This was partly born of hostility towards the British and partly of the assurances given by General Tojo, the Prime Minister of Japan, and the Indian leader, Subhas Chandra Bose. Tojo had proclaimed 'India for Indians'.[15] Bose, who had escaped from India to Berlin in January 1941, had formed there the Provisional Government of Free India with the support of the Axis powers. He was, in 1942, assuring Indians from the Azad Hind Radio, Germany, that Japan had no designs on India; 'Japan is our ally, our helper. Co-operate with the Japanese in order to eliminate British domination and establish a new order.'[16]

Wrapped in this mood of frustration, hostility, fear and hope, Congress looked to Gandhi for guidance. Gandhi, having lost faith in the physical and moral power of the British, was now in a more uncompromising mood than ever. He believed that while British domination persisted, India would not defend herself against the Japanese nor would Congress reach an agreement with Jinnah on her domestic problems. Britain, therefore, must 'quit India' immediately:

There are powerful elements of fascism in British rule, and in India these are the elements which we see and feel every day. If the British wish to document their right to win the war and make the world better, they must purify themselves by surrendering power in India.[17]

Accordingly the Congress working committee passed a resolution on 6 July 1942 asking the British to withdraw from India, otherwise Congress would be reluctantly compelled to start a civil disobedience movement.[18] The resolution, however, made it clear that Congress asked for the withdrawal of British domination and not of British forces, which might use Indian territory in their war against Japan. The resolution was endorsed by the All-India Congress Committee on 8 August 1942, at Bombay. The following day all members of the Congress working committee were arrested and Congress was outlawed. Gandhi's 'do or die' call was passionately responded to by most Indians. They rose in defiance of the *Raj* and, finding no Congress leader outside prison to guide them, they resorted to violence. Railway trains were derailed and looted, police stations set on fire and telegraph lines cut. The machinery of government was completely paralysed for a brief period in certain districts of the United Provinces and Bihar. The government called in the army which soon restored order.

With Congress outlawed and its leaders in prison the government leaned once again on the Muslim League, and Jinnah soon started counting his gains. Allah Baksh, the Muslim premier of Sind, was dismissed in September 1942 for his anti-British and pro-Congress attitude, and the Governor allowed a Muslim Leaguer to form a ministry. The League was likewise encouraged by the Governor of Assam to form a ministry there. A union of government, League, and the European members of the legislature brought about the downfall of Haq's ministry and in April 1943 a League ministry was formed in Bengal. In May 1943 a League ministry was formed in the North-West Frontier Province.

The League thus captured, though only temporarily, all the Muslim provinces except the Punjab where the Unionist party maintained its power till 1945. But the great challenger to Jinnah's Pakistan and the strong leader of the Unionist party, Sir Sikandar Hayat Khan, died in December 1942. His successor, Khizar Hayat Khan, broadly followed his policy but lacked the strength to keep the pro-League bureaucracy of the Punjab in check. The League's influences began to filter into the Punjab through the Civil Service. The formation of League ministries in these Muslim provinces, in none of which the League was in a majority, was made possible by the civil disobedience of Congress and the consequent imprisonment of the Congress leaders and the legislators of the provinces.

Jinnah's fortunes waxed steadily until October 1943, when Linlithgow laid down his seven-and-a-half year Viceroyalty – longer than that of any other Viceroy. The idea of Pakistan had by then acquired an air of feasibility. In December 1943 Jinnah asked the League to adopt the slogan: Divide and Quit.

THE GATHERING STORM, 1943–45

Lord Wavell, who succeeded Linlithgow as Viceroy, had already served India for over two years as Commander-in-Chief. Essentially a soldier, his approach to Indian problems was straightforward and honest. A man of few words, he often felt helpless among the loquacious lawyer-politicians of India. He did not understand the language of the lawyers who led Congress. An interview with Gandhi tormented him, for every sentence the Mahatma spoke, he complained, 'could be interpreted in at least two different ways'.[19] He endeavoured to reduce a complex political situation to a single question and searched for a straight answer. When he found none, he became exasperated. In a meeting with Gandhi and Nehru on 27 August 1946, when the latter remarked, 'In other words, you are willing to surrender to the Muslim League's blackmail', Wavell burst out, 'For God's sake, man, who are you to talk of blackmail.'[20] That very night Gandhi sent a cable to his emissary in London, Sudhir Ghose, indirectly asking him to tell Cripps and other Labour ministers that Wavell was unnerved and should be replaced by an 'abler and legal mind'.[21] Five months later, in February 1947, Wavell was removed from his post, though for different reasons.

In the first two-and-a-half years of his Viceroyalty, however, Wavell was very realistic in his appraisal of the Indian conditions that would soon follow the end of war. The termination of war would be followed by general demobilisation, dispersal of labour from war industries, and the winding up of war establishments, invovling large-scale unemployment and discontent.[22] He therefore thought that it would be wise to bring the Indian parties as soon as possible into the central and provincial governments to cope with post-war problems. This would also provide Indians with an outlet for their administrative and political energy. It therefore became Wavell's sole concern in the years 1944-5 to bring the leaders of the League and Congress into the central government; then to proceed to work out, with their co-operation, the problem of independence. Unlike Linlithgow, he believed that the end of the British *Raj* was near and he asked the London government to state their policy clearly so as to make the Indians believe that the British intended to leave India soon after the war. His sincere attempts, however, were foiled by Jinnah and Churchill.

Jinnah's prestige and power were on the wane in 1944. The Bengal famine of 1943-4, caused as much by war, cyclone and floods as by the mismanagement of the Bengal League ministry, resulted in the loss of nearly two million lives. Jinnah and his League lost ground in Bengal. The Muslims of the Punjab and the North-West Frontier Province began doubting Jinnah's integrity when he backed out of his promise to negotiate with Gandhi, who was then in jail.[23] A general sympathy developed among the Muslims towards Congress and its leaders for their sacrifices and sufferings. Jinnah, who had so far failed to conquer the Punjab for the Muslim League, had gone to Lahore in April 1944 to replace Premier Khizar Hayat Khan by a more amenable person. Finding Jinnah's popularity in decline and his audience reduced from a hundred thousand people to a few hundred, Hayat Khan stood firm. Jinnah retired to Kashmir for a few months, during which period his power declined.[24]

From this position Jinnah was unwittingly retrieved by his adversary, Gandhi. In May Gandhi was released from prison on medical grounds. He soon expressed his desire to meet Jinnah and discuss with him the Rajagopalachari formula.[25] This was a tactical error on Gandhi's part. It would not have happened if Congress had been clear about its policy towards the League and Jinnah. The government of India soon arranged for Jinnah's safe passage from Kashmir to Bombay, and the Gandhi–Jinnah meeting took place between 9 and 27 September. The meeting was a failure but it restored Jinnah's prestige and power. Realising that Gandhi accepted Jinnah as the only spokesman for the Muslims and was ready to discuss the partition of the country, the Muslim leaders, who were opposed to Jinnah's leadership and Pakistan, lost strength, and the Muslim masses once again looked up to Jinnah.

The breakdown of the Gandhi–Jinnah talks convinced Wavell that the initiative to solve the deadlock now decidedly lay with the British government. He sought the approval of the British Cabinet for his proposal to hold a conference in India of the representatives of the Indian parties with a view to reaching an agreement on the composition of a transitional government. He visited England in March, 1945 for consultation with the British Cabinet and returned to India in June with a plan to hold a political conference in Simla.

The 1945 Simla Conference was held from 25 June to 14 July. The basis of discussion was set by Wavell. The Viceroy's Executive Council was to have an equal number of Muslims and Hindus other than scheduled castes, and all portfolios were to be held by Indian members, except the war portfolio. The difference between Congress and the League arose over the mode of Muslim representation. Jinnah demanded that all Muslim members of the council be nominated by the League and that Congress should be denied the right to nominate any Muslim on its quota. In other words, the Muslim League should be accepted as the sole representative body of the 90 million Muslims and Congress be considered as representing solely the 250 million Hindus of British India. Jinnah's demands were untenable. Congress, which had claimed since its inception in 1885 to represent all Indians irrespective of their religions, and which had in its rank and file many Muslims, Parsis and Christians, could not accept the status of a solely Hindu organisation. The president of Congress in 1945 was a Muslim, A. K. Azad. Besides, not all other Muslims were in the Muslim League. The Unionist Party in the Punjab and its leader Khizar Hayat Khan, and the Muslim leader Fazl-ul-Haq and his Krishak Proja Party in Bengal were against the League and Jinnah. Even to Wavell Jinnah's demand seemed unjust, and he insisted that at least the Punjab Muslims should have a separate representation on the council through their Unionist Party. But Jinnah did not give in, and Wavell, being pressed by the pro-League Churchillian administration in London, could not proceed with his plan without the League's co-operation. The conference was abruptly closed and Wavell accepted, without justification, all blame for its failure.

Why did Jinnah take an extreme stand on the Muslim representation question? Why did Wavell easily accept the failure of the conference? Jinnah's stand can be explained in the light of the ministerial changes which had taken place in the early months of 1945 in the Muslim-majority provinces. As a result of Wavell's policy of the gradual release of Congressmen from prison (a general release was granted in June 1945), there had been an increase of Congress Muslim members in the provincial assemblies. This in turn had led to the defeat of the League ministries in Assam, Bengal, Sind and the North-West Frontier Province. In March 1945 a Congress ministry had been formed in the North-West Frontier Province under the Premiership of Dr Khan Sahib, a Muslim leader of Congress. Jinnah had tried and failed to bring the Punjab under his control. The easiest way of overcoming this provincial opposition to the League, Jinnah must have reckoned, was to get the League accepted by the government as the sole representative body of the Muslims of India. Once this status was acquired by the League the provincial Muslim leaders would submit to Jinnah. Further, Jinnah must have counted on the increasing Muslim mass support the League had come to command since the election of 1937. The non-League Muslim members of the provincial assemblies had gradually lost mass support in the years following their first election in 1937. Thus, counting on the Muslim masses rather than on the Muslim leaders, Jinnah must have assured himself that if a general election were held immediately the League would come to power at least in the Punjab, Sind, and Bengal, the key . provinces for Pakistan. Though justified in his reckoning Jinnah would not have been as uncompromising as he was in Simla if he had not been discreetly supported by the Tory government in London. Even a member of Wavell's executive council – an English *mullah* as Nehru called a pro-League official of the government – was advising Jinnah all the time during the Simla Conference to stand firm.[26] Of course, Wavell did not know of this.

Wavell could not implement any plan without the League's co-operation: the British government would not let him. Tory opinion in general and Churchill's sentiments in particular were in favour of the League. Jinnah and the League had refrained from undertaking any non-co-operation movement against the government during the war. Congress was the British government's enemy and Jinnah's League was the enemy's enemy, hence the fraternisation between the government and the League. Apart from this basic sympathy for the League the British government was in no hurry in June 1945 to find a solution for the Indian problem. Germany had surrendered on 7 May and the end of the war with Japan was in sight.*

A definite change in British policy, however, took place with the coming to power of the Labour government in July, 1945. The Prime Minister, Clement Attlee, the new Secretary of State for India, Lord Pethick-Lawrence, and Cripps, now President of the Board of Trade, were committed to India's independence. The Labour government had been in office before but, for the first time in 1945, they had come to power with a clear majority in the Commons. They were thus in a position to redeem their pledge. If the Tories were the supporters of the communal Muslim League, Labour was more in sympathy with Congress, which represented the national and progressive forces in India. But the Congress leaders – 'all ex-prisoners' – in view of what they had gone through were in a distrustful and suspicious mood and needed to be convinced of the *bona fides* even of a Labour government.† The veteran Liberal leader Srinivasa Sastri was telling Gandhi from his death-bed: 'Labour or Conservative, so far as India is concerned, they are all one and the same.'[27] This was unfortunate. The British government for the first time was determined to transfer power to India, but the suspicion of the Congress leaders towards them created many complications.

* Japan surrendered on 14 August 1945.
† Nehru's last term of imprisonment ended in June 1945, and he could then count 3251 days of his life spent in British Indian prisons.

The Labour government's first move was to hold a general election in India, the first since 1937. This would, the government rightly reckoned, enable them to ascertain the strength of Congress and the League. Accordingly, on 21 August 1945, Wavell announced that elections to central and provincial assemblies would be held during the winter of 1945-6. Jinnah had further strengthened the League's position by taking a decisive stand at the Simla Conference. He now felt optimistic about the outcome of the elections and declared that the League would fight on the issue of Pakistan and the title of the League to represent all Muslims. Muslims with political ambitions began to realise that their interests lay with Jinnah and the League, and many of them 'flocked to Jinnah's standard and he welcomed them like lost sheep'. Among many who now changed allegiance from Congress to the League was Abdul Qaiyum Khan, the deputy leader of the Congress party in the central government. In subsequent months he was to win the North-West Frontier Province for the League. Congress, having spent years in the wilderness, was not confident about its victory in the Muslim-majority provinces. Its Muslim president, Azad, therefore proposed that Congress should remove Muslim fears by devising a constitutional scheme in which they could feel secure. He suggested to Congress in August that India's future constitution must be federal with fully autonomous units, that the units must have the right of secession, that there must be parity of Hindus and Muslims in the central legislature and executive till such time as communal suspicion disappeared, and that there should be a convention by which the head of the Indian federation would be Hindu and Muslim in turn. Congress half-heartedly recognised in principle the right of a unit to secede from the federation but did not endorse the Azad plan in full. Congress, on the whole, was not prepared to recognise even at this late stage that the fight was now between Congress and the League and no longer between

Congress and the British *Raj*. It was on the lookout for an anti-British cause which the Indian government unwittingly provided by holding the trial of Bose's Indian National Army men in Delhi Red Fort in November 1945.* The trial provoked passionate speeches from the Congressmen and consequently caused disturbances. Fearing that Congress might unnecessarily start another struggle against the *Raj* the British government made some conciliatory and reassuring announcements in December and decided to send a British parliamentary delegation to India to gather first-hand knowledge of the views of Indian personalities.

The results of the election to the central assembly were available by the end of December.† Congress won most of the seats from the general constituencies and secured 91·3 per cent of the votes cast in non-Muslim constituencies. The Muslim League won every Muslim seat and secured 86·6 per cent of the total votes cast in Muslim constituencies. The results of the elections to provincial legislatures were announced in the early months of 1946. In all the six Hindu-majority provinces (Bihar, United Provinces, Bombay, Madras, Central Provinces, Orissa) Congress won a majority of the seats and in each of them a Congress ministry was formed. In the Pakistan provinces (provinces claimed by Jinnah for Pakistan) the Muslim League did not win all the Muslim seats but it certainly won more seats than it had in the 1937 elections. Excluding Baluchistan, which was centrally administered, in the remaining five

* These men had deserted the British Indian Army during the Japanese occupation of South-East Asia and joined Bose's National Army, which was formed to liberate India by force. During the British recapture of Burma from Japan in 1945 they were arrested and brought to India to stand trial for treason.

† The elections were held in accordance with the rules framed under the Acts of 1919 and 1935. Constituencies were divided into general and communal. Of the total 102 elected seats in the Central Assembly, Congress secured 57, Muslim League 30, Independents 5, Akali Sikhs 2, and Europeans 8. In the previous assembly Congress had secured 36 and the League 25.

provinces (Assam, Bengal, the Punjab, Sind, North-West Frontier Province), the Muslim League won a majority of seats only in Bengal. In Assam, a Hindu-majority province, Congress won a majority of seats. In the North-West Frontier Province, a Muslim-majority province, Congress won 30 seats and the League only 17. In the Muslim province of Sind Congress controlled as many seats as the League, though the League was allowed to form the ministry. In the key province of the Punjab the Congress-Sikh-Unionist coalition could claim between them 83 seats against 79 captured by the League. Thus, of the five Pakistan provinces, the Muslim League formed ministries only in two; Congress retained its control over three.

Thus the provincial elections were not very reassuring for Jinnah. The elections proved that Congress and the Muslim League were the only two major parties but they did not show that Pakistan was an absolute certainty. The future of Pakistan lay in the conquest of the Punjab and the North-West Frontier Province. The alternative for Jinnah lay in accepting an Indian union consisting of autonomous units. At the beginning of 1946, therefore, Jinnah was at the crossroads. He could accept a loose federation of India or insist on the division of the country, depending on events.

INDIA IN THE BALANCE, 1946–MARCH 1947

The all-party British parliamentary delegation, consisting of ten members and headed by Professor Robert Richards, was sent to India to fill in the time while the British Cabinet was deliberating on the next move to solve the Indian deadlock. It arrived in Delhi on 4 January 1946, and during its month's stay in India met leaders of all political parties. The delegates were sufficiently impressed by Jinnah's strength within the Muslim community but they hoped that a scheme could be found to maintain the unity of India. They unanimously reported to the British Cabinet that 'India must be guaranteed immediately her national freedom and sovereign rights'.[28] The growing feeling among British administrators that India must be made free was further strengthened by the revolt of ratings of the Royal Indian Navy ships in Bombay and Karachi from 18 to 23 February 1946. The Indian sailors, complaining of low pay, bad food and racial discrimination, hoisted the Congress and League flags on their ships and shouted the national slogan *Jai Hind* (Hail India). The soldier-Viceroy and the British generals in India were further unnerved to find that the mutineers, who had disobeyed the commands of their British officers and fought openly against the troops who had been summoned to suppress their uprising, surrendered at the call of a Congress leader, Sardar Patel. It became obvious that disaffection against the *Raj* was growing rapidly not only among the Indian civil servants and police but in the defence services of India. The growing awareness among Indians in the services that the British were soon going to leave India gave them an additional inducement to shift their loyalties from the British to the Indian national forces. Perhaps this by itself would not have galvanised them into firing on the British for there was fear of defeat and conviction. But the trial of Indian National Army men in the winter of the previous year had set a new precedent.[29] All these men had been convicted and then set free. Since then some of them had become national heroes. The Indian sailors, therefore, had no fear of losing their lives or freedom in the event of their mutiny failing. The national forces were there to protect them. But the British administration could no longer rely on these men. It was considered impossible to hold India any longer by force of arms.

On 19 February 1946 Prime Minister Attlee announced in the Commons that he was sending a special mission of three cabinet ministers to India to seek, in association with the Viceroy and Indian leaders, an agreement on the constitution of a free India. This was the first time in the history of the British *Raj* that Britain had sent such a high-powered mission to India. It showed that the Labour government meant business. The three ministers chosen were Lord Pethick-Lawrence, Secretary of State for India; Sir Stafford Cripps, President of the Board of Trade; and A. V. Alexander, First Lord of the Admiralty. The first two were important. A. V. Alexander was a mere passenger who made very little contribution to the discussions that were to follow in India. Cripps was a political theorist with a brilliant mind and a great expert in the preparation of plans. He took all factors into consideration except emotional ones. Pethick-Lawrence was emotional; he loved India and wore his heart on his sleeve. His milk of human kindness mixed with 'Cripps's cold water logic' was to be found potable by Indian leaders.[30] The cabinet mission arrived in New Delhi on 24 March 1946.

The mission met the representatives of all parties and communities but their discussions were mainly confined to the representatives of the Congress and the League, the former represented by its Muslim president, Azad, and the latter by Jinnah. Jinnah started the negotiations with his emphatic demand for a Pakistan consisting of the six Muslim provinces. The mission was equally emphatic in refusing Jinnah's demand, pointing out that Pakistan would then include many Hindu districts which in principle should belong to India. The mission argued that if Jinnah wanted a Pakistan it must be smaller than he had conceived. East Punjab, West Bengal including Calcutta, and Assam, must be excluded from Pakistan because they were Hindu-majority areas. Thus the alternatives the mission put before Jinnah were either to accept a small Pakistan with full sovereign status or a large Pakistan (consisting of all the six provinces and constituting one federal unit) within an Indian union and with less sovereign powers. Jinnah did not then want a 'moth-eaten Pakistan'. At any rate he was not prepared to lose Calcutta. But finding the cabinet mission generally against the partition of the country and decidedly against letting the Hindu areas be included in Pakistan, Jinnah modified his demand and he was prepared to accept a 'large Pakistan' within an Indian union.

Congress, too, modified its demand for a strong union and was willing to concede to the Muslim provinces as much autonomy as was consistent with the preservation of an Indian union. Now the task before the cabinet mission was to work out a constitution which struck a balance between a strong united India and an independent Pakistan. This was indeed a difficult task and the cabinet ministers were faced with Congress–League disagreement on almost every point of detail. The venue of the conference was shifted from oven-hot Delhi to the cool climate of Simla. After a week's futile struggle at Simla (from 5 to 12 May) to bring an agreement between Congress and Jinnah, the cabinet mission decided to put forward its own plan.

On 16 May the mission published its plan, rejecting the division of the country into two separate and sovereign states.[31] The creation of a larger or smaller sovereign state of Pakistan would not solve the communal minority problem, and it was inadvisable on administrative, economic and military grounds as well. At the same time the plan took into account 'the very real Muslim apprehensions that their culture and political and social life might become submerged in a purely unitary India, in which the Hindus with their greatly superior numbers must be a dominating element'. The plan thus envisaged a Union of India, embracing both British India and the Indian states, which should deal with matters of foreign affairs, defence, and communications. The Union was to have an executive and a legislature. All subjects other than the above three, and all residuary powers, were to be vested in the provinces. The provinces of British India were grouped into three sections: section *A* consisting of the six Hindu-majority provinces; section *B* consisting of the Punjab, North-West Frontier Province and Sind; section *C* consisting of Bengal and Assam. The representatives of the provinces in each section were first to meet separately, i.e. in three separate bodies to frame the constitution of the provinces in each section, and, if they so wished, also to draw up a constitution for each of the three groups. Then the representatives of all provinces were to assemble together with the representatives of the Indian states in one body to draw a constitution for the Union of India. The plan in essence provided for a three-tier governmental system – a government of the Indian Union, a group government (if the provinces in each group so wished) with an executive and a legislature, and the government for each province in each of the three groups. A province could opt out of a group if the people of the province so wished, but only after the new constitutions had been framed and inaugurated. Britain was to transfer power to India soon after the Indian constituent assembly had framed the constitution. In the meantime the administration of India was to be carried on by an interim government consisting of the representatives of the Indian political parties.

The cabinet mission's plan was the best that could be devised to maintain the unity of India at the critical period in Indian history. It removed the fears of Indian Muslims by grouping the Muslim provinces into two solid units, each autonomous except in three subjects over which the Union government was to have control. The Union government itself was to have parity between Hindus and Muslims. Jinnah, who would not budge an inch from his stand on the issue of Pakistan in 1942, had now been brought round to acceptance of an Indian Union. The success of the plan depended first on its acceptance in good faith by Congress and the League and then on their mutual trust and goodwill. Much depended on how Congress responded to the plan and how soon.

The Congress President Azad, a Muslim himself, was perhaps the only one in the Congress High Command who was aware of the fears and prejudices of the Indian Muslims, and who was not a lawyer. Nehru was still above communal issues and Gandhi was unrealistic in his approach to them. At the same time, Azad did not believe that the division of the country would solve the communal bitterness and differences which formed at least a transient phase in Indian life, for he considered that in future opposition among political parties would be based not on religion but on economic and political issues; 'class and not community will be the basis of future alignments and policies.' The cabinet mission plan, therefore, was after his own heart. But Azad, like any other Congress leader except Gandhi, did not have the status and power to pull the whole force of Congress behind him. Besides, he was not trusted by Patel – an Indian prototype of Ernest Bevin – who generally suspected the *bona fides* of the Congress Muslims.

The Congress reaction to the plan was vague and half-hearted. It did not approve the compulsory grouping of the provinces, knowing that the North-West Frontier Province and Assam, given a free choice, would opt out of sections *B* and *C* respectively. Congress disapproved of the restrictions placed on the powers and functions of the Constituent Assembly. The lawyer-leaders of Congress scrutinised the mission's plan in its multifarious implications and suspected that the grouping of the Pakistan provinces in sections *B* and *C* might induce them eventually to opt out of the Indian union and constitute themselves into one or two separate Muslim states. This suspicion was based on a wrong understanding of the mission's plan. Unlike Cripps's plan of 1942, the cabinet mission's plan of 1946 did not grant to the provinces the right to secede from the Indian union.[32] While Congress was deciding whether to accept the mission's long-term plan, a further complication arose on the composition of the interim government. On 16 June the cabinet mission and the Viceroy announced that the government would be composed of fourteen persons, six belonging to Congress, five to the Muslim League, one Sikh, one Indian Christian and one Parsi. Although Congress was opposed in principle to the League being given almost parity with the Congress, it was willing to accept the offer provided it could nominate a Congress Muslim on its quota. Jinnah, claiming that the League alone represented all Muslims, would not let the Congress nominate a Muslim. This was an article of faith with Congress. It seemed inevitable that Congress would reject both the long-term and the interim government proposals of the mission.

Cripps and Pethick-Lawrence were worried, the more so because on 6 June Jinnah and his League had accepted (with some reservations) the cabinet mission's plan and also the proposals about interim government. If Congress rejected the plan, the mission feared, the Viceroy would have to ask the League to form a government without Congress. This point was impressed upon Patel by Cripps and Pethick-Lawrence in a private meeting on 23 June.[33] Patel undertook to get the Congress working committee to agree to the mission's long-term plan provided the proposals for the interim government as they stood then were scrapped. The cabinet ministers accepted Patel's condition. Patel exercised his influence over the Congress working committee and the committee accepted the mission's long-term plan on 25 June, rejecting at the same time the short-term plan concerning the composition of the interim government.

Soon after the Congress decision the mission announced that the scheme of 16 June regarding the composition of the interim government was dropped, but a fresh start would be made to form a coalition government of the League and Congress. As both parties had accepted the long-term plan, the mission hoped that both parties would go ahead with their preparations for elections to the Constituent Assembly. On this happy note the cabinet mission left India on 29 June. The ministers, however, were not aware that there had been a change in Jinnah's mind which might destroy their plan.

The long vacillation on the part of Congress, and the secret agreement between the mission and Congress concerning the dropping of the interim government proposals, aroused Jinnah's suspicions and resentment. He felt himself the victim of collusion between the mission and Congress. He accused the Viceroy and the mission of having gone back on their word by not asking the League to form the interim government. He was now on the lookout for an excuse to back down from his earlier acceptance of the cabinet mission plan. This he found in less than a fortnight.

On 7 July the All-India Congress committee met in Bombay to endorse the working committee's resolution of 25 June. It was at this meeting that Nehru took over the Congress presidency (to which he had been elected in May) from Azad.* On that day the Congress socialists attacked the cabinet mission plan, calling it a trap laid by British imperialists, and asked the Congress committee to reject it. Nehru, with the intention of defending Congress's acceptance of the plan, chose to make an equally fiery and provocative speech which turned out to be one of the most serious tactical errors of his political life.[34] He declared that Congress was not bound by the mission's plan 'except that we have decided to go to the Constituent Assembly'.[35] This by implication meant that as soon as Congress went into the Constituent Assembly it was free to do anything, even to scrap the grouping of the provinces on which Jinnah's hopes rested. Three days later, in a press conference on 10 July, Nehru said that in all probability there would be

---

* The most formidable rival to Nehru for the Congress presidency in 1946 was Patel, but he was once again asked by Gandhi to step down. As the Congress President was to be asked by the Viceroy to form the interim government, Patel, if elected, would have been the first *de facto* Premier of India. He was 71 in 1946, while Nehru was only 56. Patel knew that he was 'robbed of the prize' and there would be no opportunity for him to become the Prime Minister of India.

no grouping of provinces because Assam and the North-west Frontier Province would decide against it. This, perhaps, was a misinterpretation of the mission's plan which gave no permission to a province to opt out of the group in which it was placed until the new constitution was framed. Nehru's statements reflected the confusion and uncertainty that prevailed then in the rank and file of Congress regarding the mission's plan. Congress should have either rejected the cabinet's plan outright or accepted it resolutely without misgivings. It did neither and drifted half-heartedly from one position to another losing in the process, as it turned out, the last opportunity to preserve the unity of India.

Jinnah quickly reacted to Nehru's statements. He inter-preted them as the complete repudiation of the cabinet mission plan. He condemned Congress for its 'pettifogging and higgling attitude'. He lamented that Congress had shown no appreciation of the League's sacrifice in accepting the unity of India under the mission's plan. The League in the circumstances had no alternative but to adhere once more to the national goal of Pakistan. He called upon the Council of the All-India Muslim League to reject the cabinet mission plan. On 28 July the Council rejected the plan without a single dissentient. Jinnah fixed 16 August as 'direct action' day and called on all members of the League to renounce government titles. On that day Jinnah declared a 'war' against the British government and Congress:

What we have done today is the most historic act in our history. Never have we in the whole history of the League done anything except by constitutional methods and by constitutionalism. But now we are obliged and forced into this position. This day we bid goodbye to constitutional methods.[36]

This was the call for a civil war.

The decision of the Muslim League soon elicited assur-ances and clarifications from Congress, but Jinnah was not satisfied. Communal tension was mounting. Only a strong interim government could guarantee peace and order. For once in the history of the national movement Congress was co-operating with the Indian administration and the Muslim League was in open defiance. The Secretary of State for India feared that Congress co-operation would soon be lost if it was not allowed to form an interim government because the League would not come in. Thus on 6 August the Viceroy invited Nehru, the Congress president, to form the government. On 8 August, the Congress working committee accepted the invitation.

Then came 16 August, the League's 'direct action day'. The League ministries of Bengal and Sind had declared the day a public holiday. The premier of Bengal, Shaheed Suhrawardy, a Muslim Leaguer, was a man with no scruples. Soon after Wavell invited Congress to form a government Suhrawardy threatened to cause bloodshed and disorder in Bengal and turn Bengal into a separate state if Congress went ahead and formed an interim government. Such speeches coming from persons in authority encouraged Muslims to commit violence on 'direct action day'. When the day came the Muslims in Calcutta attacked the Hindu shopkeepers, kicked or stabbed them, then smashed or looted their shops. The Hindus retaliated, and in forty-eight hours nearly 5000 people were killed. The 'great Calcutta killing', as it is called, was the beginning of the fierce communal riots of the civil war that spread from Calcutta to Noakhali in East Bengal, to Bihar and the Punjab and lasted until after the partition of the country, taking a toll of approximately half a million Hindu, Muslim and Sikh lives.

Wavell visited Calcutta and came back to Delhi unnerved. He realised that an interim government without the League's representatives would be a cause for more bloodshed. But he had already given the green light to Congress to form the government and the names of Congress nominees had been announced on the 24 August. In a fateful meeting on 27 August with Gandhi and Nehru he pressed Nehru rather too hard to bring the League into the government. Nehru formed a government on 2 September. Wavell kept on 'pestering' Nehru to approach Jinnah or to let him do so. In sheer exasperation Nehru agreed that Wavell should approach Jinnah.

The Calcutta killing had sobered Jinnah. Perhaps he had not envisaged the consequences of his call for 'direct action'. The entry of the Congress into the government had made him apprehensive. He thought that it would be fatal for the Muslim League 'to leave the entire field of administration of the central government in the hands of the Congress'. He feared that the League, if left in the wilderness, would die, and the Congress Muslims, who had already been brought into the interim government, might become the leaders of the Muslim community.

Jinnah was thus in a flexible mood when Wavell saw him on 16 September. He was willing to negotiate terms for the League's entry into the government. This change in his policy might soon have been followed by a change of heart if Congress had given Jinnah assurances in words as well as by deeds. The triangular negotiations – between Jinnah, Wavell and Congress – which started on 16 September progressed to a stage where Jinnah agreed to enter the government as Nehru's colleague but then differences arose between them on such a trivial point as the procedure for the nomination of a minority representative (Christian, Parsi or Untouchable) in the event of the death of any of the representatives who were already in Nehru's government and who were far younger and healthier than Nehru or Jinnah.[37] Jinnah reverted to a state of hostility towards Congress. He did not join the government. Instead he nominated five Leaguers to join the interim government, not with the purpose of co-operating with Nehru but with a determination to wreck the interim government from within, destroy the cabinet mission plan, and make the partition of India inevitable.*

A personal element was involved in this story. Unlike Gandhi, Jinnah wanted power more than glory. What position would he hold if he joined the government? Nehru was the *de facto* Premier. Would Jinnah accept a position subordinate to Nehru? Most unlikely! Perhaps for this reason Jinnah wanted the premiership (it was officially called vice-presidentship) of the interim government to be held by rotation. But Wavell firmly rejected this proposal on the grounds of inconvenience.

Soon after the League joined the interim government on 26 October 1946, the cabinet, instead of working on the principle of collective responsibility, became sharply divided into League and Congress blocs. The League had neither withdrawn its rejection of the cabinet mission plan nor had it abandoned its 'direct action' movement. It was vehemently opposed to the holding of the first session of the Constituent Assembly which was to begin on 9 December.† Wavell and Nehru urged Jinnah in vain to accept the cabinet mission plan, which was a condition to be fulfilled before a party entered the government. The League members of the government rendered its effective functioning almost impossible. Nehru demanded that the League should either co-operate or resign from the government. Wavell was reluctant to force the League to resign. If he did he reckoned that communal riots would become more intense, at least

---

* The League members opposed the Congress members on every government measure the latter proposed. The conflicts reached a climax in March 1947 when Liaquat Ali Khan, the League member in charge of finance, imposed heavy taxation on business profits which was calculated to harm the Hindu business magnates from whom Congress derived substantial financial support.

† Elections for the 296 seats of the Constituent Assembly had been completed in July 1946. The Constituent Assembly members were elected by the provincial legislatures. The Congress had won all the general seats except nine and the League all the Muslim seats except five.

in the Muslim-majority provinces. The last attempt to promote an agreement between Congress and the League was made by Attlee. In the first week of December he summoned to London, among others, Nehru and Jinnah, but the brief conference failed to reach any agreement. Nehru returned to Delhi determined to go ahead with the Constituent Assembly even without the League's participation. Jinnah came back resolved to take Pakistan, large or small.

Of the three parties involved in the last phase of India's struggle – Congress, the League and the British government – the last was faced with the biggest dilemma in January 1947. It was determined to withdraw from India, but it did not know to which Indian party or government it should transfer power. Tired and frustrated, the soldier-Viceroy Wavell did his last thinking (with the help of his chief adviser, George Abell) on the Indian deadlock and produced what was called 'Operation Ebb-Tide'.[38] It was a scheme to withdraw British troops and British administration stage by stage, province by province, from India, handing over power to provincial governments. The plan was condemned by both Churchill and Attlee as 'an ignoble and sordid scuffle' which in effect would either Balkanise India or leave it to chaos and anarchy. The plan thus led to nothing but Wavell's recall.

The Labour government announced its own plan on 20 February 1947. The plan was based on the reasoning that the Indian parties would come to an agreement if they were told that the British would withdraw from India by a definite date. On that day Attlee made the statement in Parliament that the British government intended to transfer power to Indian hands by a date not later than June 1948. If the Indian parties had not worked out an agreed constitution by that date then the British government would have to consider to whom it should transfer the powers of the Indian central government: 'Whether as a

whole to some form of central government for British
India, or in some areas to the existing provincial governments, or in such other way as may seem reasonable and
in the best interests of the Indian people.'[39] By implication
the plan meant that in the event of the League and
Congress not agreeing to a constitution for the Union of
India the British government might transfer power separately to Muslim and Hindu provinces of India. In other
words, the British government would rather agree to the
creation of Pakistan than delay any longer than June 1948
the withdrawal of British power from India. Churchill
condemned the government for its resolution to hand over
power to the Indian politicians who were 'men of straw of
whom in a few years no trace would remain'.[40] Cripps, however, told the House that, apart from other considerations,
Britain, even if it wanted to maintain its power in India,
could not do so because it lacked sufficient British military
and administrative personnel to hold India.[41] On the same
day Attlee announced that Wavell was to be replaced by
Lord Mountbatten.

Attlee's announcement induced Jinnah and his lieutenants to intensify their struggle to capture control of the
Muslim provinces, especially the Punjab and the North-
West Frontier Province. In February–March 1947 all eyes
turned to the Punjab. The Muslim League had stolen a leaf
from Gandhi's book and started a civil disobedience move-
ment in the Punjab, with the sole aim of overthrowing the
Unionist–Sikh–Congress administration under Khizar Hayat
Khan. The intensely communal movement of the League
aroused the fears and anger of the Sikhs and the Hindus.
Each of the three communities formed private armies.
The Sikhs, who were scattered all over the Punjab, were to
lose in either case whether the whole of the Punjab went to
Pakistan or whether it was divided and its eastern part, a
Hindu-majority area, remained with India and the western
part, a Muslim-majority area, went to Pakistan. The leader

of the Sikh community, Master Tara Singh, asked both the Hindus and the Sikhs to unite, fight and 'finish the Muslim League'.[42] The scramble for the Punjab began and soon the cities and towns of the province fell victim to communal riots. The Muslims, comprising about 56 per cent of the total population of 29 million, scored a major victory. Khizar Hayat Khan resigned, the governor took over the administration, and the Muslim–Sikh–Hindu coalition came to an end.

Congress feared that if the worst came to the worst and Pakistan was created the Hindu–Sikh-majority areas in the Eastern Punjab and Hindu-majority areas in West Bengal would be permanently swallowed by a Muslim state. Thus on 8 March the Congress working committee demanded a partition of the Punjab. The Congress leaders suggested a similar partition of Bengal as well. The partition of these provinces, Congress ostensibly suggested, would put a stop to the continuing communal riots. By suggesting the division of the provinces on communal grounds the Congress betrayed its willingness to accept the partition of the whole country rather than to allow it to drown in a pool of blood. In some measure, therefore, the foundation for India's partition was established before Mountbatten arrived in Delhi on 22 March 1947.

[1] *P.I.S.P.*, M. Mujeeb.

[2] Zetland, *Essayez* (1956), p. 248. Also Khaliquzzaman, p. 207.

[3] Menon, *Transfer of Power in India* (1957), p. 78.

[4] See Jinnah's speech, March 1940. Jamil-ud-Din Ahmad, vol. i, p. 161.

[5] Parl. Papers, x, Cmd. 6196.

[6] *P.I.S.P.*, H. T. Lambrick.

[7] Ibid.

[8] *P.I.S.P.*, R. J. Moore.

[9] Menon, *Transfer of Power*, p. 85.

[10] *P.I.S.P.*, B. R. Nanda.

[11] Menon, *Transfer of Power*, p. 98.

[12] *P.I.S.P.*, B. Shiva Rao.

[13] Ibid.

[14] Quoted in *P.I.S.P.*, B. Shiva Rao.

[15] *Selected Speeches of Subhas Chandra Bose*. Broadcast from the Azad Hind Radio, Germany, 6 April 1942, p. 138.

[16] Ibid., p. 141.

[17] Tendulkar, *Mahatma* (1951–4), vol. 6, p. 123.

[18] Sitaramayya, vol. ii, pp. 340–3.

[19] Mosley, *The Last Days of the British Raj* (1962), p. 19.

[20] Ibid.

[21] Ghose, *Gandhi's Emissary* (1967), pp. 19–20.

[22] Menon, *Transfer of Power*, p. 167.

[23] *P.I.S.P.*, H. Kabir.

[24] Ibid.

[25] Ibid.

[26] Menon, *Transfer of Power*, p. 214.

[27] *P.I.S.P.*, B. R. Nanda.

[28] *P.I.S.P.*, Lord Sorensen. He was a Labour member of the Delegation.

[29] Tuker, *While Memory Serves* (1949), p. 89.

[30] Mosley, p. 21.

[31] *India, Statement by the Cabinet Mission*, Cmd. 6821 (1946).

[32] *P.I.S.P.*, A. G. Noorani. In fact it was Patel who was most suspicious of all.

[33] Ghose, pp. 168–9.

[34] Brecher, *Nehru* (1959), p. 316.

[35] *Indian Annual Register* (1946), vol. 2, pp.145–4.

[36] Ahmad, p. 314.

[37] *P.I.S.P.*, H. Kabir.

[38] Mosley, p. 50. Also Campbell-Johnson, *Mission with Mountbatten* (1951), p. 17.

[39] Parl. Debates, H.C., vol. 433 (1947), cols. 1395–8.

[40] Ibid. vol. 434 (1946–7), cols. 497–508.

[41] Ibid.

[42] Khosla, *Stern Reckoning* (1949), p. 100.

7 India Divided,
March–August 1947

> 'Let us gratefully acknowledge while our achievement is in no small
> measure due to our own sufferings and sacrifices, it is also the result
> of world forces and events, and last though not least it is the
> consummation and fulfilment of the historic tradition and demo-
> cratic ideals of the British race.'
>
> RAJENDRA PRASAD, 15 August 1947

THE thirty-fourth and last of the British Governors-General
of India, Lord Mountbatten, was also the first to arrive in
India with a definite mission. His mandate was to wind up
the 182-year-old British Indian empire in fifteen months
by June 1948. To accomplish this gigantic task he asked for
more powers (plenipotentiary powers to act in his own way
and without interference from London) and privileges (to
take with him men of his own choice to work on his personal
staff in Delhi).* He also demanded a guarantee that after
the termination of his Indian assignment he be taken back
into the navy without loss of seniority so that he could
pursue his life-long ambition to become First Sea Lord.
Attlee personally granted all his demands.

Attlee had chosen Mountbatten for his 'extremely lively,
exciting personality'. The Indian deadlock, it was believed,
could be broken by closer personal contacts with the Indian
leaders. Attlee thought that Mountbatten had 'an extraordinary faculty for getting on with all kinds of people', and
he was 'also blessed with a very unusual wife'. Mountbatten

---

* Mountbatten took with him to India, among others, Lord Ismay
as his Chief of Staff, Sir Eric Miéville, Captain R. V. Brockman and
Lt.-Colonel V. F. Erskine Crum as secretaries, and Alan Campbell-
Johnson as Press Attaché.

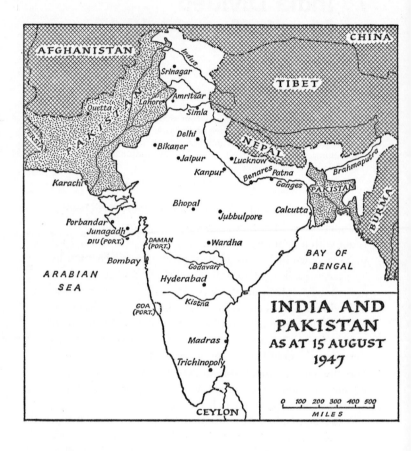

AFGHANISTAN

CHINA

TIBET

Srinagar

Quetta

Lahore

Amritsar

Simla

PAKISTAN

NEPAL

Delhi

•Bikaner

•Jaipur

•Lucknow

Kanpur

Benares Patna

Ganges

Brahmaputra

Karachi

PAKISTAN

Calcutta

BURMA

Bhopal

•Jubbulpore

Porbandar

Junagadh

DIU (PORT.)

DAMAN
(PORT.)

•Wardha

BAY OF
BENGAL

Bombay

Godavari

ARABIAN
SEA

Hyderabad

GOA
(PORT.)

Kistna

Madras

Trichinopoly

INDIA AND
PAKISTAN
AS AT 15 AUGUST
1947

0 100 200 300 400 500

MILES

CEYLON

was, in fact, the opposite of Wavell. His royal ancestry (he was a cousin of King George VI) and the success of his naval career (he was the Supreme Commander of the South-East Asia Command in the last years of the war) gave him an enormous self-confidence, and 'a sense of dominance over events'.[1] He had a political flair which enabled him to know instinctively 'who was important and what was important'. Unlike Wavell, he loved to talk and discuss and was ready to change his mind. Above all he had 'a great speed of adjustment and decision'. He possessed an acute sense of detachment which easily turned him into a keen and sometimes ruthless implementor of policies. He arrived in India somewhat like a time-and-motion-study expert who had been 'called into a factory to knock off the wasteful minutes and get out the product before the target date.'[2]

Mountbatten spent the last week of March and April in meeting the Indian leaders individually. His wife and their seventeen-year-old daughter, Pamela, worked on social diplomacy – establishing personal relationships with some of the Indian leaders through their daughters or sisters.* The first interview with Nehru was rewarding. Mutual confidence and friendship were established between them. At the end of the interview Mountbatten said:

'Mr. Nehru, I want you to regard me not as the last Viceroy winding up the British Raj, but as the first to lead the way to the new India.'

Nehru was intensely moved, and said:

'Now I know what they mean when they speak of your charm being so dangerous.'[3]

The first interview with Gandhi started in an atmosphere of friendliness, the Mahatma placing his hand on Lady Mountbatten's shoulder and treating her as he treated his

* Nehru, Patel and Jinnah were widowers. Indira Gandhi, Nehru's daughter, Patel's daughter Maniben, and Jinnah's sister Fatima were the constant companions of their fathers and brother respectively.

own granddaughters, and the Mountbattens listening to his life-story for two hours. The following day, 1 April, Gandhi met Mountbatten again and put forward his somewhat academic plan for solving the Indian deadlock. It was nothing less 'than to dismiss the present cabinet and call on Jinnah to appoint an all-Moslem administration'. Gandhi promised to persuade Congress to accept this plan. As it turned out Congress did not accept the plan and Gandhi withdrew it. The first interview with Jinnah, however, was different. Reserved, tense, haughty and aloof, Jinnah started off the conversation quite blankly:

'I will enter into discussion on one condition only.'

Mountbatten interrupted:

'Mr Jinnah, I am not prepared to discuss conditions or, indeed, the present situation, until I have had the chance of making your acquaintance and knowing more about you yourself.'[4]

As soon as the interview was over and Jinnah had gone Mountbatten remarked to a member of his staff:

'My God, he was cold. It took most of the interview to unfreeze him.'[5]

Mountbatten might have brooded over what Nehru had told him the other day about Jinnah. The secret of Jinnah's success – which came to him very late in life, at over sixty – 'was in his capacity to take up a permanently negative attitude'; he had got so far by saying 'no' so often.[6] Jinnah was more emphatic then in his demand for Pakistan than ever before. Attlee's statement of 20 February 'was a public open licence for the creation of Pakistan'. Jinnah knew that if he kept the League outside the Constituent Assembly, made the working of the interim central government impossible, and kept his followers around him, then the Labour government would have to give him Pakistan even though it was 'moth-eaten'.

During these interviews Mountbatten made up his mind

on two vital issues. On the question of a United India versus Pakistan the decision was made for the latter. It was, however, not a difficult decision to make. The Congress High Command – specifically, Nehru and Patel – 'had reconciled themselves to partition in some form by December, 1946'.[7] The constant harassment and opposition which Nehru and Patel had to suffer at the hands of the League members of the interim government had broken their spirit. They had grown old and tired, and now that they were at the threshold of power they felt inclined to accept Pakistan rather than to go back and continue their struggle for India's unity. By conceding Pakistan to Jinnah they would 'hear no more of him and eliminate his nuisance value' or, as Nehru put it privately, by 'cutting off the head we will get rid of the headache.'[8] Further, Patel had privately accepted in December–January the counsel of V. P. Menon (1899–1966) that it was better to accept the division of the country than to let her gravitate towards civil war.[9] This distinguished Hindu civil servant, who in 1947 was to play an important role from behind the scenes, was the Reforms Commissioner and Constitutional Adviser to Linlithgow, Wavell and Mountbatten. He did not believe that the Cabinet mission plan of 1946 with its three-tier constitutional set-up would ever work. In this assumption he might have been wrong but, nonetheless, he succeeded in impressing upon Patel that the plan was an illusion and the only alternative left was to accept the division of the country. In a public speech made on 20 April, Nehru declared: 'The Muslim League can have Pakistan, if they wish to have it, but on condition that they do not take away other parts of India which do not wish to join Pakistan.'[10] This, in fact, meant that Jinnah could have his Pakistan minus the Hindu areas of Assam, West Bengal, East Punjab and possibly the North-West Frontier Province.

Having sensed the Congress stand on the first question Mountbatten refrained from asking Jinnah whether he would accept a truncated Pakistan, 'because I have felt he could certainly have said no, in the mistaken belief or hope that I would go further and recommend to H.M.G. the full Pakistan that he desires'.[11] Instead, he went ahead evolving his own plan for the transfer of power. The plan was completed by the end of April and on 2 May it was sent to London with Lord Ismay and George Abell for the approval of the British Cabinet. It was not shown either to Nehru or Jinnah but Mountbatten was confident that the former would accept it. He had, however, doubts about Jinnah's reaction, for the plan was more damaging to Jinnah's concept of Pakistan than to Nehru's united India of Hindu provinces.

The essence of Mountbatten's plan lay in transferring power to the existing Constituent Assembly of the six Hindu provinces (Madras, Bombay, Orissa, United Provinces, Central Provinces, Bihar) but giving an option to each of the six Pakistan provinces (Assam, Bengal, Punjab, Sind, Baluchistan, North-West Frontier Province) either to join the existing Constituent Assembly of the Hindu provinces (which would mean joining the Indian union) or to form one, two or three independent states; the non-Muslims in the Punjab and Bengal having the additional option of demanding the partition of each province and then joining the Indian union with their Hindu-majority areas of West Bengal and East Punjab.

This plan, if approved and implemented, would either have divided the country into India and Pakistan, each including their present territories, or it would have created three, possibly four, independent countries out of the Pakistan provinces, while maintaining the union of six Hindu provinces, plus Assam. This analysis is, of course, based on the assumption that whereas the Hindu provinces would have chosen to remain together, among the Muslim provinces, which then lacked strong common bonds, Bengal and possibly the Punjab might have opted for separate independent status and the North-west Frontier Province, still somewhat under Congress influence, might have either joined the Indian union or stood out for an independent Pathan state. In this eventuality Jinnah would have been left with a Pakistan consisting only of Sind and possibly Baluchistan.

It is, therefore, no matter for surprise that Mountbatten, after despatching the plan to London, was worried whether Jinnah would accept it. What would he do if Jinnah did not accept the plan? In that case, as he was advised by Abell and Ismay, he should transfer power to the central government which was then headed by Nehru, leaving Jinnah to the 'tender mercy of the Hindus' or if Jinnah changed his mind within three years, giving him a much more truncated Pakistan.[12]

In the light of the political realities then existing in India, it may be rightly argued that the prospect of two or three independent states emerging out of the Pakistan territories was very remote. It may also be argued that the Labour government would not have consented to power being transferred to Nehru's central government in the event of Jinnah's non-acceptance of the plan. But the fact remains that Congress was in no way a loser under the plan. Congress could lose only if Bengal and the Punjab each opted first for remaining undivided and then for either joining Pakistan or constituting two separate independent states. In that case the Indian union would have lost the Hindu-majority areas of West Bengal and East Punjab. But this was very unlikely to happen. The non-Muslim representatives in each of the provinces must have voted in the first instance for the partition of the provinces rather than have leaped into the dark by voting for unity, for there was no guarantee against Bengal or the Punjab eventually joining Pakistan.

The second question which emerged during the month of April, while Mountbatten was evolving his plan on the first vital issue, related to the time-limit for the transfer of power. Should the date, June 1948, as laid down in Attlee's statement of 20 February, be adhered to or should the transfer of power be implemented much sooner? In view of the progressively deteriorating situation in the country, the Viceroy decided that power should be transferred sooner than stipulated. As soon as it became definite that the British were withdrawing from India and the country was to be partitioned, signs of imminent disintegration appeared. The Indian members of the civil and police services, now facing a state of uncertainty regarding their future citizenship (whether of India, Pakistan, or say, an independent Bengal), slackened in their duties. The British members of the services became disheartened, and were 'anxious only to get the sickening task of departure done with, and somehow to carve out fresh careers for themselves and new homes for their families elsewhere'.[13] Consequently, law and order became practically non-existent over large tracts of the sub-continent. Various movements for other would-be separate independent states sprouted. An extremist section of the Sikh community demanded 'Khalistan' – a sovereign state for the Sikhs. The Pathans in the North-West Frontier Province asked for a Pathan state. The Muslims in the Hindu provinces claimed a right of self-determination. The Nagas on the Assam-Burma border, the Adibasi tribesmen of Bihar and Orissa, the Mongoloid inhabitants of the hill tracts of the Darjeeling area, the Dravidians of the far south – each claimed a separate state. In these circumstances it seemed imperative that the interim period of uncertainty between the British and the Indian *Raj* be cut to the minimum. Subsequently it was shortened by ten months and the date of the transfer of power was fixed for 15 August 1947.

Having resolved his mind on the two vital issues, Mountbatten went up to Simla in the first week of May for a short respite. Nehru arrived as the Viceroy's guest on 8 May. On the night of 10 May Mountbatten had a sudden hunch about his plan which by then was nearly approved by the British cabinet. He showed his plan to Nehru and, to his utter surprise, found that Nehru vehemently disapproved of it. It was, in fact, Nehru who had told the Viceroy earlier in one of his interviews that each of the Pakistan provinces should be given the choice to decide whether or not to join the Indian union.[14] What now frightened Nehru and caused him to turn against Mountbatten's plan?

Nehru's objections (which he gave in writing to the Viceroy the following morning) were vague. He feared that the plan 'would encourage disruptive tendencies everywhere and chaos and weakness' and would lead to the 'Balkanisation of India'.[15] It has been observed earlier that the plan might, if anything, have led to the Balkanisation of the Pakistan provinces, but certainly not of the Hindu provinces of India. Perhaps Nehru's fear arose from the 'option of independence' the plan gave to each of the provinces of the Punjab and Bengal. This was very unlikely to occur as the non-Muslims in each of the two provinces would have opted for the partition of the provinces. Perhaps he objected to the plan because it left the Indian States free either to opt for independence or choose between India and Pakistan. It is also possible that he did not know precisely what he wanted and was still emotionally attached to the concept of a united India.

Nehru's emotional reaction to the plan caused a crisis which was, however, soon resolved. V. P. Menon, who had been from the start opposed to the Mountbatten plan (in the drafting of which he had not been consulted), had evolved a plan of his own and privately secured Patel's approval of it. His plan was not radically different from Mountbatten's except that it provided for the transfer of power on a Dominion status basis. In Mountbatten's scheme power was to be transferred to two or three or even more sovereign independent states, outside the British Commonwealth. This would delay the transfer of power until the Constituent Assembly of each state had framed a constitution. In Menon's plan India was to be divided, if at all, into two Dominions (not independent states) of Pakistan and India, both remaining members of the British Commonwealth. The acceptance of Dominion status [even for a short period] by India and Pakistan, Menon argued, would bring them many advantages.[16] First, power could be transferred immediately to the two central governments instead of delaying it until the constitutions of each state were framed and implemented. Secondly, it would be warmly welcomed by Britain whose goodwill and friendship were needed, as all the services then were officered by Britons who might have created trouble if they knew that India was to opt for complete independence and sever all connections with Britain. By staying within the Commonwealth as a Dominion India would get all the advantages without compromising its sovereignty, for after all the test of sovereignty lay in drafting and amending one's constitution. The Indian Constituent Assembly would be a sovereign body and it could later decide to withdraw from the Commonwealth.

Menon came to Mountbatten's rescue and amended the latter's plan in less than three hours. Among other amendments, the 'independent option' given in the Mountbatten plan to Bengal and Punjab was dropped. The amended plan was shown to Nehru before he left Simla on 11 May. Nehru accepted it; Mountbatten 'regained his buoyant spirit and good cheer' and returned to Delhi on 14 May.

The Viceroy had communicated to the British Cabinet an outline of the alternative plan. Faced with a new situation Attlee invited the Viceroy to London for personal consultations. Before going to London Mountbatten wanted to secure written acceptance of the plan by the leaders of the three parties (Congress, the League and the Sikhs). Baldev Singh on behalf of the Sikhs and Nehru on behalf of Congress accepted the plan, the latter on condition that the

League accepted the plan as a final settlement. Jinnah signified his acceptance of the general principles of the plan but he refused to commit himself in writing. He persisted in his ambiguous stand on the plan until it was actually implemented. Why did he adopt this strategy? His followers might react against Pakistan if they knew in advance its exact shape and size and fully realised its implications. How would the middle-class Bengali Muslims react when they found out that a 'truncated' Pakistan, which at the most the plan conceded to Jinnah, would not include Calcutta? Most of them lived and carried on their business or profession there. What would be the reaction of the millions of Muslims residing in the Hindu-majority provinces, especially the Muslims of the United Provinces, when they realised that they, who had been the staunch supporters of Pakistan, would be left out of it? The one way to avoid their disappointment, Jinnah might have reckoned, was not to disclose to them the contents of his Pakistan bag, to which his explicit acceptance of the plan would have virtually amounted. Further, by treating the plan as a compromise and not as a final settlement, Jinnah could bargain for more concessions, not with an intention of getting them but with a view to keeping his followers believing (until it was safe to disillusion them) that there was something more to come.* Then there was the personal factor. Under the plan there was to be a single Governor-General for both the Dominions. Jinnah had worked hard for power and he was now seventy-one years old and suffering from a mortal disease of which only he and possibly his sister were aware, and from which he was to die in September 1948. He wanted to be the head of the Pakistan state and he could not afford to wait until the termination of the interim joint

---

* A few days after the plan was announced on 3 June, the Khaksars, a group of militant Muslim fanatics who demanded an undivided Pakistan from Karachi to Calcutta, made an attempt on Jinnah's life because they believed he had betrayed Muslim interests.

Governor-Generalship of the Dominions. An equivocal acceptance of the plan on his part, therefore, might have cost him his long-cherished ambition.

For these reasons Jinnah might have decided to keep his cards close to his chest. Soon after Mountbatten left for London on 18 May, Jinnah demanded a 'corridor' across Indian territory to link West and East Pakistan. His demand might have aroused the hopes of the United Province Muslims that there was still a prospect of their being taken into Pakistan territory. The Congress leaders strongly opposed it. A crisis point was once again reached when Mountbatten returned to India on 31 May having obtained approval of the revised plan from the British government. The Viceroy told Jinnah that his demand was unreasonable and he must not persist in it, otherwise the Congress would go back to the Cabinet mission plan of 1946 and insist on power being transferred to the existing interim government. Jinnah yielded.

The Menon–Mountbatten plan was presented by the Viceroy to the Indian leaders at the historic conference held on 2 June in Delhi. Nehru, Patel and J. B. Kripalani accepted the plan on behalf of Congress. Baldev Singh accepted the plan on behalf of the Sikhs. On 3 June the leaders again met the Viceroy to convey the formal acceptance of the plan by their respective parties. On this occasion Jinnah signified his unequivocal acceptance by just nodding his head.[17] As arranged, Attlee announced the plan in the House of Commons on 3 June.

The purpose of the plan was to let the people of the 'Pakistan provinces' themselves decide whether they wanted a partition of the country. The elected members of the legislative assembly of Sind and the chosen representatives of Baluchistan were to decide whether they wanted to join the existing Constituent Assembly (which would mean remaining in the Indian union) or 'a new and separate Constituent Assembly' (which would mean opting for

Pakistan). In the North-West Frontier Province a referendum was to be held and the electors invited to choose one of the alternatives. In the Punjab the members of the existing legislative assembly were to meet in two parts, one representing the Muslim-majority districts and the other the rest of the province. The members of the two parts sitting separately were to decide whether they wished to remain in the Indian union or wanted to opt for Pakistan. They were also to decide whether the province was to remain united or be partitioned into separate Hindu and Muslim areas, the former joining the Indian union and the latter Pakistan. If a simple majority of either part decided in favour of partition, the province was to be divided. The same procedure was laid down for Bengal. The people of Sylhet (a predominantly Muslim district in the Hindu province of Assam) were to decide whether they wanted to join East Bengal (that is East Pakistan) or to remain with Assam. As for the Indian states, they were left free either to remain independent or to join either of the two Dominions.

Attlee's announcement of the plan was followed in India by a succession of All-India Radio broadcasts made by Mountbatten, Nehru, Jinnah and Baldev Singh. The concentration of press and radio interests on the events of 3 June in Delhi was heavier 'than for any single development in Asia since the surrender of Japan'.[18] The acceptance of the plan meant for Congress the acceptance of the division of the country, for the Muslim League the acceptance of the partition of Bengal and the Punjab, and for the Sikhs the loss of their homes and livelihood. At the same time the acceptance of the plan brought the culmination of the national movement of Congress, the end of a sixty-two-year struggle for independence, and the beginning of a new era. Nehru, in his broadcast on 3 June, artistically reflected on himself and his comrades in the memorable words: 'We are little men serving great causes, but because the cause is great something of that greatness falls upon us also.'[19]

It was a day of mixed feelings – of frustration and achievement, of remembrance and apprehensions. But a continent had at last made a decision.

For the chief implementer of the plan, Mountbatten, it was time only to look forward, for the sands were running out of the hour-glass. It was now assumed that the verdict of the Pakistan provinces would be in favour of the partition. The government, the Civil Service, the armed forces, the assets, the furniture, the files and records – all these, among thousands of other things, had to be divided. The boundaries of Pakistan and India had to be demarcated. The future of over 600 Indian states had to be settled. The task was enormous and the time short – only two-and-a-half months to go. Such a task had never been performed in world history within such a short period and with so much bloodshed.

The verdict of the Pakistan provinces was secured in less than a month, from 20 June to 17 July. In the Punjab and Bengal the decision went for the division of each province into the Muslim and non-Muslim areas. Thus West Punjab, East Bengal and Sylhet opted for Pakistan. East Punjab and West Bengal joined the Indian union. Sind and Baluchistan joined Pakistan; in the absence of a legislative assembly in Baluchistan the decision was made by members of the Quetta municipality. In the North-West Frontier Province only 50 per cent of the electorate voted,* of which 289,244 were for Pakistan and 2874 for India. Pakistan was born.

Operations were at once started on all fronts for the partition of India. On 4 July Attlee introduced in the House of Commons the Indian Independence Bill intended to transfer power to the new Dominions on 15 August.[20] The

* The Muslim Congress leader of the province, Khan Abdul Ghaffer Khan, asked his followers to boycott the referendum because they were not given the option to vote for the creation of an independent Pathan state. Congress, however, had lost its strong hold on the province and the Muslim Leaguer, Abdul Quaiyum Khan, had succeeded in tipping the scales in favour of Pakistan. *P.I.S.P.*, A. Q. Khan.

Bill was passed within a fortnight on 18 July. In India, the interim government was divided into two sections, a Partition Council and an Arbitral Tribunal were set up, a Joint Defence Council under Field-Marshal Sir Claude Auchinleck was constituted to divide the armed forces,* and two boundary commissions under the chairmanship of Sir Cyril (now Lord) Radcliffe were appointed – one to demarcate the boundaries of East and West Bengal and the other to separate East from West Punjab. Each commission, consisting of two Hindu and two Muslim judges, failed to arrive at an agreed solution. Hence the chairman, Radcliffe, took it upon himself to make the final award. This was sub-mitted to the Viceroy on 13 August. Mountbatten rightly assumed that the award would not be satisfactory to either party because their demands were conflicting. As he did not want the Indian leaders to suffer a disappointment before the celebration he did not make the award public until 17 August, two days after the celebration of indepen-dence in Delhi and Karachi.†

Communal riots started in the Punjab soon after the award was made public. As for the joint Governor-General-ship of India and Pakistan, Jinnah, who had evaded giving a definite reply to Mountbatten, finally told him on 2 July that he himself wanted to be Governor-General of Pakistan. Congress, on the other hand, invited Mountbatten to become Governor-General of free India. Though dis-appointed at Jinnah's self-appointment as the head of

* It was decided that the armed forces should be divided on a territorial and not communal basis.

† Congress had claimed for West Bengal about 59 per cent of the area and 46 per cent of the population of the province. The Radcliffe Award gave to West Bengal 36 per cent of the area and 35 per cent of the population. Of the total Muslim population of Bengal only 16 per cent came under West Bengal, while as many as 42 per cent of non-Muslims remained in East Bengal. The Award gave 38 per cent of the area and 45 per cent of the population of the Punjab to East Punjab and 62 per cent of the area and 55 per cent of the population to West Punjab. Menon, *Transfer of Power*, 402–3.

Pakistan the Viceroy gracefully accepted India's offer.

The only big question which remained to be resolved before 15 August was the future of the Indian states – six hundred of them, occupying two-fifths of the land of the country and containing one hundred million people, just under a quarter of India's total population. On 15 August British paramountcy was to lapse and the states were to become free. It was up to the rulers to decide whether they should continue as independent states or join either of the two new Dominions. Most of these states were inhabited by Hindus and situated within or adjoining Indian territory. Congress naturally expected that the rulers would accede to the Indian union. But the matter was complicated by Sir Conrad Corfield, the Political Adviser to the Viceroy, who was decidedly anti-Congress and determined to make things difficult for India. As soon as the prospect of India's independence became certain, Corfield began advising the princes to declare themselves independent. With this encouragement the rulers of Travancore, Hyderabad, and Bhopal signified their intention of becoming sovereign states after 15 August. A small number of rulers headed by the Raja of Indore, on the other hand, were willing to join the Indian union. But a large number of rulers were, in the months of June and July, undecided.

Congress was alarmed at the prospect of two-fifths of the Indian territory becoming Balkanised. It was, however, running branch organisations in most of the Indian states under Patel's guidance. Patel could also count on the support of the people in creating, if necessary, internal disorder in the princely states. On 25 June Nehru's interim government created a States Department. Two days later the department was allotted to Patel. Patel appointed V. P. Menon as secretary of the department. The operation began. Menon evolved a scheme for the integration of the states. They were to be asked to accede to India only on three subjects – external affairs, defence and communication.

The states had never exercised full control over any of these subjects. Hence, in acceding to India on these matters, they would not be parting with any power they had really exercised before. Such mild terms would induce them to join the Indian union. When they had been brought in, Menon advised Patel, 'the basic unity of India would be achieved and, when the new constitution was framed, we could thrash out the necessary details concerning the relations between the centre and the states at our leisure.'[21] Patel agreed. Menon then proposed that the active co-operation of Mountbatten should be secured, for 'apart from his position, his grace and his gifts, his relationship to the Royal Family was bound to influence the rulers.'[22] Patel whole-heartedly agreed. Menon then approached the Viceroy with his plan and pointed out that 'the wounds of partition might to some extent be healed by the states entering into relationship with the Government of India and that he would be earning the gratitude of generations of Indians if he could assist in achieving the basic unity of the country.'[23] This remark touched Mountbatten deeply and he agreed himself to sponsor the Instrument of Accession. 25 July was fixed for a conference with the princes. On that fateful day Mountbatten, dressed in full uniform with an array of orders and decorations, addressed altogether twenty-five of the major ruling princes and seventy-four state representatives.[24] He 'used every weapon in his armoury of persuasion' and made it clear that the offer made by Congress was most generous, leaving the rulers as masters in their domestic affairs, and that the offer was not likely to be repeated. He would be unable to mediate between them and the Congress after 15 August. So this was their last chance and if they did not sign the Instrument they were finished. One by one the princes signed on the dotted line, but not all of them. Hyderabad, Kashmir, Junagadh, Travancore, Jodhpur, Bhopal and Indore, as well as five others, held back. The last four, however, subsequently yielded to Indian pressures and acceded to India before 15 August. The only states which had not acceded to either of the Dominions by Independence Day were Hyderabad, Junagadh and Kashmir*. The Menon–Patel–Mountbatten team succeeded in integrating nearly 600 Indian states in less than three weeks. It was, perhaps, their greatest achievement.

In this last episode of the British *Raj* Jinnah played, surprisingly enough, a non-communal role. He held out to the rulers, Hindus or Muslims, the prospect of joining Pakistan on any terms they chose. This was a well calculated move. The rulers knew that their feudal powers and privileges would disappear in Congress's democratic and socialist India. In Jinnah's Pakistan, on the other hand, their future prospects seemed brighter. Had not Menon come forward in time with his scheme, which promised internal sovereignty to the rulers. Jinnah might have succeeded in fishing a few tormented Rajas from the troubled water. In choosing to give to the prince and not his people the absolute right to decide about the future of a state, Jinnah, however, ran a risk he was perhaps not aware of in the beginning. Pakistan had a stake in only one of the large Indian states – Kashmir. What if the Hindu ruler of Kashmir decided to opt for India? In this game, as it turned out, Jinnah lost all along the line. Kashmir was lost and none of the Hindu states joined Pakistan. And, at the same time, Jinnah seemed to have virtually renounced the two-nation theory (Pakistan

* Hyderabad's population consisted of 85 per cent Hindus but the ruler (Nizam) was a Muslim. The Nizam struggled to maintain the independence of the state. Negotiations with the Indian government broke down in June 1948, when Mountbatten left for Britain. The Indian army marched on the state and the Nizam's forces surrendered on 17 September 1948. The Hindu ruler of Kashmir, the population of which consisted of 80 per cent Muslims, evaded accession to either Dominion until October 1947, when tribal levies from Pakistan invaded the state. The Maharaja then acceded to India and the Indian army recaptured the major part of the state. Junagadh's population consisted of 85 per cent Hindus. The Muslim ruler of the state acceded to Pakistan. The people of the state opposed their ruler's decision. The ruler fled to Pakistan and the Indian army occupied the state in October 1947.

for Muslims and India for Hindus) on the basis of which he had created Pakistan. Could he do otherwise? Perhaps not. When he left Delhi for Karachi a few days before the birth of Pakistan he left behind more Muslims in India than there were in West Pakistan.

The British *Raj* finally reached its last moment. Mountbatten flew to Karachi on 13 August. On the following day the Dominion of Pakistan was inaugurated. That very day Jinnah assumed for himself all powers. In effect, he became 'Pakistan's King Emperor, Archbishop of Canterbury, Speaker and Prime Minister'. The Mountbattens then flew back to Delhi. It was in India and at Delhi that the ceremony of the transfer of power had some real meaning for the Britons. It was India that they had conquered and it was from Delhi they had ruled the empire since 1912. The Indian Constituent Assembly was convened late on the night of 14 August to assume sovereignty at midnight, the exact moment of India's independence. At the approach of the hour, Nehru said:

Long years ago we made a tryst with destiny, and now the time comes when we shall redeem our pledge, not wholly or in full measure, but substantially. At the stroke of the midnight hour, when the world sleeps, India will awake to life and freedom.[25]

The midnight hour struck and celebrations started all over India. Nehru and Prasad drove from the Assembly House to Viceregal Lodge to offer Mountbatten formally the Governor-Generalship of an independent India.* The ceremony itself was informal. In the early hours of the day Mountbatten drove in state to the Assembly House to administer the oath of office to Nehru and his cabinet.

The ceremony was over and the Mountbattens drove home. On their way back to Government House they were cheered by millions with cries of 'Jai Hind', 'Mountbatten

* Mountbatten remained Governor-General of India until June 1948 when he was succeeded by Rajagopalachari.

H

Ki Jai' and even 'Pandit Mountbatten'.[26] It was a unique day. A nation had forgotten its sorrows and sufferings of yesterday and warmly offered its hand in friendship to its erstwhile master. On her part Britain had acted differently from other colonial powers and transferred power to India and Pakistan without strings. The two countries became genuinely independent and no effort was made by Britain to set a limit on their independence. Britain's example was soon followed by other colonial powers (Holland and France) in South and South-East Asia, and within a few years Western dominance over Asia came to an end.

Thus 15 August 1947 marked the beginning of the end of European empires. For the countries of South and South-East Asia the struggle for freedom was nearly over but a greater struggle was to begin in coping with the problems of independence.

[1] *P.I.S.P.*, H. V. Hodson.

[2] Mosley, p. 54.

[3] Campbell-Johnson, p. 45.

[4] Ibid., p. 57.

[5] Ibid., p. 56.

[6] Ibid., p. 44.

[7] *P.I.S.P.*, H. V. Hodson.

[8] Campbell-Johnson, p. 98.

[9] Menon, *Transfer of Power*, p. 358.

[10] Quoted in Menon, *Transfer of Power*, p. 354.

[11] Mountbatten's telegram to Ismay, May 1947. Govt. of India Records. Quoted in Mosley, p. 114.

[12] Govt of India records. Quoted in Mosley, p. 115.

[13] *P.I.S.P.*, Ian Stephens.

[14] *P.I.S.P.*, H. Tinker.

[15] Menon, *Transfer of Power*, p. 362.

[16] Ibid., pp. 358–9.

[17] Campbell-Johnson, p. 103.

[18] Ibid., p. 105.

[19] Ibid., p. 107.

[20] 10 and 11 Geo. VI, c. 30.

[21] Menon, *Integration of the Indian States*, p. 93.

[22] Ibid., p. 94.
[23] Ibid.
[24] Campbell-Johnson, p. 140.
[25] Nehru, *Independence and After*, pp. 3–4.
[26] Campbell-Johnson, p. 159.

8 In Retrospect

QUEEN VICTORIA (1819–1901) bequeathed to her son, Edward VII, the richest and most powerful empire in the world. Britain then was the torchlight of the modern world, but the British *Raj* was essentially conservative. The preservation of the empire was the political manifesto of the British *Raj*, profit for Britain its economic justification, and conservation of the old social order its social policy. Constituted as it was, the British administration could not sufficiently release the forces of industrial civilisation which might have demolished the old values, levelled the social barriers, and transformed a medieval into a modern society. Perhaps the only shining era of reform and innovation during the whole period of British *Raj* was from 1828 to 1856. But this came to an abrupt end with the outbreak of the mutiny of 1857, after which the Government became irrevocably committed to the policy of non-interference in social matters. The Indian middle classes then took the initiative and started various socio-religious movements. But these movements were not simultaneously backed by economic changes. Furthermore, they subsided at the turn of the nineteenth century with the rise of Indian nationalism. The nationalists argued that the National Movement would become disrupted if it joined hands with the social reform movement. India should first attain political freedom and then concentrate on the reform of its society. The reform movements thus made little impact on traditional society.

At the close of the Victorian era India was a curious mixture of the ancient and the modern. Modern ideas and ways of life had descended upon a few English-educated middle-class Indians, who were animated with the idea of nationalism, who travelled from one end of the country to the other in steam-driven railway carriages, who preached (but did not always practise) the equality of all human beings, and who cautiously attacked the old order and its institutions – caste, untouchability – though many of them married their daughters and sons within their own caste. A marriage between a Hindu and Muslim was rarer than marriage between an Indian and a Briton. While the Indian middle class was staggering along the new path of modernity, the illiterate Indian masses lay firmly under the grip of religion and wallowed in its superstitions and prejudices. They cultivated their land with the ancient plough and travelled to the local bazaar (or furthest to the district town) on foot or in an ox-drawn cart. They faithfully believed in social segregation based on religion, caste, race, language, diet, and even province. Their village was their country and their family their highest form of association. Between them and their middle-class countrymen there was no communication, no political, economic or social link. Yet, it was on their support that the progress of the National Movement was to depend. Gandhi succeeded in involving the masses in his non-violent national movement but with results which shocked him more than any other nationalist.

Though Hindus and Muslims did not intermarry and inter-dine there were areas of social intercourse between them. In villages and small towns they lived harmoniously. However, the Hindu and Muslim socio-religious reform movements (in particular the Aligarh movement of Syed Ahmad Khan and the Arya Samaj movement of Dayanand), instead of promoting integration between the two communities made each community conscious of its separateness from the other. Even so, the Hindu–Muslim relationship at the beginning of the present century was flexible. Leaders could either set both communities apart by playing on their social differences or bring them closer by promoting common political and economic interests. The Muslim League adopted the former and Congress the latter course.

The Muslim community on the whole was nearly half a century behind the Hindu community in the race for modernisation. This accounted for the slow growth of the middle classes in the Muslim community. At the turn of the last century there was only a handful of professional men among the Muslims. The upper-class Muslims, most of whom belonged to the landed aristocracy, were therefore the leaders of the Muslim community. They were genuinely concerned about the backwardness of their community. They feared that with free competition for government posts, and general election for seats in legislatures, this community would be the loser, and a certain measure of political and administrative power that the British administration might concede to Indians would certainly be appropriated by the middle-class Hindus. Thus, there should be some considerations for the distribution of power other than merit and number. The Muslims, though in the minority, should be given weightage and allotted more seats in the legislatures and more posts in the government than their population warranted. This scheme for the distribution of power, based as it was on communalism, needed for its sustenance a perpetual division of society on religious grounds. It was a contradiction of nationalism and democracy and consequently a formidable challenge to the Congress movement. If implemented it would not only separate Muslims from Hindus but create various subdivisions among the Hindus themselves. A crop of communal leaders would spring up all over the country and a mighty force of communalism would rise against the national movement of Congress.

If discouraged by the British administration, the upper-class Muslims might have abandoned the idea of communal electorates and safeguards for the minority. It was obvious that only a few armchair politicians were to benefit under this scheme at a tremendous cost to Indian unity. But the British *Raj* was antagonistic to the national movement of Congress, which was considered a threat to the empire. Basically conservative and lacking in vision, the *Raj* chose to ally with communalism. Hence communal electorates were granted in 1909.

The introduction of communal electorates revived communalism in all sections of Indian society. It was exploited by politicians more for political gains than for the preservation of the cultural entity of each communal group. From now on the Indian National Congress had to fight against colonialism in front and against communalism at the rear. In this fight Congress committed many errors. Perhaps its greatest blunder lay in not recognising communalism as a formidable enemy. It failed either to combat or pacify it. Consequently communalism was more ignored than fought. Gandhi wanted to kill colonialism and communalism at one stroke, by raising the moral character of the masses. Nehru believed that democracy and socialism would destroy communalism. When frustrated in their hopes, both put the blame on the British *Raj* as the originator and perpetuator of communalism. Communalism would disappear with colonialism. Hence all efforts, they argued, must be concentrated on the frontal battle against colonialism.

The British *Raj* was not the originator of communalism. But it did nourish Muslim separatism as a useful ally against Congress nationalism. Muslim separatism was born in the Aligarh school of Syed Ahmad Khan, baptised in 1906 as the All-India Muslim League, and blessed with the communal electorate in 1909. It staggered on alone from 1910 to 1912, leaned on and fraternised with the Congress movement from 1913 to 1919, and was swallowed up by the Khilafat movement from 1920 to 1923. It was revived in 1924, though only on paper, reinforced in 1927 at the prospect of new constitutional reforms, was split in 1928, and led a divided and dormant existence until 1935 when it was uplifted by the strong hands of Jinnah. Jinnah's re-entry into politics was motivated by the 1935 Act which transferred power to Indian hands in provincial adminis-tration. Embittered by Congress non-acceptance of his League as a healthy partner, Jinnah fed and fattened the League on raw communalism and turned it by 1939 into a major rival to Congress. He raised the Pakistan slogan in 1940 and by the end of 1946 succeeded in bringing a majority of upper- and middle-class Muslims under his leadership. Jinnah's success was due in no small measure to his strategy and to the ready support of the British govern-ment which he received until 1945, but in greater measure it was due to the miscalculated actions and omissions of Congress. Linlithgow's August Offer of 1940, Cripps's plan of 1942 and Wavell's Simla Conference of 1945 gave body and soul to Jinnah's Pakistan. Congress gave it life and strength by resigning from the provincial ministries in October 1939, by launching the 'Quit India' movement in 1942, by persisting in its distrust of the British government in the year 1945–6, and finally by misinterpreting and virtually sabotaging the cabinet mission plan of 1946. British policy made Pakistan feasible and Congress, by lacking a definite policy towards the League, made it attainable. After the failure of the cabinet mission plan, the outbreak of the civil war, and Attlee's announcement of the withdrawal of British power from India by a specified date, the partition of India became inevitable.

Chronological Table

1857–8	Indian mutiny and widespread rebellion in Northern India.
1858	East India Company's rule in India replaced by the British Crown.
1875	Dayanand (1824–83) founds the Arya Samaj at Bombay.
	Syed Ahmad Khan (1817–98) founds Muhammadan Anglo-Oriental College at Aligarh.
1877	Queen Victoria proclaimed Empress of India.
1885	Indian National Congress inaugurated in Bombay.
1893	Hindu missionary Vivekananda (1862–1902) addresses the First World Parliament of Religions at Chicago. M. K. Gandhi (1869–1948) starts his career in South Africa.
1899–1905	The Viceroyalty of Lord Curzon.
1905	Partition of Bengal. The rise of anti-partition movement in Bengal. The rise of Extremist Party in Congress under B. G. Tilak (1856–1920).
1906	
1 October	Muslim deputation led by Aga Khan (1875–1958) presents address to Viceroy Minto (1905–10).
30 December	Inauguration of the All-India Muslim League at Dacca.
1907	Split in Congress at Surat. Beginning of terrorist movement in India.
1908	The Extremists excluded from Congress.

1909 May	Morley–Minto Reforms (The Indian Council Act) grant Muslim demand for separate electorate.
1910	Birth of Hindu Mahasabha.
1911	Visit of King George V and Queen Mary and the Delhi Durbar.
	Partition of Bengal annulled.
	Transfer of Indian Capital from Calcutta to Delhi announced.
	Italy and Turkey at war in Tripoli.
	Growth of anti-British feeling among Indian Muslims.
1912	Turkey gets involved in the first Balkan war.
1913	Rabindranath Tagore (1861–1941) awarded Nobel Prize for his *Gitanjali*.
1913	Balkan War concluded by the Treaty of London.
1914	
4 August	The First World War breaks out.
4 November	Turkey joins Germany against Britain. The growth of Pan-Islamism in India.
1915	
January	Gandhi returns to India from South Africa.
February	The liberal leader of Congress, G. K. Gokhale (born 1866) dies.
December	Beginning of the alliance between Congress and the Muslim League.
1916	
August–September	Tilak and Mrs Annie Besant (1847–1933) found the Home Rule Leagues.
December	The Extremists are taken back into Congress. The Muslim League and Congress reach an agreement at Lucknow and jointly demand for India a national legislative assembly to be elected on communal basis.

1917

April	Gandhi starts his first *Satyagraha* in Champaran, Bihar.
20 August	Edwin Montagu, Secretary of State for India (1917–22) defines British policy towards India.
November	Montagu arrives in India.
December	Indian government appoints Rowlatt Committee.

1918

April	Rowlatt Committee submits its report.
July	Montagu and Viceroy Chelmsford (1916–21) publish their joint constitutional report.
November	Allies secure victory in the First World War.

1919

March	Rowlatt Acts passed.
6 April	Gandhi starts his first All-India civil disobedience movement in protest against the Rowlatt Acts.
13 April	Jalianwala Bagh (Amritsar) massacre. Gandhi suspends civil disobedience movement.
23 December	The Government of India Act (incorporating Montagu–Chelmsford Report) is passed by Parliament.

1920

January	House of Lords rejects censure motion on General Dyer, the perpetrator of the Amritsar massacre.
March–May	Official and non-official reports on Amritsar massacre published.
1 August	Gandhi launches non-co-operation movement on behalf of Khilafat party. Tilak dies.

1921

February	Central Legislature is inaugurated.
August	Moplah rebellion in Malabar.

| November | Boycott of the Prince of Wales on his arrival in Bombay. |
| | Riots follow. |

1922

4 February	Policemen murdered at Chauri Chaura by mob.
6 February	Gandhi suspends the non-co-operation movement.
10 March	Gandhi arrested.
December	Birth of Swaraj Party and split in Congress.

1923

| September | Differences between Swaraj Party and Congress resolved. |
| November | Swaraj Party contests elections on behalf of Congress. |

1924

January	Central Legislative Assembly inaugurated.
March	Kemal Pasha abolishes Caliphate.
May	The Muslim League revived at its Lahore session.
September	Hindu–Muslim riots at Kohat.
November	All-Parties Conference held in Bombay to settle Hindu–Muslim problem.

1925

| October–November | Split in the Swaraj Party. |
| December | Hindu Mahasabha revived. |

1926

March	The Swarajists walk out of the Central Legislature.
	The end of the Swarajist interlude.
April	Communalism at its peak.
	Third general election held.

1927

| April | First airmail arrives in India from Croydon in under 54 hours' flying time. |

| November | All-white Simon Commission is appointed to recommend further constitutional advancement for India. Congress decides to boycott the commission. |
| December | Congress undertakes to draft a constitution for India independently of the Simon Commission. |

1928

February	Simon Commission arrives in India.
May	Congress appoints a committee under Motilal Nehru (1861–1931) to draft a constitution for India.
August	The Nehru committee completes its report.
December	The Nehru report accepted by Congress and the All-India Convention.
	Jinnah's (1876–1948) opposition to Nehru's report is outvoted and he parts company with Congress.

1929

| September | Jawaharlal Nehru (1889–1964) is elected the President of Congress. |
| December | At its annual session held at Lahore Congress demands complete independence for India. |

1930

26 January	Congress celebrates this day as Independence Day.
March	Gandhi launches the civil disobedience movement.
May	Gandhi arrested.
June	Congress is outlawed
	Simon Commission report is published.
November	First Round Table Conference meets in London.
	Congress boycotts the Conference.

1931

January	The Round Table Conference is adjourned.
	Congress leaders released.
17 February– 4 March	Viceroy Irwin (1926–31) starts peace talks with Gandhi and a pact is made. The civil disobedience movement is suspended.
23 March	Hindu–Muslim riots at Kanpur.
September	Gandhi attends the Second Round Table Conference held in London.
December	The Conference yields no further results and Gandhi returns to India.

1932

3 January	Gandhi threatens to resume civil disobedience movement.
4 January	Gandhi and other Congress leaders arrested.
17 November– 24 December	The Third and the last Round Table Conference.
	Jinnah abandons politics and settles down in London.

1933

March	White Paper is issued formulating proposals for Indian constitution.
December	Liaquat Ali Khan (1895–1951) persuades Jinnah to return to India.

1934

May	Congress suspends the civil disobedience movement.

1935

2 August	Government of India Act receives Royal Assent.
28 December	Congress celebrates its Golden Jubilee.

1936

April	Inauguration of the new provinces of Orissa and Sind. Congress decides to contest elections under the new constitution.

| May–June | Congress President Nehru and the Muslim League President Jinnah start their election campaigns. |

1937

January–February	Elections held for the provincial assemblies.
1 April	Provincial responsible government comes into force.
July	Congress ministries are formed in Bihar, Orissa, C.P., U.P., Bombay and Madras.

1938

| March | Congress ministry is formed in Assam. |

1939

3 September	Viceroy Linlithgow (1936–43) announces that India is at war with Germany.
14 September	Congress demands a declaration of war aims from the British government.
22–23 October	Congress calls on Congress ministries to resign.
31 October	All Congress ministries resign by this date.
22 December	The Muslim League observes this day as 'Deliverance Day' from Congress rule.

1940

February	Jinnah declares that Western democracy was unsuited for India.
March	Congress demands complete independence and a constituent assembly. At its Lahore session the Muslim League demands the division of India into autonomous national states.
10 May	Winston Churchill replaces Neville Chamberlain as Prime Minister.

17 June	The fall of France.
7 August	The Viceroy makes a statement on India's constitutional development – the August Offer.
17 October	Congress starts the individual civil disobedience movement.

1941

27 January	Subhas Chandra Bose (1897–1945) escapes to Germany.
August	'Atlantic Charter': Joint declaration by Roosevelt and Churchill.
December	Civil disobedience prisoners set free.

1942

February–March	Fall of Singapore and Rangoon.
22 March	Sir Stafford Cripps arrives in Delhi.
30 March	Cripps proposals published.
April	Congress and the Muslim League reject the Cripps mission plan. Cripps returns to London.
8 August	Congress demands the withdrawal of British power from India and sanctions the beginning of mass struggle under Gandhi's leadership.
9 August	Congress leaders are arrested and Congress is declared unlawful. Beginning of disturbances throughout India.

1943

March–April	Muslim majority provinces come under the control of the Muslim League.
August–November	Bengal famine.

1944

March	The Japanese advance into Assam assisted by the Indian National Army of Bose.
6 June	Allied armies land in France; D-Day.

June	Japanese defeated at Imphal. C. Rajagopalachari's formula made public for the first time.
9–27 September	Gandhi–Jinnah talks.

1945

7 May	Germany surrenders.
14 June	Viceroy Wavell (1943–7) announces a conference to be held in Simla.
15 June	Congress leaders released from prison.
25 June–14 July	Simla Conference and its failure.
26 July	Labour government under Clement Attlee comes into power in Britain.
14 August	Japan surrenders.
November	The I.N.A. trials begin in the Red Fort, Delhi.
December	Results of elections to the Central Legislative Assembly announced.

1946

January	Parliamentary delegation arrives in India.
18–23 February	Royal Indian Navy mutiny.
19 February	The British government announces that a cabinet mission is to visit India.
25 March	Cabinet mission arrives in Delhi.
5–12 May	Second Simla Conference between Cabinet mission and Indian leaders.
16 May	Cabinet mission presents its constitutional plan.
6 June	Muslim League accepts Cabinet mission plan.
16 June	Cabinet mission presents its interim government plan.
25 June	Congress accepts mission's constitutional plan but rejects interim government plan. Cabinet mission drops its interim government plan.
29 June	Cabinet mission leaves India.

6 July	Nehru interprets the Cabinet mission's constitutional plan.
29 July	Muslim League retracts its acceptance of the Cabinet mission plan and calls for 'direct action'.
16 August	Muslim League starts its direct action and the riots begin in Calcutta.
2 September	Congress forms interim government without the Muslim League.
25 October	Muslim League joins the interim government.
9 December	Constituent Assembly meets without the League.

1947

20 February	Attlee announces in Parliament the British intention of leaving India by June 1948.
22–23 March	Mountbatten replaces Wavell as Viceroy.
April	Congress accepts the principle of partition.
10 May	Nehru rejects Mountbatten's plan in Simla.
11 May	V. P. Menon amends Mountbatten's plan. Nehru accepts it.
18–31 May	Mountbatten discusses the amended plan with the British government in London.
2–3 June	The plan for the partition of India accepted by Congress, Sikhs and the Muslim League.
20–23 June	The Bengal and the Punjab Legislative Assemblies opt for partition.
26 June	The Sind Legislative Assembly opts for Pakistan,
June	Baluchistan opts for Pakistan.
6–17 July	Sylhet and North-West Frontier Province decide to join Pakistan.

18 July	The Indian Independence Act receives Royal Assent.
25 July	Mountbatten addresses the Chamber of Princes.
7 August	Jinnah flies to Karachi.
13 August	Radcliffe Award completed.
15 August	India and Pakistan become independent. Jinnah is sworn in as Governor-General of Pakistan and Mountbatten as Governor-General of India. The Pakistan cabinet is headed by Liaquat Ali Khan and the Indian cabinet by Nehru.

Bibliography

I. UNPUBLISHED PRIVATE PAPERS

THE Private Papers of British rulers and Indian nationalists will always remain the most useful source for the Indian National Movement and British policy. The 'gaps' and the 'dark patches' of history which cannot be explained by official records and newspapers are often illuminated with the aid of Private Papers. The first phase of the National Movement from 1885 to 1910 (the birth of Congress and the growth of Muslim separatism) is fortunate to have many legacies of Private Papers. Of the five Viceroys who ruled India from 1885 to 1910 (Dufferin, 1884–8; Lansdowne, 1888–94; Elgin II, 1894–9; Curzon, 1899–1905; Minto II, 1905–10), each has left behind a mass of private correspondence which explains his policies, prejudices, and attitude towards the national or sectarian aspirations of the Indian middle classes. Added to this are the Private Papers of two Secretaries of State for India, a Conservative G. Hamilton, 1895–1903, and a Liberal J. Morley, 1905–10. The India Office Library, London, houses the Private Papers of Dufferin (microfilm copy), Lansdowne (Mss. EUR. D558), Elgin II (Mss. EUR. D558), Curzon (Mss. EUR. F111), Hamilton and Morley (Mss. EUR. E233); Minto papers are in the custody of the National Library of Scotland, Edinburgh.

From the Private Papers of Indian nationalists, however, emerges a somewhat fuller picture of the early national movement. The papers I have usefully consulted are of G. K. Gokhale, V. S. Srinivasa Sastri, G. S. Khaparde, R. C. Dutt, N. B. Khare, B. Tyabji and P. D. Tandon, all housed in the National Archives of India, New Delhi. The massive collection of Gokhale's papers throws new light on the working of the Congress movement from 1898 to 1915 and on his own role as the leader of the moderate party in Congress. Although the *Letters of S. Sastri* are edited and published by T. N. Jagadisan (1963) it is rewarding to look into the original collections. The Private Papers of Tilak's right-hand-man Khaparde give an insight into the working of the extremist party in Congress up to 1920 and enable us to assess the personalities of Tilak and B. C. Pal. The Papers of Khare and, to a lesser extent, of Tandon explain in some measure the role of the Hindu Mahasabha in the 1930s and 1940s in the National Movement. The papers of Tyabji, the first Muslim president of the third Congress in 1887, are most valuable in assessing the growth of Muslim separatism and its pressure on the nationalist Muslims.

2. OFFICIAL PUBLICATIONS, NEWSPAPERS AND PERIODICALS

These are referred to in the chapter references.

The government publications are massive and fall into various categories. Of these the Parliamentary Debates are valuable for a study of the British policy, and the Indian Census Reports and Moral and Material Progress Reports (published annually since 1858) for some understanding of the social changes.

The Indian National Congress published the proceedings of each of its annual sessions. These Reports are indispensable for a specialised study of the Congress Movement up to 1936. Among periodicals H. N. Mitra's *Indian Annual Registers* (starting from 1919 and turning into *Quarterly Register* from 1924 to 1929) are an authentic record of the main political events up to 1947.

3. BIOGRAPHIES, MEMOIRS AND DIARIES

The works consulted may be divided into three categories according to their usefulness for the understanding of the persons, periods or subjects. The place of publication is London unless stated otherwise.

Max Mueller's *Biographical Essays* (1884) and C. Isherwood's *Ramkrishna and his Disciples* (1965) contain sympathetic appraisals of the ideas and personalities of the Hindu renaissance including Dayanand and Vivekananda. W. Wedderburn's *Allan Octavian Hume* (1913), though not critical, is the only accurate account of the life and works of the founder of the Congress movement. Similarly G. F. T. Graham's *The Life and Works of Syed Ahmad Khan* (Edinburgh, 1885) still holds the field as the standard English biography of the founder of Muslim separatism. Of the many biographies of Gokhale and Tilak, the two great leaders of the first phase of Indian nationalism, S. A. Wolpert's *Tilak and Gokhale, Revolution and Reform in the making of the Modern India* (Berkeley, 1962) is by far the best. Gandhi has a number of biographers each differing from the other in his interpretations of the mysterious Mahatma. His own account of his life, *The Story of my Experiments with Truth* (first published at Ahmedabad, 1927), though more reflective than factual, is by far the best source on his life and activities up to 1920s. U. N. Pyarelal's *Mahatma Gandhi: The Last Phase* faithfully describes Mahatma's last struggle against communal violence in the 1940s. D. G. Tendulkar's *Mahatma* (Bombay, 1951–4) in eight formidable volumes is the most authentic account of his life from 1869 to 1948 told mostly in his own writings and speeches. Jawaharlal Nehru's *An Autobiography* (first published in London, 1936; a cheaper edition published in India, 1962) is as much a story of his life as of Indian politics from 1912 to 1935. This may be supplemented with M. Brecher's *Nehru: A political biography* (Oxford, 1959), which surpasses previous writings on Nehru in authenticity and depth. B. R. Nanda's *The Nehrus; Motilal and Jawaharlal* (1962) is a brilliant and scholarly study of the father and son up to 1931. Rajendra Prasad in his *Autobiography* (Bombay, 1957) narrates his role in politics to the 1940s, in particular the Right–Left tension of the 1930s in Congress. N. D. Parikh's *Sardar Vallabhbhai Patel* (Ahmedabad, 1953) and K. L. Panjabi's *The Indomitable Sardar: A Political Biography* (Bombay, 1962) authentically describe the life and works of the iron man of Congress until his death. H. Bolitho's *Jinnah: Creator of Pakistan* (1954) provides a character study of the Muslim leader. M. A. H. Ispahani's *Qaid-e-Azam Jinnah as I Knew Him* (Karachi, 1966) furnishes some intimate details about Jinnah's conquests in Bengal and the Punjab. M. H. Saiyid's *Mohammad Ali Jinnah: a Political Study* (Lahore, 1945), still remains a detailed record of Jinnah's political achievements.

Of the works which describe periods rather than portray characters Sir Stanley Reed's *The India I Knew 1897–1947* (1952) is anecdotal, also containing some glimpses of the early twentieth-century social lives of the *Sahebs* in India. B. C. Pal's *Memories of my Life and Times* (2 vols., Calcutta, 1951) and Sir S. N. Banerjea's *A Nation in the Making* (1925) are relevant to the period from 1900 to 1920. M. N. Das's *India under Morley and Minto* (1964), R. S. Wasti's *Lord Minto and the Indian Nationalist Movement 1905–1910* (Oxford, 1964), S. A. Wolpert *Morley and India, 1906–1910* (California, 1967), Mary Minto, *India, Minto and Morley 1905–10* (1934), and John Viscount Morley's *Recollections*, vol. ii (1917), together provide a definitive study of the Minto–Morley period of Indian history and the growth of Muslim separatism.

Edwin Montagu's *An Indian Diary* (1930) is a Secretary of State's diary written day by day during his visit to India in 1917–18. The Earl of Halifax's *Fulness of days* (1957), Viscount Templewood, *Nine Troubled Years* (1954), Marquess of Zetland's '*Essayez*' (1956), S. Gopal's *The Viceroyalty of Lord Irwin 1926–31* (Oxford, 1957) and the Earl of Birkenhead's *The Life of Lord Halifax* (1965) are valuable works on the crucial period roughly from 1926 to 1935 – Gandhi's civil disobedience movement of 1930, Round Table Conferences and the origin of the 1935 Act. A. K. Azad's *India wins Freedom* (Bombay, 1959) contains his critical analysis of Congress's attitude towards the Muslim League in 1930s and 1940s. S. Ghose's *Gandhi's Emissary* (1967), though self-centred, gives some new facts on the Cabinet Mission's activities in 1946. Alan Campbell-Johnson's *Mission with Mountbatten* (1951) is a diary of the events and is indispensable for the last phase of the British Raj – March–

August, 1947. Lord Ismay's *Memoirs* (1960) is relevant for the same period though it yields very little.

M. R. Jayakar's *The Story of my Life*, 2 vols. (Bombay, 1958) is essentially an account of Maratha politics from 1895 to 1922 and the rise of Hindu Mahasabha from 1922 to 1925. See also C. H. Setalvad's *Recollections and Reflections* (Bombay, 1946). India's leading businessman and industrialist, G. D. Birla, in his work *In the Shadow of the Mahatma: A Personal Memoir* (Calcutta, 1953) gives an account of his association with Gandhi from 1916 to 1945, and provides glimpses of economic nationalism. Aga Khan's *Memoirs* (1954) describes his role in Muslim politics especially in the nine troubled years of 1900–9 and again during the Round Table Conferences in the 1930s.

4. GENERAL WORKS

Hindu Renaissance 1828–1900

On Ram Mohan Roy the best study is S. D. Collet's *Life and Letters of Raja Rammohun Roy* (3rd ed.) (Calcutta, 1962). *The English Works of Raja Ram Mohan Roy* (Allahabad, 1906) is the primary source. On Arya Samaj movement the basic work is Dayanand's *Satyarth Prakash* (English trans. by Dr. Bharadwaja, Allahabad, 2nd ed. 1915). Lajpat Rai's *A History of Arya Samaj* (rev. ed. Calcutta, 1967) and H. B. Sarda's *Dayanand Commemoration volume* (Ajmer, 1933) are the standard works. The primary source on the thoughts of Vivekananda is *The Complete Works of Vivekanand*, 8 vols. (Almora, 1923–51). A critical appraisal of his ideas is provided by D. G. Dalton in his unpublished University of London Ph.D. thesis, 'The idea of freedom in the political thought of Vivekanand, Aurobindo, Gandhi and Tagore'.

For general works covering various aspects of Hindu renaissance Charles H. Heimsath's *Indian Nationalism and Hindu Social Reform* (Princeton, 1964) is excellent. T. de Bary's edited *Sources of Indian Tradition* (Columbia University, 1958) can still be used as a source book. J. N.

Farquhar's *Modern Religious Movements in India* (New York, 1918) remains a standard general work. *Encyclopaedia of Religion and Ethics*, vol. ii (New York, 1909), provides authentic accounts of Arya Samaj and Brahmo Samaj movements. *Indian Social Reform* (ed. C. Y. Chintamani) (Madras, 1901) contains standard articles on individual social problems, and also some of the speeches of Ranade. There is no standard work on the impact of renaissance on Hindu society though S. Natarajan's *A Century of Social Reform in India* (Bombay, 1959) is a modest attempt.

British Policy and Economic Development 1858–1947

Documentation on policy and change is adequately provided by C. H. Philips *et al.* (eds.) *The Evolution of India and Pakistan: Select Documents, 1858–1947* (Oxford, 1962), and M. Gwyer and A. Appadorai (eds.), *Speeches and Documents on the Indian Constitution 1921–47*, 2 vols. (O.U.P., 1957). T. R. Metcalf's *The Aftermath of Revolt: India 1857–1870* (Princeton, 1965) is an excellent standard work on the period its title suggests. S. Gopal's *British Policy in India 1858–1905* (1965), mainly based on the Private Papers of the Viceroys, is a mine of valuable information.

The standard works on economic development are Vera Anstey's *The Economic Development of India* (1957), R. C. Dutt's *Economic History of India*, 2 vols. (1901–5) and D. R. Gadgil *The Industrial Evolution of India* (1934).

Indian Nationalism

General

B. B. Misra's *The Indian Middle Classes* (Oxford, 1961) is a pioneer scholarly work. K. Dwarkadas's *India's Fight for Freedom 1913–1937: An eye-witness story* (Bombay, 1966) is a critical and invaluable study of Congress and the League to 1937 when they drifted apart. S. R. Mehrotra's *India and the Commonwealth 1885–1929* (1965) is an authentic and scholarly interpretation of British–Congress–League policies. Anil Seal's *The Emergence of Indian Nationalism* (Cambridge,

1968) provides an excellent analysis of Indian politics in the three Presidencies to 1888. D. A. Low (ed.), *Soundings in Modern South Asian History* (London, 1968)–a collection of eleven articles–shifts the focus from the all-India to the regional politics. J. H. Broomfield's *Elite Conflict in a Plural Society; Twentieth-Century Bengal* (University of California, 1968) provides an insight into Bengal politics from 1912 to 1927.

Congress 1885–1947

P. Sitaramayya's *The History of the Indian National Congress*, 2 vols. (Bombay, 1946) is the official account, and is factual and accurate though provides dull reading. C. F. Andrews and G. Mookerjee's *The Rise and Growth of the Congress in India* (rev. ed. Meerut, 1967) and B. and B. P. Mujumdar's *Congress and Congressmen in the Pre-Gandhian Era 1885–1917* (Calcutta, 1967) fills in a few gaps but lacks scholarship and depth.

Dadabhai Naoroji's *Speeches and Writings, etc.* (Madras, 1910), G. K. Gokhale's *Speeches* (Madras, 1920), H. W. Nevinson's *The New Spirit in India* (1908), and P. C. Ghosh's *The Development of the Indian National Congress, 1892–1909* (Calcutta, 1960) are useful for the early period to 1910. V. C. Joshi (ed.), *Lala Lajpat Rai: writings and speeches*, 2 vols. (Delhi, 1966) explains the reasons for the rise of Hindu communalism in the 1920s. Dorothy Norman's *Nehru. The First Sixty Years* (1965), the writings and correspondence of J. Nehru as contained in *Independence and After* (Delhi, 1949), *India and the World* (1936) and *A Bunch of Old Letters* (Bombay, 1958), S. C. Bose's *Selected Speeches of Subhas Chandra Bose* (Gov. of India, 1962) and Rajendra Prasad's *India Divided* (3rd ed. 1947) – these are very useful for the 1930s and 1940s. On Sikhs K. Singh's *A History of the Sikhs*, 2 vols. (Princeton, 1963, 1966) is authoritative and readable.

Muslim Politics 1870–1947

S. A. Khan's *An Essay on the Causes of the Indian Revolt* (Calcutta, 1860) and W. W. Hunter, *The Indian Mussalmans*

(1871) are the basic works causing a change in British policy towards the Muslims of India. W. C. Smith's *Modern Islam in India* (1946) provides an economic interpretation of Muslim politics. S. M. Ikram's *Modern Muslim India and the Birth of Pakistan* (Lahore, 1965) provides biographical sketches of Muslim luminaries from Hali to Jinnah. R. A. Symonds's *The Making of Pakistan* (1950) is a dispassionate study. Lal Bahadur's *The Muslim League: Its history, activities and achievements* (Agra, 1954), based on archival materials, and Ram Gopal's *Indian Muslims: A political history 1858–1947* (1959), are biased but valuable general works on Muslim politics. Choudhry Khaliquzzaman's *Pathway to Pakistan* (1961) is a self-centred and apologetic work by a provincial Muslim leader personally involved in the high politics of Congress and the League. K. K. Aziz's *Britain and Muslim India* (London, 1963) concentrates mainly on the British attitude towards Muslim nationalism from 1857 to 1947. Jamil ud-Din Ahmad's *Speeches and writings of Mr. Jinnah* 2 vols. (Lahore, 1960, 1964) is an indispensable collection on the career of Jinnah from 1935 to 1948, C. M. Ali's *The Emergence of Pakistan* (Columbia University Press, 1967) provides intimate details about the League block in the interim government of 1946–7. The author, then a financial adviser to the government, became the Prime Minister of Pakistan from 1955 to 1956.

Transfer of Power 1945–7

V. P. Menon's *The Transfer of Power in India* (Calcutta, 1957) and *The Story of the Integration of the Indian States* (first published 1956; cheap ed. Madras, 1961) are authoritative, accurate and dispassionate accounts by a high civil servant who played an important role in the great events of the last years of the Raj. Of the three works on the same theme E. W. R. Lumby's *The Transfer of Power in India, 1945–47* (1954), Michael Edwardes's *The Last Years of British India* (1963) and L. Mosley's *The Last Days of the British Raj* (1962), the last is by far the best in style and documentation though a little biased in the interpretation of Mountbatten's role. G. D. Khosla's *Stern Reckoning; a survey of the events leading up to and following the partition of India* (New Delhi, 1949) mainly deals with the violence in the Punjab.

Most valuable are the Papers delivered by participants in the Partition of India Seminar organised and presided over by Professor C. H. Philips at the School of Oriental and African Studies, University of London. The papers concentrate on the period from 1935 to 1947. They are to be published shortly.

Index